P9-DFU-242

Toronto & Niagara
COLOURGUIDE

2nd Edition

Edited by Mark Grzeskowiak

Formac Publishing Company Limited
Halifax

Contents

Copyright © 2010 by Formac Publishing Company Limited
All rights reserved. No part of this book may be reproduced or transmitted in any
form or by any means, electronic or mechanical, including photocopying, or by any
information storage or retrieval system, without permission in writing from the
publisher. For photo credits and CIP data, see pages 256 and 3 respectively.

Library and Archives Canada Cataloguing in Publication

Toronto & Niagara colourguide / edited by Mark Grzeskowiak ;
photography by Breanne Thomas. -- 2nd ed.

(Colourguide series) Includes index.
ISBN 978-0-88780-899-9

1. Toronto (Ont.)—Guidebooks. 2. Niagara Peninsula
(Ont.) Guidebooks. I. Grzeskowiak, Mark II. Thomas, Breanne III. Title:
Toronto and Niagara colourguide. IV. Series: Colourguide series

FC3097.18.T667 2010   917.13'541045   C2010-900304-7

Formac Publishing Company Limited	Distributed in the United States by:	Distributed in the United Kingdom by:
5502 Atlantic Street	Casemate	Portfolio Books Limited
Halifax, Nova Scotia B3H 1G4	2114 Darby Road, 2nd Floor	2nd Floor, Westminister House
www.formac.ca	Havertown, PA 19083	Kew Road, Richmond,
Printed and bound in Hong Kong		Surrey TW9 2ND

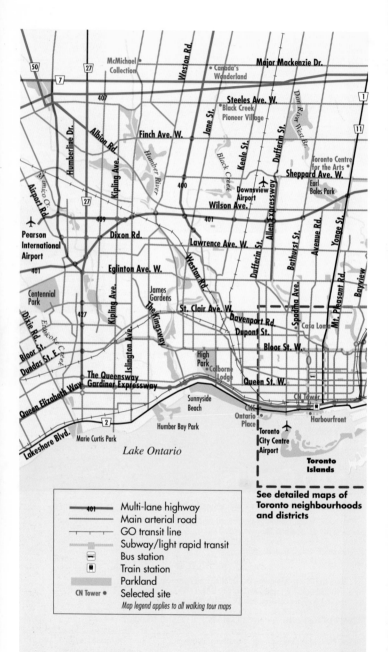

See detailed maps of
Toronto neighbourhoods
and districts

401	Multi-lane highway
	Main arterial road
	GO transit line
	Subway/light rapid transit
	Bus station
	Train station
	Parkland
CN Tower •	Selected site

Map legend applies to all walking tour maps

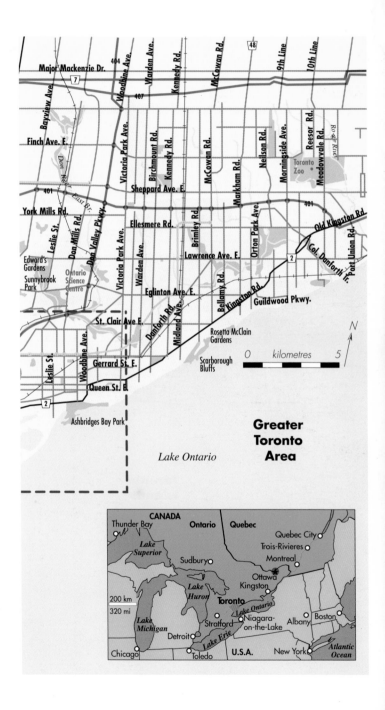

Greater
Toronto
Area

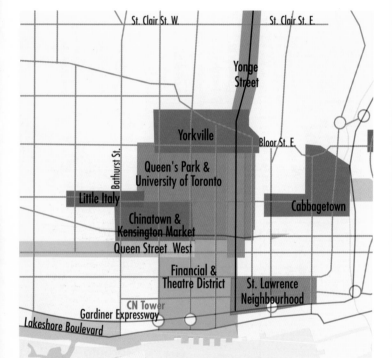

▲ Toronto Accommodation Map

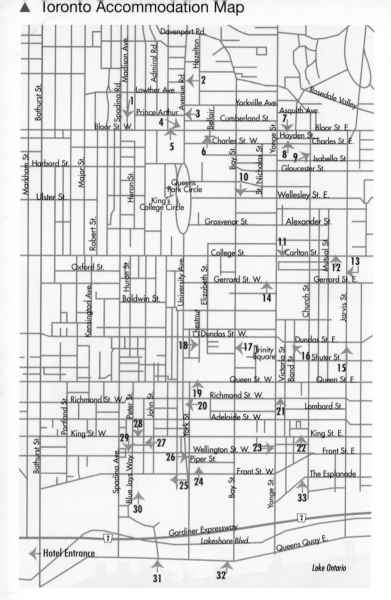

1. Madison Manor
2. Howard Johnson Inn Yorkville
3. Four Seasons Hotel
4. Park Hyatt Hotel
5. Hotel Inter-Continental
6. Windsor Arms
7. Toronto Marriott Bloor Yorkville
8. Comfort Hotel Downtown
9. Town Inn
10. Sutton Place
11. Days Inn
12. Best Western Primrose Hotel
13. Ramada Hotel & Suites Downtown.
14. Delta Chelsea Inn
15. Grand Hotel & Suites
16. Bond Place
17. Marriott Eaton Centre
18. Metropolitan Hotel
19. Sheraton Centre
20. Hilton Toronto
21. Cambridge Suites
22. Le Royal Meridien King Edward Hotel
23. Hotel Victoria
24. Royal York Hotel
25. Intercontinental Toronto Centre
26. Strathcona Hotel
27. Hotel Le Germain
28. Holiday Inn on King
29. SoHo Metropolitan
30. Renaissance Toronto Hotel at Roger's Centre
31. Radisson Plaza Hotel Admiral
32. Westin Harbour Castle
33. Novotel Toronto Centre

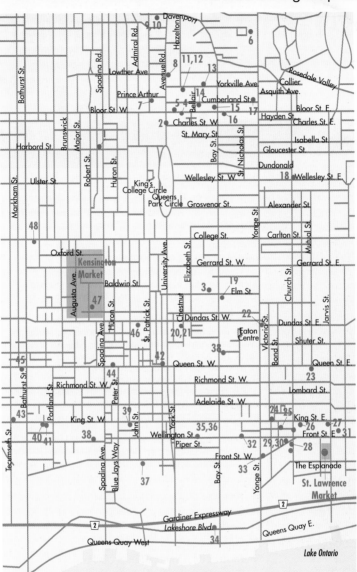

Restaurants with very similar locations are shown with a single dot and locator number.

1. Splendido Bar & Grill
2. C5
3. Barberians
4. Dynasty
5. Prego Della Pizaa
6. Rebel House
7. Opus
8. Spice Room and Chutney Bar
9. Mistura
10. Sopra
11. Remys Restaurant
12. Bellini's Ristorante
13. Crêpes à Gogo
14. Sassafraz
15. Pangaea
16. Panorama Lounge and Restaurant
17. Pilot Tavern
18. Kaiseki Sakura
19. Oro
20. Hemispheres
21. Lai Wah Heen
22. Hard Rock Cafe
23. George Restaurant
24. Le Méridien King Edward
25. Colborne Lane
26. La Maquette
27. Biagio Italian Restaurant
28. Hot House Cafe
29. Cafe Moroc
30. Sultan's Tent
31. Hiro Sushi
32. Jump Cafe and Bar
33. Biff's
34. Harbour Sixty Steakhouse
35. Canoe Restaurant and Bar
36. Bymark Restaurant
37. 360 Restaurant
38. Le Select Bistro
39. Joe Mamas
40. Conviction
41. Lee
42. Nota Bene
43. Amuse-Bouche
44. Ultra Supper Club
45. Rosebud
46. Frank
47. La Palette
48. Plaza Flamingo Restaurant

About This Guide

Toronto waterfront

Anyone who has ever flown into Toronto's Pearson International Airport has a good idea of the city's enormous size. Spreading out from the shores of Lake Ontario, its skyscrapers, buildings and streets dominate the horizon. Toronto is truly a "mega-city." This guide's modest goal is to introduce visitors to the best in arts, culture, shopping and dining that the City of Toronto and the nearby Niagara region have to offer.

The maps in the opening pages of the guide are intended to help navigate the Greater Toronto Area (GTA) and the Niagara region. The Overview map provides a broader view of the city's main highways and roads. The legend used for this map applies to others used in later sections of this book. A similar overview is provided in a map of the Niagara region on pages 144 to 145. We have also included additional maps at the start of this guide with a selection of Toronto's best hotels and restaurants.

The first and largest section of this guide includes a history of the City of Toronto, a description of its top attractions and chapters devoted to the city's best museums, galleries, theatre, music, nightlife, shopping, parklands and sports, as well as chapters devoted to Gay Toronto and the city's many annual events. The second section is devoted to the Niagara region. Again, there is a description of the region's top attractions, as well as a chapter devoted to its specialty — wine and food. The third section outlines the best in history, art, theatre and nature that can be found just outside the City of Toronto. The final section of this guide contains listings of all the attractions, sites and restaurants mentioned in the book, as well as information on accommodations and travel.

This is an independent guide and its contributors are all local experts. Their recommendations and suggestions are intended to do no more than introduce you to the best attractions, theatres, museums, galleries and restaurants in the City of Toronto and the Niagara region. No payments of any kind have been solicited or accepted by the creators or the publisher of this guide.

Please keep in mind that things always change, and this is especially true for a dynamic city like Toronto. Before visiting any of the attractions or venues presented in this guide, it is best to confirm details with a quick call. If anything you encounter doesn't match our listings, we'd like to hear about it. Please contact us at the address on page 3.

Some of the local experts who have contributed to this guide are:

CHRISTINE BEEVIS has been hiking, running and skiing through Toronto's many parks and trails for the last 30 years and has paddled the Don River twice. Her writing has been published in *ON Nature*, *Pathways* and *UnderCurrents*. (Parklands)

BRUCE BELL is a well-known Toronto historian, playwright and author. Official Historian of St. Lawrence Hall and St. Lawrence Market, Bruce is also the official tour guide of St. Lawrence Market. (St. Lawrence Neighbourhood)

JENIVA BERGER is a long-time Toronto theatre critic and cultural journalist. She has been a regular theatre columnist for *Toronto Calendar Magazine*, *The Canadian Jewish News*, *Toronto Tonight*, *The Buffalo News* and *Scene Changes* magazine. She is the co-founder and founding president of the Canadian Theatre Critics Association. (Excursions for The Theatre Lover)

JULIA BROWNE is a freelance writer, specializing in travel, personal profiles and history. She has travelled widely and lived in France for many years where she created a tour company offering historical walking tours. (Excursions for The Historian)

MICHAEL CRABB is an arts writer and broadcaster, the award-winning host of CBC Radio's *The Arts Report* and currently covers opera and dance for CBC Radio's *Here and Now*. He is also dance critic of *The National Post*. (Symphony, Chamber Music and Opera)

MARK GRZESKOWIAK is an editor, writer and teacher who has called the city of Toronto home for over 30 years. A former university lecturer, Mark currently works as an editor in educational publishing and teaches in local private schools.

DANNY GLENWRIGHT is a Canadian journalist who spent many years investigating Toronto's nightlife. He has lived in Canada, the United Kingdom and Namibia. He is currently working for Journalists for Human Rights, a Canadian non-governmental organization, in Freetown, Sierra Leone. (Gay Toronto)

DEIRDRE HANNA has written extensively on art, design, literature and cultural issues for Canadian and international media including Amazon, *Canadian Architect*, *Canadian Art*, *Details*, *The Globe and Mail*, *Images*, *Masthead*, *Opera Canada*, *Saturday Night*, *Salon*, *The Toronto Star*, *Vanguard*, *The Walrus* and *NOW*, where she was art editor for fourteen years. (Museums and Galleries)

MARICHKA MELNYK is a radio producer for CBC Radio One, specializing in arts and entertainment coverage. She was the voice of "Go2it" events on the CBC Radio One program *Here and Now* and now produces the program. (Theatre and Dance)

SHAUN SMITH is a freelance food writer in Toronto. A former chef, he has been cookbook reviewer for *Quill & Quire* magazine for more than ten years and is a restaurant reviewer for *Toronto Life*. (Dining)

Exploring Toronto

Berczy Park

Visitors to Toronto can take heart — despite its mega-size, the city is relatively easy to get around in. Its streets are clean and safe, and although Torontonians like to claim otherwise, there is an excellent transit system that will take you to the doorstep of just about every top attraction Toronto has to offer. For people planning on staying in the city — and perhaps foregoing the excursions outside Toronto that are outlined in this guide — all that is needed is a bus ticket.

Visitors planning a longer stay in Toronto will, of course, want to do a little research before arriving in the city. Information on attractions, special events or accommodations in Toronto can be gathered from any number of official sources. The Toronto Convention and Visitors Association's website (www.seetorontonow.com/) is the first and best stop for information on Toronto events, goings-on and happenings — as well as other essential matters, like accommodations and maps. The Government of Ontario's tourism website (www.ontariotravel.net/) is also worth a look, especially for anyone who is considering travelling outside the city.

For travellers arriving by air, a cab ride from Lester B. Pearson International Airport to the downtown core will cost around $30 Canadian, and is typically a flat rate charge. A cheaper (albeit slower) option is to take local transit. Although there is no fixed link between the airport and the city, the Toronto Transit Commission (TTC) operates a bus service out of the airport. It's a short ride across the highway and through the west end of the city to Kipling subway station, and from there the subway runs directly downtown in about thirty minutes. Visitors arriving in the city by train will be dropped off at Union Station, which is already in the heart of downtown Toronto.

Subway systems in large cities can be daunting — one need only think of Paris's multi-layered Metro or London's similarly intricate Tube system. The nice thing about Toronto's subway system is that it is relatively simple. There is an east-west line called the Bloor-Danforth line, and two north-south lines, jointly known as the Yonge-University-Spadina line. (A recently added Sheppard line at the north end of the city isn't really of interest to visitors; locals call it the "subway to nowhere.") Of course, the downside to such a simple subway system is that it doesn't necessarily take you directly to every place you want to go, but that's where the TTC's buses and streetcars come in. And viewed as a whole, the city's transit system is convenient and dependable.

Toronto subway cars

Guided tours of the city are available through companies such as Toronto Hippo Tours (www.torontohippotours.com) and Toronto Trolley Tours (www.torontotours.net). The former touts itself as an "urban safari" and interestingly provides its

Boat tour on the Toronto Harbourfront

passengers with a land and water experience — its buses float. Another, and depending on the time of year, much more spectacular perspective on the city is available via any one of the many Toronto Harbour tours (www.torontotours.com).

In fact, there is no better way to enjoy the city's skyline on a warm summer's evening than from a boat on Lake Ontario, while watching the setting sun reflect off the CN Tower and the city's skyscrapers.

St. George subway station

The city's waterfront is also worth noting for the presence of the Martin Goodman Trail, a recreational trail that runs along the shoreline of Lake Ontario. In the warmer months, it is an excellent option for cyclists who want to see Toronto — although it is best to pick up the trail either west of Spadina Avenue or east of Yonge Street. The stretch in between, around Harbourfront, isn't really bicycle-friendly due to the busy traffic.

Toronto is also a great city for walking. The downtown core certainly has its hustle and bustle, as might be expected of a city of this size, and there are times of the day and city blocks (for example, weekdays at 5:00 p.m. around Union Station) where the less nimble will find themselves at serious risk of being trampled by office workers hurrying home. But overall, when put to the test, Torontonians — like most Canadians — tend to be courteous and helpful to strangers. And Toronto has the added bonus of having a 27-km-long network of pedestrian tunnels, known as the PATH, located directly under the city's skyscrapers, for those days when the weather is inclement.

Finally, for planning outings, it may be worthwhile picking up a free local magazine such as *NOW magazine* or *eye weekly* for listings of events, movie times, theatre and concert times and restaurants available to visitors.

Toronto waterfront

A Short History of Toronto

Erin Phelan

Understanding Toronto today requires a look back in time. Compared to European cities of a similar size, Toronto's history is young; however, it is a history rich in culture and filled with stories of change. A number of factors have influenced and shaped the Toronto of today.

Fort York with view of city skyscape

Toronto's First Settlers

The land on which Toronto and its surroundings sit has always been important for trade. Thousands of years before European settlers came to the area trade routes established by the native population covered the land where Lake Ontario, Lake Huron and Georgian Bay converge. Although some have argued that Toronto translates from Huron as "meeting place," its actual name stems from Iroquois, and translates as "where the trees meet the water."

Historians do not know for certain when the first Europeans reached the Toronto area, but believe it was sometime in the seventeenth century. Not only did the Europeans bring increased strife to the region, they also brought new diseases across the Atlantic Ocean: between 1634 and 1640, half of the aboriginal population perished from these diseases. Various indigenous groups fought alongside Europeans and against each other for control of the land. After the Dutch had settled what is now New York they

Toronto streetcars

Fort York canon

struggled with the French for control of the fur trade, and the Toronto portage became a route for war parties. Finally, in 1649, the Huron and their French allies won a decisive victory. They continued to bolster their trade in fur and other goods over the next century and by 1750 the volume of trade had exceeded their expectations. The French built Fort Rouille between 1750 and 1751 as a protective trading post and destroyed it in 1759 to prevent it from falling into the hands of the British during the Seven Years' War. After gaining control of the region the British decided the land would be suitable for a settlement and less than twenty years later purchased approximately 400 square miles from the Mississauga people in what was known as the "Toronto Purchase." The cost? About 1700 pounds, some barrels of flour and other miscellaneous goods.

Battle Scars

Colonel John Simcoe was an important figure in Toronto's history. A veteran of the American Revolution, he became the first Lieutenant-Governor of Upper Canada (now Ontario) and chose Toronto as the provincial centre. In 1793, on hearing news that France had gone to war with Britain, Simcoe ordered the construction of Fort York to defend Toronto Bay against a possible invasion from the Americans, who were allies of the French. Many historians cite this moment as the creation of urban Toronto. Over the next few years Simcoe laid out the town, establishing a north-south, east-west grid that remains to this day, and

St. James Park

started construction of Yonge Street for swifter transportation of goods and soldiers.

The citizens of York suffered three attacks during the War of 1812, the worst on April 27, 1813 when the US army, supported by naval ships, pushed towards Fort York. The six-hour battled ended when the British blew up the fort's gunpowder magazine, causing casualties on both sides, and retreated to Kingston. The US forces occupied York for six days and, in spite of capitulation terms between the two countries, the embittered victors robbed houses and torched the governor's home and parliament buildings (the British retaliated the next year by burning the White House, Congress and other buildings when they captured Washington).

The British returned to York and rebuilt. The town's status changed from a threatened frontier to an important administrative and commercial centre in a growing colony. Many newcomers from Britain crossed the Atlantic from 1815 onwards in search of a better life. In addition, the opening of the Welland Canal in

1824, which linked Lake Erie and Lake Ontario, made the town an important trade centre along the Montreal-Chicago axis. From a small population of 720 souls in 1815 the town grew into a metropolis of nearly 10,000 in 1834, when Toronto re-adopted its original name, and was incorporated as a city.

The City Grows

During the 1820s and 1830s the economy went through many ups and downs, in line with periods of recession. A horrific typhus epidemic in 1847 and 1848 claimed 1,100 lives, many of them Irish immigrants who had fled the potato famine. The British united Upper Canada and Lower Canada in 1841, and the capital status was moved away from Toronto, eventually settling in Ottawa in 1865. In 1867 Toronto became a city within a country when the Dominion of Canada was founded. By then Toronto had established itself economically as the largest urban centre in the most populous province of a new nation.

Corso Italia neighbourhood

The city continued to handle an influx of immigrants. Although the majority came from the United Kingdom, increasing numbers came from other parts of Europe. By the 1901 census, eight per cent of Toronto's 208,000 people were of non-British origin. By 1922 the population had grown to 522,000. During this rate of expansion, many of the Edwardian buildings that survive today were established. Streetcar tracks were laid down to support the popular mode of transit, and car ownership rose from 10,000 in 1916 to 80,000 in 1928.

Responding to a sense of uninspired urban bleakness, philanthropists and reformers worked to enrich Toronto's cultural side. The Art Gallery of Toronto (now the AGO) began construction in 1900, followed by the Royal Ontario Museum in 1912. Toronto music venues such as the Royal Alexandra and the Winter Garden theatres were built around this time, providing more theatrical settings for people's amusement. Sports flourished, and the city's first shrine to hockey, Maple Leaf Gardens, opened in 1931.

Dundas Square at night

Following the Second World War, Toronto changed dramatically. The area that made up the city and its environs exploded, doubling in population from just over one million people in 1945 to more than two million in 1971. After 1951, immigrants and refugees, skilled and unskilled workers and students flocked to Toronto from Italy, Greece, Central Europe, the British Commonwealth, the Caribbean and the Indian subcontinent, transforming the face and soul of Toronto and providing an important foundation for today's cosmopolitan city. People's motivations for moving to Toronto were varied: many were "displaced persons" who could not return home after the war. Others were refugees from some other trauma, such as Hungarians who fled when the Soviet Union invaded their country

Cycling over streetcar tracks

in 1956 or the Vietnamese who began to arrive in the late 1970s after the fall of Saigon. Many families came in the hope of achieving a better life for their children. In addition to immigrants, a significant proportion of Toronto's new population consisted of Canadians from other parts of the country, choosing to seek their fortune in the big city. By 2001, more than 2.5 million people found themselves living in one of the most diverse — but relatively harmonious — places in the world.

The Toronto Transit Commission struggled to keep up with the burgeoning population, opening the first subway line in 1954, while retaining the streetcars and buses. In the latter decades of the twentieth century, and continuing today, anti-car and pro-cycling advocates have worked to establish bike lanes and convince people to leave their cars at home. However, the rate of automobile ownership in contemporary Toronto is among the highest in North America and with that comes pollution and congestion issues — ongoing headaches for citizens and politicians alike.

The city skyline has been transformed dramatically from the 1950s onwards. Toronto had become a moneymaking centre, and after the Toronto-Dominion Centre was completed in 1963 other skyscrapers quickly sprang up. At the time of this growth, many heritage buildings were demolished, including the old downtown Chinatown, which was destroyed as "a sanitary measure." Many people fought to protect their neighbourhoods from high-rise development, and with the liberalizing attitudes of the 1960s and 1970s developers converted many underutilized factories and other properties into new condominium or townhouse projects — a trend that continues today with the conversion of such heritage sites as the Tip Top Tailor factory.

Maple Leaf Gardens

And what about that looming spire in the centre of the city, for many years the world's tallest freestanding structure? In the 1970s, Toronto's building boom brought about a serious problem: people were experiencing poor television reception. The pre-skyscraper transmission towers were not high enough anymore. In 1972 Canadian National (CN) began construction on a tower that would solve this problem — and also serve as a world-class tourist and entertainment destination — the CN Tower.

Toronto Today

Toronto is very different today than it was in its early days. With a population of more than 2.5 million in the Amalgamated City of Toronto, it is North America's fourth largest city, and Canada's economic capital. Like any large city it faces challenges, but at the same time it flourishes, and for residents and visitors alike it is a beautiful, exciting city, rich in culture and heritage.

Toronto

Top Attractions

Miles Baker, Jean Paul Pelosi, Marichka Melnyk, Melissa Brazier, Regan Ray, Bruce Bell, Grant Gaspari, Todd Aalgaard, Mark Grzeskowiak, Lonny Knapp

Toronto Harbourfront

Art galleries, museums, theatre, music, first-class restaurants, lively nightlife and great shopping, as well as a host of annual festivals and events — Toronto has a lot to offer visitors. The attractions described in the following pages are the best in the city. From the CN Tower to Casa Loma, from Harbourfront to the Toronto Zoo, Toronto's top attractions provide visitors with a range of activities and historic sites to make their stay in the city a memorable one.

CN Tower glass floor

CN Tower

The tallest free-standing tower in the world (the Guinness Book of World Records recently decided that its closest competitor, the Burj Dubai in the United Arab Emirates is the world's tallest building) continues to be a source of pride for Torontonians, one that offers a truly spectacular view of the City of Toronto. That's no small honour when one considers similar vantage points in other great cities. Indeed, the London Eye may be more fun, and the view from Montmartre in Paris more romantic, but neither compares to the almost mathematical joy of following the pattern of Toronto's parks, streets and buildings as they spread out into seeming oblivion to the north, east and west.

The CN Tower, a true feat of engineering, has defined Toronto's skyline since the 1970s. Construction began in February 1973, and over the next three years the tower inched its way skyward, as concrete, wire and steel rose endlessly from a massive base made up of 7,000 cubic metres of concrete. The rooftop antenna was put in place by a heavy-lift helicopter in 1975, and the CN Tower opened to the public one year later.

View of Toronto, CN Tower observation deck

Officially a communications tower, it is used by numerous broadcast media companies, including many of Toronto's local radio and TV stations. But this functional raison d'être has never detracted from the CN Tower's significance as an entertainment venue.

The fun doesn't come cheap. Depending on how much of the tower visitors want to experience, the trip will cost between $20 and $35, and there is a line-jumper special at $65. The inclusive packages include a visit to the observation deck located at 330 metres, a film about the tower's construction, a "movie ride" and a trip up the elevator with its glass windows offering a view of the city as you ascend. It's one of the very few times an elevator trip is actually exciting.

Besides enjoying the unique view, brave or double-dared youngsters will enjoy jumping on a large glass floor on the main deck, which is approximately 348 metres above the ground. The main deck of the CN Tower also has the appropriately named 360 Restaurant. Dinner for two without wine can cost more than $100, but there is no other dining experience like it in the city. A table by the window offers a panoramic view of the city as the restaurant revolves. A less expensive meal is available at the Horizon Cafe, which offers lighter fare, or possibly drinks — as visitors afraid of heights may want a stiff one!

But for most visitors, the majority of time at the CN Tower will probably just be spent in awe of Toronto's topography. The southern side of the tower, with its views of the Toronto Islands and Lake Ontario, is also spectacular. On a clear day it's even possible to see as far as Niagara-on-the-Lake, near the American border, with the naked eye.

Rogers Centre

Rogers Centre (formerly SkyDome)

Near the shore of Lake Ontario sits Toronto's Rogers Centre, a world-class arena that hosts the city's major professional sports teams as well as concerts, trade fairs and conventions. Built in 1989, the stadium was the first in North America with a fully retractable roof and a built-in hotel. Seventy of the hotel rooms actually overlook the field. The Centre also houses retail stores, lounge bars and a Hard Rock Cafe.

The arena's 31-storey roof loops across the cityscape like a giant sail. The bold design has become a Toronto landmark and commonly appears on postcards together with its neighbour, the CN Tower (the tower can be seen from inside the stadium when the roof is open). The golden statue protruding from the northwest wall of the arena — Michael Snow's "Audience" sculpture — of a fan with binoculars, another eating a hot dog and one other giving the "thumbs down," adds a unique touch and some personality to the Centre's otherwise grey exterior.

Michael Snow's *The Audience*, Rogers Centre

Watching a sports fixture in the 50,000-seat Rogers Centre can be both thrilling and noisy. If the roof is closed, which is usually the case on chilly days, the arena assumes a gladiatorial atmosphere. There's something dramatic about indoor sports: echoes of the action down on the field, the smell of hot dogs and peanuts, and a crowd that always seems larger than it is. It's the perfect setting for an Argonauts football game.

During the summer, the dome's roof usually retracts, opening the blue Toronto sky over the spectators. Summer means Blue Jays baseball, warm July breezes, cold beer and a lower-deck seat along the third base line. The Jays dance team flip and twist atop the dugout, urging the team on: "Go Jays, go!"

In 2005, Ted Rogers, CEO of Rogers Communications and owner of the Blue Jays, announced that he would increase the team payroll and change the stadium's original name of SkyDome to the Rogers Centre. Once the deal was complete, Rogers refurbished the arena, installing the world's largest TV screen (at the time) and building other monitors into the outfield wall. The

Rogers Centre

"fire" graphic that lights up these screens is an especially nice touch during games.

The Rogers Centre's main entrances are best accessed from John or Front Street, or via the Skywalk pedestrian tunnel, which begins at Union subway station. Tours of the Centre are available.

Harbourfront

Toronto's highest concentration of cultural offerings is available at Harbourfront Centre, located at the foot of York Street below the Gardiner Expressway and sprawling across 4 hectares along the water's edge. Harbourfront is a non-profit cultural centre that provides a diverse menu of activities and offerings any day of the week, year round, many of them free.

The complex comprises three buildings converted from their original industrial purposes into multi-use spaces. These venues allow Harbourfront to provide a full spectrum of events and entertainment for all ages in all forms of the arts: author readings, gallery exhibitions, studio workshops, film screenings, musical and theatrical performances and more. There are also restaurants, shopping and outdoor activities at the water's edge, regardless of season. A quick look at local listings or online will provide a comprehensive overview of what's on at Harbourfront.

The visual centrepiece of the Harbourfront area is the Queen's Quay Terminal building, a 1926 warehouse converted in an award-winning redesign into a shopping, entertainment and residential complex. More than twenty-five stores, cafés and restaurants welcome visitors to the sunlit, glass-walled atrium, and the patio features some of the city's best

Toronto
Harbourfront Centre

New Simcoe Street
Wave Deck

South boardwalk, Harbourfront

waterfront dining. On the third floor is the Premiere Dance Theatre, a 450-seat venue with proscenium stage. The Premiere has been used for everything from conventional theatre to corporate rentals, but its primary function is to host modern dance performances in an intimate setting.

Next door to the Queen's Quay Terminal building is the Enwave Theatre. Originally used as an ice house for the warehouse stores, it has been dramatically renovated into a convertible space notable for its acoustics. The Enwave provides a year-round stage for theatre, dance, concerts and other events.

The York Quay Centre, formerly a truck garage, has been renovated into a venue for workshops, exhibitions and performances in ten different areas of the building, both indoors and out. Along the old loading bays visitors can stroll past craftspeople and artisans creating art pieces out of metal, ceramics and glass. Many of these works are available at Bounty, a gallery and craft shop at the front of the building, which offers a range of one-of-a-kind pieces for sale.

Power Plant, Harbourfront Centre

Performances in the York Quay Centre take place in several of the available spaces, primarily in the Studio Theatre, a small stage space seating about 200 people, which is also used for readings and film screenings. The Brigantine Room is an open space that is easily adjusted to accommodate anything from readings and panel discussions to cabaret-style club and musical performances, all in an intimate and changeable setting. A number of other community spaces in the building house speakers, shows and activities at different times.

The York Quay Gallery is the central exhibition area for visual arts, presenting ongoing collections and installations by visiting artists. Other spaces in the building offer different shows and presentations throughout the year. At the back of the building the Lakeside Terrace offers cafeteria-style eating in an indoor setting, with an outdoor patio that is often used for musical performances.

The York Quay Centre backs onto a man-made pond that is used year round. In the summer, Harbourfront offers canoe lessons. In November, the pond becomes Canada's largest artificially cooled outdoor rink, staying open in temperatures as warm as 8°C. Visitors can rent skates and enjoy skating day and night, accompanied by music.

In warm weather, the outdoor Concert Stage holds free concerts and movie screenings, with seating for some 1,300 people and standing room for 2,000 more in an open-sided space under a canopy. In the summer, the International Market and World Cafe are set up nearby, providing a selection of wares and menus from all over the globe for visitors to sample.

The Power Plant Contemporary Art Gallery, housed in a reclaimed and renovated industrial site, is Harbourfront's focal point for contemporary art. As a non-collecting gallery, the Power Plant is able to operate as a showcase for world-class art in a variety of media, complemented with lectures and guest speakers.

A short walk along the shoreline from the central Harbourfront complex is Toronto's unique Music Garden. Acclaimed cellist Yo-Yo Ma, inspired by the music of Johann Sebastian Bach, designed this landscaped park space. Visitors can join a guided tour or pick up audio devices from Harbourfront for an aurally enhanced walkabout of the garden. In summers, the Music Garden features free concerts and dance programming.

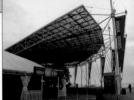

Molson Bandshell at Harbourfront

Harbourfront pays tribute to the city's marine tradition with various institutions and programs. In the summer, a variety of craft such as Canadian Coast Guard vessels, historical tall ships from around the world and Greenpeace ships dock here and are open for public tours. Several boat and charter companies dock along the shoreline and offer tours of the city from the water, including nighttime dinner and entertainment in warm weather. The Nautical Centre offers activities and rentals for water sport enthusiasts. Berthing for craft of varying sizes is available in three locations along the Inner Harbour.

Dennis Griots,
Harbourfront World
Stage Festival

Andrea Nann,
Dreamwalker
Dance Company,
Harbourfront's
NextSteps

Events and Activities at Harbourfront

Harbourfront not only presents cultural events, it also supports new work in the arts by awarding commissions through its Fresh Ground awards program. This program provides funding for creations and installations in all disciplines of the arts, which then become part of the programming at the Centre and keep the rotation of material fresh and current. The HATCH incubator program encourages original new work in the performing arts through residencies and expertise, showcased in a springtime series at the Studio Theatre.

Harbourfront also hosts several diverse cultural festivals throughout the year. Different communities hold weekend-long ethnic festivals that incorporate music, theatre and dance into their lineups. These include the Ashkenaz Jewish Festival, the Mexican Day of the Dead celebrations, Carnivallissima and more. Each festival immerses the visitor in activities, music and presentations all over Harbourfront Centre, and offers ethnic food, for a holistic experience of that particular community, both in Toronto and from the world at large.

The Centre has a dramatic spring lineup, with the World Stage Festival, which gives audiences a chance to enjoy boutique productions selected from around the world. In a springtime series of productions at the York Quay Centre, HATCH presents the results of the Harbourfront's program to encourage new theatrical and performance pieces. Spring is also the season for the Milk International Children's Festival, which includes events and activities as well as theatre and musical performances geared for both children and families.

The highlight of the fall season is the International Festival of Authors (IFOA), a world-class series that brings writers from all over Canada and around the globe to Toronto for talks, soirees and readings. Also in the fall, HarbourKIDS provides an ongoing series of child-friendly activities meant to engage young imaginations and raise kids' interest in the arts. The lineup includes film shorts, crafts workshops, shows and interactive exhibits all day long over the course of a weekend.

From fall through spring, the

relatively new NextSteps festival showcases local talent, reflecting the diverse origins of Toronto's population and its fusion of sensibilities in the Canadian milieu.

Distillery District

A national historical site, the Distillery District was founded in 1832 and spans more than 5 hectares of downtown Toronto. Here pedestrians roam the cobblestone walks to take in the art, culture and entertainment of this focal point of creativity.

Once the Gooderham and Worts Distillery, the largest distillery in the British Empire, the more than forty buildings today offer something for everyone. The centre displays the 175 plus years of the district's history, including artifacts and memorabilia. It also offers informative walking and audio tours that can be reserved ahead of time. And visitors can sign up for a Segway HT tour to take a spin around this historically rich area.

As for retail, the area boasts everything from home furnishings, denim and handmade jewellery to automobile memorabilia, hand-crafted tiles and home audio/video systems.

The galleries cover a wide spectrum of the arts. Visitors can soak up the masterpieces of new and established artists including photographers, painters and sculptors at: Arta Gallery, Artcore, The Blue Dot, Bravo-sud, Corkin Gallery, distill, Gibsone Jessop, Julie M. Gallery, le laboratoire d'art (LABO), Monte Clark, Pikto, PROOF Studio Gallery, Redeye Studio, Shao Design and Thompson Landry. The Deaf Culture Centre pays homage to internationally known deaf artists and has an interactive sign-language centre, and the Sport Gallery celebrates the art and history of sports photography.

Those who like to relax after touring around can do just that at the Oasis Wellness Centre and Spa, with hot-stone massages, facials, manicures, pedicures and body wraps. This area also has several cafés and restaurants where diners can take in the best-preserved Victorian industrial architecture in North America or a brewery tour at the Mill Street Brew Pub. And there are sixteen theatres where after-dinner performances can be enjoyed.

Top: Balzac's.
Centre: Goodherham Worts sign.
Bottom: Mill Street Brew Pub

Civic Centre: City Halls Old and New and Osgoode Hall

Ice-skating at Nathan Phillips

Osgoode Hall

Old City Hall

New City Hall

Square is a winter ritual for any Torontonian, but the public space that rolls out in front of New City Hall is a central beacon for outdoor events in any season. Concerts, farmers' markets, exhibitions and, of course, skating go on all year round outside, while the city's civic activities take place inside the uniquely designed building. City Council's chamber is situated in a saucer-shaped pod that sits between two curved towers. The architecture was a radical shift for the city, as was the design competition that brought it forward. Mayor Nathan Phillips put out an international call for submissions, and the winning design was from Finnish architect Viljo Revell, who sadly died one year before the building was completed in 1965.

Old City Hall, still standing next door to its modern successor, celebrated its centennial in 1999 and now houses municipal courts. The Romanesque revival building was constructed using local stone from the Credit River Valley and features a massive clock tower and stone caricatures representing politicians of the time. The monument faced demolition in the 1960s when nearby Eaton Centre was under construction and New City Hall had already been built. Citizens vehemently protested, and Old City Hall was ultimately declared a national historic site in 1989.

Revell's radically designed structure separates Old City Hall from its architectural mate, Osgoode Hall down the street. Osgoode is also a nineteenth-century design and currently boasts immaculate gardens behind an elaborate wrought iron gate that was originally erected to keep out grazing cows from nearby farms.

Named after Ontario's first chief justice, William Osgoode, it has been in the hands of the Law Society of Upper Canada and the Ontario Government since 1840. The heritage building housed Osgoode Law School until 1969 and is currently home to the Ontario Court of Appeal and the Superior Court of Justice. The structure has seen a number of restorations and expansions over the years, and many architectural achievements have resulted. The Great Library, for example, with its cork floors, magnificent ceiling and etched glass has been touted as the most beautiful room in Canada.

Queen's Park
Standing at the head of University Avenue, the Ontario Legislative building — often referred to

simply as Queen's Park — is a masterpiece of carved red sandstone. Built between 1888 and 1892 by British-born (but American-based) architect Richard Waite, it is the seat of Ontario's government and houses the Legislative Assembly of Ontario.

Walkway, Queen's Park

Open to the public on weekdays when the Legislature is sitting, and throughout the week during the summer, Queen's Park is also a fascinating museum and art gallery filled with statues, oil paintings and monuments to Ontario's incredible history.

In 1910, after fire destroyed the Legislature's west wing, Toronto architect E. J. Lennox (Old City Hall, Casa Loma) added a white and grey marble stairwell pier that rises to the top, giving the newly rebuilt west wing a light, airy feel. He also added a luxurious apartment at the rear of the wing that to this day is the official residence of Ontario's Lieutenant-Governor.

Behind the Legislature Building is Queen's Park itself — one of the oldest urban parks in Canada, opened in 1860 by the Prince of Wales (later King Edward VII) and named for his mother, Queen

Looking downtown from Queen's Park

Victoria. The equestrian statue of Edward VII that stands in the middle of the park originally stood in Delhi, but was removed along with all other British commemorative statuary when India was granted independence in 1947. A war memorial dedicated to the 48th Highlanders of Canada is located at the northern end of the park, and the Ontario Veterans

University College,
University of
Toronto

Munk Centre for
International
Studies, U of T

MUNK CENTRE
FOR INTERNATIONAL STUDIES

Memorial was recently opened at the park's southern end at Queen's Park Crescent, in front of the Legislature building.

The Legislature offers guided and self-guided tours, and for the hungry visitor there is a cafeteria in the basement that offers very good food at modest prices — as one might expect in a place of work for Parliamentarians!

University of Toronto

The St. George main campus of the University of Toronto is situated downtown, bordered by Bay Street and Spadina Avenue to the east and west, and by Bloor and College Streets to the north and south. The campus presents many different options in the realms of art, design, discussions and lectures, film and theatre, as well as incredible walking opportunities in a parklike setting surrounded by a rich display of architectural styles.

The main campus is home to numerous galleries, catering to a diverse range of interests. The University of Toronto Art Centre comprises eight galleries of permanent and travelling exhibitions featuring architecture, contemporary and historical objects, decorative and fine arts and photography.

The Eric Arthur Gallery, on the main public level of the Faculty of Architecture, Landscape and Design, presents exhibitions of architecture, landscape architecture, urban design and allied design fields. Opened in 2001, the gallery consists of three spaces, including a dramatic bay window that cantilevers from the historic building and overlooks

College Street. The Justina M. Barnicke Gallery at Hart House specializes in Canadian art exhibitions, both historical and contemporary. And the Thomas Fisher Rare Book Library houses special collections including books, manuscripts and other materials and features exhibits on these works.

U of T Varsity Stadium

Numerous concerts, film festivals and screenings and theatrical productions run throughout the year, catering to a wide range of tastes. The MacMillan Theatre was designed for the presentation of operas, concerts and recitals, and Convocation Hall — built in 1907 — has hosted contemporary pop and rock performances in addition to lectures, ceremonial functions and movie screenings.

For film buffs, Innis Town Hall and the Isabel Bader Theatre have played host to the annual Canadian Film Centre's Worldwide Short Film Festival. Innis Town Hall also hosts regular screenings, lectures and film festivals (Indie Can Film Festival, Macedonian Film Festival, After Dark Film Festival and others). Every Friday night since 1978, storytellers and listeners have been gathering for an open evening of stories in the Innis Cafe for the unique 1001 Nights of Storytelling.

Walkway, University of Toronto

Several U of T venues play host to the annual Nuit Blanche festival — art installations, all-night exhibits, live performances and creative programs presented from sunset on Saturday to sunrise on Sunday during late September.

For a brief escape from the bustling downtown without having to go too far, or simply for a little outdoor fix, the St. George campus is also perfect for leisurely strolling and sightseeing in all seasons, and provides an abundance of photography subjects: new blossoms in spring, the full canopy cover in summer, a bright array of autumn colours or dazzling snow-covered branches and rooftops.

Founded in 1827 and continuously growing, the University exhibits classic and modern architectural styles. Ranging from mid-nineteenth-century Romanesque revival architecture to 1960s minimalist modernism and beyond, the grounds display the U of T's past and present and its harmonious blending between styles, as befits a place of coming together, learning and experiencing life in all of its forms.

The University of Toronto is within walking distance of the Royal Ontario Museum, the Gardiner Museum, the Bata Shoe Museum and the Art Gallery of Ontario and is accessible by subway, streetcar, bus and car.

Casa Loma and Spadina House

Casa Loma

In 1912, after making a fortune selling electricity at an enormous profit to the Province of Ontario, Sir Henry Pellatt set out to build himself the definitive dream home: Casa Loma. Situated at the top of a hill where Spadina and Davenport Roads cross, this castle-like mansion overlooks the city's downtown core. A tribute to the Faustian ambitions of one Toronto's most famous businessmen, Casa Loma is truly spectacular. But, in its own way, it is also a warning to those who haven't learned to temper their dreams.

Casa Loma steps from Davenport

To construct his castle, Pellatt hired one of Toronto's greatest architects, Edward James Lennox. Together, the pair travelled to Europe gathering ideas for the businessman's vision. It was Lennox — whose previous architectural work in Toronto included City Hall (opened in 1899 and now known as Old City Hall) and the King Edward Hotel (1903) — who managed to rein in Pellatt's ambitious idea of building a massive home not only for himself and Lady Pellatt, but for visiting British Royalty too.

Lennox's calming influence over the towering figure of Pellatt (he stood 6 ft 5 in) ultimately made the castle more appealing. This monumental home had everything a self-styled baron of industry could want, including ninety-eight rooms, three bowling alleys, twenty-five fireplaces, state-of-the-art electric power, a telephone exchange (connecting sixty in-house telephones) and an elevator.

At a cost of $3 million, it took 300 workers three years to build Henry Pellatt's magnificent home, complete with stables that were more luxurious than many of the finest homes in the city. Sadly Pellatt, the romantic adventurer, athlete, military leader and financier, only lived in the great home for less than ten years, losing his entire fortune to bad business deals after the First World War. In 1939, the once wealthy Sir Henry died almost penniless. Torontonians — inspired by the businessman's passionate if not somewhat Quixotic

Casa Loma

Casa Loma

vision — still accorded him the largest funeral Toronto had ever seen.

For a while, the castle on the hill was turned into a hotel but was taken over in the late 1930s by the Kiwanis Club of Toronto, which still operates it as a major tourist attraction for the City of Toronto, attracting half-a-million visitors a year. Guided tours of Casa Loma are available for visitors.

Spadina House

Once the hilltop estate of the powerful Austin family, this Victorian mansion is an exquisite reminder of how the very rich lived in Toronto at the height of the Victorian era.

The first house to stand on the site was built in 1818 by William Warren Baldwin, who constructed a small one-storey Georgian-style cottage. When that house burned to the ground in 1835, a larger home was built and passed on to Baldwin's son Robert, the man who would introduce responsible government to Parliament (the system in which members of the

Hippopotamus at the Toronto Zoo

Cabinet are responsible to the elected House) and thereby paved the way for the Dominion of Canada to be created in 1867. In 1866 James Austin, a prominent nineteenth-century Toronto businessman, bought the house, demolished it and began to build what eventually became the imposing home that stands there today.

The name of the home is pronounced correctly as Spa-deen-a, and is derived from a First Nation's word meaning "rise in the hill." Most Torontonians, however, refer to it as Spa-dine-a House — a quirk of local pronunciation that visitors should be aware of when asking for directions.

With its glass-roofed *porte cochère* and brilliant palm room overlooking a sweeping lawn, Spadina House was once the centre of social activity for Toronto's elite. And unlike its grander, more imposing neighbour next door, Casa Loma, which was abandoned after only twelve years, Spadina House was occupied from the time it was first constructed until 1982.

Today, Spadina House is a museum showcasing the life of the gentry in early Toronto. Supervised tours of this grand home are included with the price of admission.

Toronto Zoo

To keep the kids entertained for hours on end, or for an enjoyable time in the great outdoors at a leisurely pace, Toronto Zoo is the place. Lions, tigers, bears and other favourites grace the grounds of the zoo, along with many lesser-known species.

Elephant at the Toronto Zoo

First opened in 1974, the Toronto Zoo was designed to house animals in outdoor and indoor enclosures that reflect the geographic regions they come from, as opposed to grouping them by type. A Siberian Tiger, for example, is not housed right next to an African lion. The two species live in the Eurasia and Africa pavilions respectively. One of the first zoos to be created in this fashion, it gives visitors a sense of which animals coexist in what environments. It also provides habitats that are more accommodating to its furry,

feathered or scaled residents. The drawback is that it can be very difficult to spot some animals at times in some of the larger outdoor enclosures. In addition to the great care that is put into its animal conservation efforts, the Toronto Zoo is heavily involved in leading-edge reproductive, veterinary and behavioural research.

Summer is the best time to enjoy all of the outdoor activities and enclosures that the zoo has to offer, but it is also the busiest time of year — crowds and lineups are to be expected. Regardless of crowds it is almost impossible to cover the entire zoo in one day, especially with children in tow. With more than 5,000 animals, displays, shows, rides and 10 km of walking trails spread over 287 hectares, the zoo experience can easily cover two days.

Constant improvements to the habitat areas mean that some animals are not on display at times, but if that is a factor in choosing a time to visit, the zoo's website does list what environments are undergoing renovations and what animals may be unavailable. It also lists special and feature exhibits to further assist in planning a visit.

For meal and refreshment breaks the zoo has several fast-food locations, cafés and restaurants. Visitors are also permitted to bring in their own picnics, and will find many picnic tables situated throughout the zoo site.

Below: The Molson Amphitheatre; Bottom: Ontario Place entrance

Ontario Place
Ontario Place is one of Toronto's busiest and most renowned entertainment destinations, attracting both visitors and long-time residents. South of Exhibition Place, on the shores of Lake Ontario, the theme park operates on a seasonal schedule,

35

Ontario Science Centre, exterior

IMAX Theatre, Ontario Science Centre

traditionally intended to draw a family audience with activities for children as its focus. Opened in 1971, Ontario Place remains an agency of the province, subsidized to keep its venues, rides and attractions accessible to the public at a cost lower than most similar amusement parks.

Toronto's rapid development throughout much of the twentieth century had a negative effect on the city's waterfront, with much of the lakeside area heavily industrialized and cut off from the city proper. The idea to build an aesthetically vivid park on Lake Ontario evolved out of the need to remedy that problem and renew the city's potential.

Ground was broken on March 17, 1969, and following two years of construction Ontario Place finally opened to great acclaim, heralded as a modern, futuristic architectural achievement. The construction phase involved the sinking of three decommissioned Great Lakes freighters, the hulls of which would serve as a bulwark against the erosive effect of the lake itself. Covered in concrete and anchored to Lake Ontario's stone bottom, the result was three man-made islands, each measuring 20 hectares, accommodating the many venues and facilities to follow.

The design of Ontario Place was fitting for the early 1970s, with kaleidoscopic, flashy colours splashed across its walls, walkways and grounds. Many of the attractions that were featured at the park's opening no longer exist, including the HMCS *Haida*, a Second World War destroyer that remained at the site until 2002. Today, *Haida* is in Hamilton, Ontario, restored and reopened as a maritime museum. The Forum, one of Ontario Place's earliest landmarks, was lauded for its architectural innovation. It was dismantled in 1995 to make way for the Molson Amphitheatre, a larger open-air concert venue.

Among Ontario Place's other attractions is one of

the city's most visually iconic landmarks, the Cinesphere. Its domed design houses the world's first permanent IMAX theatre, with a towering sixty-foot screen and seating capacity for 752 people. Its presence at the park is a focal point for Toronto's residents, a symbolic structure reminiscent of places like "Spaceship Earth" at Walt Disney World's Epcot Center.

Challenge Zone, Ontario Science Centre

Ontario Science Centre

Entertaining and educational? Sounds like a tall order, but for more than thirty-five years the Ontario Science Centre has delivered — and shows no sign of slowing. With nine exhibition halls spanning five levels down the slope of the picturesque Don Valley, the Centre has enough visuals, displays, live demonstrations and interactive areas to suit the preferences of any child or adult.

Diverse exhibition halls to explore include "Living Earth," containing a walk-through jungle, whale skeleton, tornado chamber and other natural science wonders; "Sport," where visitors can actually test mind and body in athletic situations such as a baseball pitching cage, judge a figure skating competition and learn how technology is changing athletics; and "KidSpark," an area designed for children aged eight and under that teaches through play. Demonstrations of papermaking, rock polishing, punch-card loom designs, short-wave radio operation and the ever-popular Electricity Demo (how high will your hair stand up?) are held at various times daily. Also on-site is the only

Ontario Science Centre activity

IMAX Dome theatre in Canada (admission extra), where visually stunning and educational films are shown on a screen 4,500 times bigger than an average TV.

In addition to its permanent lineup, the Centre hosts many temporary and travelling exhibits. In 2007 it featured the Marvel Super Heroes Science Exhibition and Titanic: The Artifact Exhibition, both of which drew the attention and wonder of kids and adults of all ages.

Although the Centre, a barrier-free facility, is suitable for all ages, children should be at least eight to ten years of age to

Toronto Eaton Centre, Dundas and Yonge

get the most out of their day as there is a fair amount of reading material and complexity. Crowds are steady during the summer, and school trips to the Centre are the norm on weekdays during the school year. Food options consist of a café and a cafeteria-style hall providing pizza, burgers, sandwiches and salads. Bring-your-own lunches are permitted, with outdoor picnic tables and a designated indoor dining hall.

Yonge Street & Eaton Centre

At the corner of Queen Street West and Yonge Street is the Toronto Eaton Centre, one of the largest shopping malls and office complexes in the city.

With more than 300 stores the Eaton Centre is one of the most-visited tourist attractions in the city. The Centre retains its original name despite the demise of the Eaton's shopping chain itself in 1999. It rests on the site of the original Eaton's store, neighbouring Old City Hall and the Church of the Holy Trinity, among the few exceptions to Eaton's prior ownership of nearly every parcel of land at the intersection of Queen and Yonge Streets. Another notable exception is the Bay on Queen West's south side, one of the first retail branches of the Hudson's

Pedestrian scramble at Yonge & Dundas Streets

Bay Company, and the physical location of a major rivalry between the two companies.

The Eaton Centre has undergone some major changes in recent years, transforming it from just another urban mall to a major metropolitan shopping centre. This downtown haven, which runs along Yonge

Street from Queen to Dundas, has recently seen the inclusion of stores such as Coach, Lucky Brand Jeans, Lacoste and Danier Leather, as well as cosmetics retailer Sephora and the Apple Store. Old favourites such as Banana Republic, GAP, Jacob, Zara and Club Monaco remain located among the Centre's three floors. Swedish retail giant H&M has built at the corner of Yonge and Dundas, and the immense, three-level store includes a children's section and two sections for women's clothing. High-end jewellers Birks and Swarovski raise the glamour quotient in the Eaton Centre, as does the St. Regis Room, which stocks brands like Armani and is located in the Bay at the Queen Street entrance. Visitors looking up to the Eaton Centre's ceiling at the south end of the mall will notice a flock of fiberglass Canada Geese. This sculpture, *Flight Stop*, was designed by Canadian artist Michael Snow and over the years has become the shopping mall's iconic symbol.

Michael Snow's *Flight Stop* sculpture, Toronto Eaton Centre

Exiting anywhere along the east side of the Eaton Centre puts the visitor on Yonge Street, a designated national historic site and — according to the Guinness Book of World Records — the longest street in the world. Yonge Street stretches from Toronto's lakeshore all the way to Rainy River, Ontario, near the border with Minnesota, a distance of approximately 1,896 km. The Canon Theatre (formerly known as the Pantages Theatre and onetime home to the long-running Phantom of the Opera musical) is located across from the Eaton Centre, as is Massey Hall, one of Toronto's premier concert venues, dating back to the nineteenth century. The southeast corner of Yonge and Dundas Streets, directly across from the north end of the Eaton Centre, is dominated by Dundas Square, a public square that was officially opened to Torontonians in November 2002. The square is frequently the site of free public concerts and festivals. Its most notable design feature is a set of ten fountains built directly into its granite slabs — the perfect place to cool down on a hot, humid summer's day. A retail and cinema complex on the north side of Dundas, currently called 10 Dundas East (it has

Dundas Square looking north to new AMC Theatre

gone through a few names so far), adds to the area's appeal and includes restaurants and movie theatres. Other notable attractions nearby range from the Hard Rock Cafe to the Elgin and Winter Garden Theatres, closer to Queen Street. For those who like to scramble across the street, a scramble or diagonal intersection that stops all traffic and allows pedestrians to cross any which way they please, is now in place at the corner of Yonge and Dundas streets.

The stretch of Yonge Street north of Dundas to Bloor is mainly known for its shopping, although the range and quality of stores here varies. Head shops mix with large retailers such as the HMV music store and the electronics giant, Future Shop. Unless you're looking for a 1970s era concert t-shirt or a bargain on a new plasma TV, the neighbourhood doesn't have that

much to offer. Torontonians have come to accept this unfortunate reality, despite their constant bellyaching about the state of this central Toronto neighbourhood. Architecturally, there is a building at the corner of Yonge and College Streets worth noting. College Park is a retail, residential and office complex originally built by Eaton's department store in the late 1920s. Designed in the art deco style, its seventh floor is home to the Carlu, an historic event space that was reopened in 2003, following a long period of decline. The restoration of this art moderne masterpiece — a real throwback to Toronto's past — may just be a harbinger of better times to come for this stretch of Yonge Street.

Massey Hall

CNE

The Canadian National Exhibition (CNE) is the largest annual fair in Canada and the fifth largest in North America. This eighteen-day fair takes place every August, concluding on Labour Day, and attracts a reported 1.3 million visitors every year.

One hundred thousand people lined up and shelled out twenty-five cents for admission to the inaugural fair in 1879. The fair was originally founded to promote the development of agriculture, industry and the arts, and visitors to the CNE in the early years enjoyed equestrian shows, strolled through art galleries and marvelled at new technology. In fact, many Canadians first listened to radio and watched television at the CNE when these technologies were unveiled at the 1922 and 1939 fairs respectively.

These days, the main attraction of "the Ex," as it is popularly known, is the midway. Blood curdling screams fill the air as thrill seekers are flipped, spun and dropped at tremendous speeds on rides with names like the Mega Drop, the Polar Express and the Fire Ball. Rides for children and less adventurous adults can be found at the kiddie midway.

The fair offers more than eighty skill-testing midway games. Visitors can knock down a stack of milk bottles with a softball or bust a balloon with a

CNE's popular
swing ride

dart and walk away with a life-sized, stuffed
SpongeBob SquarePants toy.

In addition to the midway and its rides, the CNE
hosts a stunning lineup of Canadian and international
performers to entertain the entire family each year.
Concerts by popular musicians, Broadway-themed
musical shows and death-defying acrobatic
performances are just a few of the
attractions on offer. On the Labour
Day weekend the Canadian National
Exhibition concludes with the
Canadian International Air Show, the
largest over-the-water air show in the
world, featuring the Snowbirds,
Canada's precision flying team. For
many visitors this three-day
aeronautical celebration is the
highlight of the fair.

Cotton candy, corn dogs and
popcorn are available from vendors on
the midway, and more substantial and
sophisticated fare can be purchased at
the CNE Food Building from more
than ninety vendors who offer foods
from around the world.

The Canadian National Exhibition
has been putting smiles on the faces of
Toronto's children for more than a
century. For many families a trip to
"the Ex" is a summer tradition that
spans the generations.

CNE Princess
Gates

Museums and Galleries

Deirdre Hanna

Peter Paul Rubens'
Announcement, Art
Gallery of Ontario

Toronto's major museums entered the twenty-first century with a series of ambitious, must-see architectural makeovers. The Art Gallery of Ontario (AGO) and the Royal Ontario Museum (ROM) have both been transformed, but the city's museums are more than just eye candy. They boast a wealth of treasures that eclipse their pretty new façades. The ROM's collections of Chinese antiquities, for example, remain unrivalled outside Asia, and Britain's premier sculptor, Henry Moore, bequeathed his personal studio collection of art to the AGO. Either could justify a special trip to Toronto.

Other must-see collections are housed in the city's jewel-like selection of smaller, more idiosyncratic museums with highly specialized mandates — ceramics, textiles, even shoes — which make a strong case for the notion that perfection lies in the details.

Conveniently compact, the city's museum district clusters around the University of Toronto's main downtown campus. Most lie within easy walking distance of each other (in good weather), with direct public transit connections as an alternative.

Tom Thomson's
The West Wind,
1916-17, Art Gallery
of Ontario

Art Gallery of Ontario

International architecture superstar Frank Gehry grew up within sight of the Art Gallery of Ontario, so it is only fitting that the first project to be completed in his native land by the Los Angeles-based, Pritzker Prize winner, who became a household name with his design for the Guggenheim Bilbao museum, should be the latest renovation of the AGO.

After a "dark" year in which 5,000 pieces in the AGO's 68,000-object collection were being reinstalled in the 110 galleries, the AGO reopened in late 2008 with more space for its collections in Gehry's inspired expansion of the building.

The gallery owns an outstanding collection of contemporary and historical Canadian art. Tom Thomson, Emily Carr and the members of the Group of Seven and their followers are well represented, as well as major nineteenth-century figures Cornelius Krieghoff and Royal Canadian Academy founder Lucius R. O'Brien. The AGO also safeguards a series of encyclopedic study collections acquired from the estates of twentieth-century Canadian artists Paterson Ewen, Greg Curnoe and David Milne and is aggressively working to expand its holdings of art by Canada's First Peoples.

Henry Moore Sculpture Centre, Art Gallery of Ontario

Frank Gehry's Art Gallery of Ontario

The sculptures, drawings and working maquettes given to the AGO by British sculptor Henry Moore (more than 900 in all) have been displayed in their own wing since 1974, when the collection came to the AGO as a thank-you to the people of Toronto for raising funds to purchase Moore's Archer, which is displayed in front of Toronto City Hall.

The AGO's Print and Drawings Study Centre holds a weekly open house on Wednesdays, during which visitors can enjoy informal and intimate displays of works normally held in the vaults: on any given week these thematically linked selections could feature Rembrandt etchings or rococo figure studies.

Other significant European holdings include some destination-worthy recent

43

The Michael Lee-Chin Crystal, Royal Ontario Museum

acquisitions, notably the life-sized bronze "Christ Crucified" that Italian baroque sculptor Gian Lorenzo Bernini created to use as a devotional object in his own home, and Peter Paul Rubens' "Massacre of the Innocents". When late Canadian newspaper magnate Kenneth Thomson purchased the spectacular Rubens in 2002, he set a record for the highest price ever paid for an old master painting.

Thomson's gift to the museum included not only the Rubens but also the majority of his substantial personal art collection, as well as cash to kick-start the construction of Frank Gehry's dynamic new façade and expansion for the gallery. Gehry himself has remarked that the AGO project has had profound personal resonance, noting that, "the Art Gallery of Ontario is where I first experienced art as a child…. The building we envision will connect the city and its people to great art and art experiences."

The AGO has endeavoured to keep open to visitors, at least partially, during most phases of the construction. And its original home — the Grange — has been preserved as an early nineteenth-century historic house. The Ontario College of Art and Design's over-the-top vertical extension by Will Alsop, completed in 2005, is visible from Grange Park.

Royal Ontario Museum

Canada's largest museum, and the fifth-largest in North America, the Royal Ontario Museum possesses more than six million artifacts in its world cultures and natural history collections.

The Royal Ontario Museum

The ROM's new exterior and Michael Lee-Chin Crystal expansion were designed by German architect Daniel Liebeskind, who subsequent to winning his Toronto commission won the bid to design the World Trade Center Memorial in Manhattan. Completed in 2007, the Crystal has drawn controversy since its inception, literally bursting

Engraving, Royal Ontario Museum

through the ROM's beaux-arts exterior (Darling and Pearson's original 1914 structure and Chapman and Oxley's 1933 expansion) to realign its façade with the vibrant retail strip along Bloor Street. This restores the ROM to its orientation of almost a century ago. Increasing the museum's exhibition space by 80,000 square feet, the Lee-Chin Crystal represents a significant benchmark in the museum's growth. The physical expansion complements an aggressive acquisition campaign, begun in 2000, to augment the museum's already substantial collections. Liebeskind, whose studio has designed other noted museum projects, including the Jewish Museum in Berlin, says of the ROM, "the foundation of virtually all of my work is a firm belief in culture as the driving force behind vital, creative cities and, indeed, nations."

The ROM's history has, in fact, been one of constant growth and evolution, each phase accompanied by its own controversy, including the 1968 break from the formal stewardship of the University of Toronto. Starting in the 1980s the ROM started replacing its static natural history displays with kid-friendly installations, notably a popular interactive reconstruction of a bat cave and a stunning display of birds mounted as a single flock in flight. These have been maintained on the second floor of the main building, while the substantial dinosaur display is slated to occupy a prime spot in the new Crystal.

Royal Ontario Museum ceiling

The ROM is particularly noted for its extensive collections of Middle Eastern and East Asian art, which include one of the largest collections of Chinese antiquities outside China, Canada's most extensive Japanese art collection and the nation's only collection of Korean artifacts — which contains pieces from the stone age through to the twentieth century. Other highlights include the galleries of Ancient Egypt, European history and Canadian history. The latter incorporates both

European influences and the heritage of Canada's aboriginal peoples.

Recent purchases include important fossil specimens; significant antiquities from South Asia, Persia and Egypt; artifacts from Canada's First Peoples and aboriginal communities across the globe; and "the Light of the Desert," at 900 carats the largest faceted cerussite gem in the world.

These new objects are being integrated into the ROM's existing displays as well as galleries that were being reinstalled, through 2009, following the architectural expansion. The ROM also opened galleries of artifacts from China, many of them brought to Canada with some secrecy by Anglo-Irish trader George Crofts, who was able to export thousands of objects out of the country during the political upheaval of the 1920s; a gallery of Canada's First Peoples; and galleries focusing on Judaica and the cultures of Africa (notably Egypt) ancient Cyprus, bronze-age Greece, Japan, Korea and Europe. Natural history displays include galleries of birds, mammals and reptiles and a hands-on biodiversity discovery gallery.

Galleries that recently re-opened include dinosaurs, mammals, South Asia, Middle East, textiles, Africa, the Americas and Asia Pacific. The ROM's innovative Institute of Contemporary Culture (ICC) presents a regular program of temporary exhibits that combine artifacts from the museum's vaults with contemporary art. Shape Shifters, opened in the fall of 2007, combines works by contemporary Canadian First Nations artists with aboriginal artifacts, and in 2008 an ICC display examined Charles Darwin.

Top and bottom:
Gardiner Museum
of Ceramic Art

Gardiner Museum of Ceramic Art

Works by Sèvres, Meissen, Pablo Picasso — the Gardiner Museum of Ceramic Art holds a treasure trove of exceptional pottery artifacts from Europe as well as Asian and New World antiquities.

From the time it opened its doors in 1984, directly across what was then the ROM's main entranceway on ceremonial Queen's Park Crescent, the Gardiner Museum of Ceramic Art has borne the personal stamp of it founders. Helen Gardiner remains active on the museum's board of directors. Her husband, the late financier and philanthropist George R. Gardiner, amassed a fortune through a wide-ranging career during which he founded Canada's first discount brokerage house, brought Kentucky Fried Chicken to Canada and enjoyed stints as the director of the Toronto Stock Exchange and on the committee that controlled Maple Leaf Gardens.

The Gardiners started collecting ceramics in the 1970s to embellish their home and in 1984 endowed the initial construction costs of the small, elegant museum to which they donated their — by then — extensive personal collection. This core collection consists primarily of pre-Colombian American antiquities — some dating from as early as 3000 B.C. — and an encyclopedic selection of decorative eighteenth-century European porcelain. Occupying the museum's entire second floor, the European porcelains include first-rate examples from virtually every significant European region noted for its ceramics, from Sèvres to Meissen and from Bristol to Delft. A circular display of Commedia dell'arte figurines allows visitors to carefully study the subtle stylistic differences between objects from the various European centres of production, and their chronological development through the 1700s.

The Gardiner spent a decade, from 1987 to 1997, under the management of the Royal Ontario Museum, a phase that ended with a further endowment of $15 million by its founders. The museum underwent an expansion, designed by Bruce Kuwabara of Toronto firm Kuwabara Payne McKenna Blumberg and completed in 2006, which doubled its exhibition space. This physical expansion allowed the museum to significantly increase the extent of its holdings, including pottery of the Ancient Americas; Chinese, Japanese, English and European porcelain; English Delftware; Italian Renaissance Majolica; and modern and contemporary ceramics. A new third storey holds a spacious gallery dedicated to special exhibitions and touring shows, as well as a restaurant operated by famous Canadian chef Jamie Kennedy, while a working ceramics studio in the basement level is open to members of the public on Sunday afternoons for a nominal fee that includes the cost of firing their own creations in a kiln.

Bata Shoe Museum

Bata Shoe Museum

Toronto boasts the world's only museum dedicated entirely to footwear, and contains a singular collection of more than 12,000 shoes and shoe-related objects dating from the past 4,500 years, with everything from Princess Diana's high heels and Michael Jordan's basketball shoes to the fashionable silk footwear of Louis XIV's

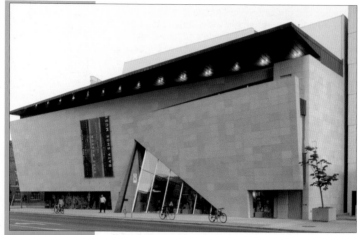

Bata Shoe Museum

well-heeled courtiers to the heart-breakingly tiny hand-embroidered shoes made by wealthy Chinese women to wear on their bound feet.

The Bata Shoe Museum, which opened at its permanent location in 1995, was designed to resemble a shoebox with its lid slightly askew by Raymond Moriyama (of Moriyama and Teshima Architects), who also designed the Ontario Science Centre in Toronto and the National War Museum in Ottawa. The Bata resides a short walk — one subway stop — west of the Royal Ontario Museum.

The museum's core collection was amassed over decades of passionate study by Sonja Bata, a Swiss-trained architect who, in 1946, married a Czech "shoe man" whose family business was nationalized by the communist government in what was then Czechoslovakia. From their base in Canada the Batas rebuilt the international company and, while travelling on business, Sonja Bata picked up an extensive collection of traditional and historic shoes. In 1979 she created the Bata Shoe Museum Foundation and started funding research trips to study the traditional footwear of circumpolar regions including the Canadian Arctic, Greenland and Siberia. These boots, along with Mrs. Bata's personal collection, form the museum's core collection.

At any given time the museum displays as many as half a dozen rotating exhibits examining in depth various aspects of the museum's collection, while a permanent exhibit on the lower level provides a survey of the collection.

During the construction of the current building the shoe museum briefly operated out of the mezzanine-level space in the Colonnade, a mixed-use retail and residential structure in the same city block as the Gardiner Museum. This space is now occupied by the Japan Foundation, a cultural arm of the Japanese government, which regularly hosts first-rate exhibitions of historic and contemporary Japanese art and design.

University of Toronto Art Centre

Toronto's museums tend to cluster around the University of Toronto's downtown facilities, but the University of Toronto Art Centre operates as a small but satisfying museum at the heart of the St. George campus. With more than 550 square metres of exhibition space and 5,200 objects in its collection, the U of T Art Centre ranks as the third-largest fine art gallery in Toronto. Special exhibitions tend to alternate between displays of historic art — past examples include a survey of Renaissance Marion art from the former Peruvian empire and highlights from the National Gallery of Bermuda — to contemporary exhibits such as working drawings by architect Frank Gehry or recent projection-based imagery.

Founded in 1996 and housed in a wing of University College's fine nineteenth-century Romanesque revival compound, the Art Centre is the official repository of the Lillian Malcove, University College and University of Toronto art collections. Collection highlights include Lucas Cranach the Elder's 1538 "Adam and Eve", more than 100 Byzantine and post-Byzantine icons and substantial holdings of art by important Canadian artists. A selection from the permanent collection is always on display, and at any given time visitors can expect to see an eclectic mix that could include works by members of the Group of Seven plus pieces by Cathy Daley, Kazuo Nakamura and Harold Town.

Kimono, Japan, early 20th century, Textile Museum of Canada

Festival Hat, China, late 19th to early 20th century, Textile Museum of Canada

Textile Museum of Canada

Hidden behind an unlikely façade — the side door of a hotel and condo development just north of Toronto City Hall — lies the lush world of tapestries and carpets, ikats and indigo-dyed fabric, lace and embroideries that make up the core of the Textile Museum of Canada collection.

While the exterior doesn't look particularly promising, Canada's only textile museum offers

some of the most consistently insightful and provocative programming in the city. In 2006, for example, the museum won six awards from the Ontario Association of Art Galleries, including "Exhibition of the Year" for Jennifer Angus's *A Terrible Beauty*, which featured thousands of insects pinned to the walls in repeating patterns.

Visitors can expect to see a mix of displays that illustrates aspects of contemporary fibre-art practice, traditional textile techniques and historic treasures from some of the 200 cultures represented in the collection, as well as provocative glimpses at how textile technologies reflect — and often create — the social and industrial history of the human race. The crafty side of textiles is on view, too, and the museum shop sells an impressive array of fibre-based crafts by Canadian artisans and textiles from around the world.

The Textile Museum of Canada was founded in 1975 by Simon Waegemaekers and Max Allen, the latter of whom continues as the gallery's director. In 1989 the museum moved from its original tiny space in Mirvish Village to its current four-storey, 2,300-square-metre suite of galleries.

Max Leser's *Circular Scent Bottle*, 1982, Design Exchange

Design Exchange

Housed in the stylish 1937 moderne George and Moorehouse-designed structure built to house the Toronto Stock Exchange, North America's only design

promotion centre, the Design Exchange — or DX — is located in the heart of Canada's largest financial district, at Bay and King streets. Opened as a museum after the stock exchange relocated in 1983, the Design Exchange does double duty as a convention centre, and is particularly popular for professional events held within the industrial and graphic design communities.

A ground-floor exhibition space showcases selections from the DX's permanent collection of exemplary Canadian design from 1945 to the present, such as Torontonian Julian Rowan's iconic 1955 electric kettle or Nova Scotia's Clairtone stereo speakers. Additional entry-level displays, which can be seen free of charge, typically include finalists and winning entries from recent industrial design competitions. More ambitious touring exhibitions, which include shows of anything from Japanese graphic arts to industrial products designed to enhance accessibility for disabled people, are mounted in a spacious suite of third-floor galleries overlooking the bustle of Bay Street. In recent summers these main galleries have been taken over by design-oriented theme camps for children. Even when the main galleries are "dark," however, the DX merits a visit, as the original 900-square-metre trading floor, located one storey above street level, is open for viewing. It is a prime example of a period interior and is decorated with murals

Museum of Contemporary Canadian Art

by Canadian painter Charles Comfort, who also designed the relief limestone frieze that graces the DX exterior. And the light fixture suspended in the stairwell leading up to the trading floor is a fine example of deco design — the first fluorescent light to be installed in Canada.

Museum Of Contemporary Canadian Art

Since moving from North York to its new digs in the nexus of Toronto's booming West Queen West gallery district in 2005, the Museum of Contemporary Canadian Art wasted no time in establishing itself as a prime destination to view cutting-edge Canadian and international contemporary art. MOCCA presents works by established and emerging Canadian artists in an international context. Between 2005 and 2007 this ambitious institution mounted more than 40 exhibitions and projects in its elegant Queen West digs and at offsite locations in Canada and the USA, China, France, Italy, Germany, Spain and Taiwan. Crowds of more than 800 regularly attend MOCCA's openings.

While its name implies a collecting mandate — and between its foundation in 1985 (as the Art Gallery of North York) and 1998 it amassed a collection of 400 works by 150 contemporary Canadian artists — MOCCA's acquisitions program remains on hold.

Installation view of *Unholy Alliance: art + fashion meet again*, Museum of Contemporary Canadian Art

Currently, MOCCA operates as an arms-length agency of the City of Toronto's Culture Division. It's a radical — and welcome — diversion from its roots as an adjunct to now-disgraced theatrical impresario Garth Drabinsky's LiveEnt empire, when it was housed in a wing of the North York Centre for the Performing Arts and funded by a surcharge on every ticket sold.

Independent Galleries

Tanya Gulliver

Kinsman Robinson Galleries, Yorkville

Toronto's art scene is continually changing and growing at a tremendous rate. Galleries are opening up throughout Toronto, as the city increasingly becomes a hot spot for international art. In addition to the traditional areas such as Yorkville, which continue to draw attention to local and international artists, amazing new art districts are popping up all over the city.

From Canada's oldest fine art gallery — the Roberts Gallery at 641 Yonge Street was established in 1842 — to Toronto's Art and Design District on Queen Street West, Toronto has something for everyone. Many galleries in Toronto are closed on Monday, and it's a good idea to call ahead for the hours of operation.

Yorkville

Founded in 1830, Yorkville has transformed from primarily a residential area, first to a bohemian/hippie locale and then to the area of upscale and trendy stores, condos, hotels and galleries it is today. The first gallery district in Toronto, Yorkville continues to showcase high-end art from many well-known Canadian and international artists.

The Mira Godard Gallery (22 Hazelton Avenue) is one of the largest commercial galleries in Canada. Printmaker Stu Oxley, abstract artist Yves Gaucher and sculptor Joe Fafard are just a few of the many well-known and award-winning Canadian artists Goddard represents. Songwriter Leonard Cohen has exhibited annually for the past few years, including 2009's exhibition "Re-Visit," at The Drabinsky Gallery at 114 Yorkville Avenue, in the heart of Yorkville. Featuring contemporary art, the gallery focuses on emerging and mid-career Canadian artists.

Godard, Drabinsky and their counterparts, the Ingram Gallery, the Hollander York Gallery and many others, showcase mainstream and senior artists.

West Queen West — Art and Design District

Queen Street from Bathurst west to Dufferin is Toronto's "Art and Design District," but most people just call it West Queen West. It's a dynamic breeding ground for emerging and diverse artists that blossomed in the early 1990s. Often compared to SoHo for its mix of lofts, cafés, funky shops and galleries, Queen Street West is home to more than forty galleries, as well as the Museum of Contemporary Canadian Art. Just off the main drag the side streets are also crowded with galleries, especially Ossington Avenue, which is home to Lennox Contemporary, Xpace, Gallery TPW and InterAccess, among others.

West Queen West early adopters Katharine Mulherin and Jamie Angell are joined by newer gallery owners such as Clint Roenisch and youngster Thrush Holmes of Thrush Holmes Empire. Mulherin's Contemporary Art Projects has grown from one storefront location in 1998 into three galleries at two locations: 1082 and 1086 Queen Street West. An ongoing presence on Queen, Mulherin focuses on the work of emerging and mid-career artists, including the stunningly detailed ink drawings of Oscar De Las Flores and the mixed-media found artistry of Clint Griffin.

Spadina-Richmond-King

A trip down Spadina towards King finds another diverse group of galleries set in the midst of Toronto's Chinatown.

80 Spadina plays host to a range of galleries, including the Ryerson Gallery and the Leo Kamen Gallery. The former showcases the work of students from Ryerson's School of Image Arts, whereas the latter focuses on contemporary Canadian artists, including John Kissick and Patrick Mahon. The Moore Gallery is also at this location.

At 451 King the

Katharine Mulherin Contemporary Art Projects

Nicholas Metivier Gallery represents award-winning photographer Edward Burtynsky, the subject of the award-winning film *Manufactured Landscapes*, which explores the effects of industry in China. Metivier, who spent twenty-two years at Yorkville's Mira Goddard Gallery, also represents Montreal-based Sanchez brothers Carlos and Jason, whose often disturbing, yet always powerful photographs capture disconcerting scenes of death and life.

401 Richmond houses 140 cultural producers and small businesses, including many art galleries. It is home to many of Toronto's oldest established member-run galleries, including A Space, WARC Gallery (Women's Art Resource Centre), and YYZ Artists' Outlet. WARC offers interesting exhibits but goes further by developing educational programs for schools and operating a Curatorial Research Library on women artists. Also at 401 Richmond is the Wynick/Tuck Gallery, which represents many established artists including Dyan Marie, Sara Angelucci, David Askevold and Lawrence Weiner.

Closeup, Hang Man Gallery

The quirky Ydessa Hendeles Art Foundation is at 778 King Street West and only opens Saturdays from noon to 5:00 p.m. Hendeles has an impressive collection of avant-garde art and creates unique, long-running exhibits based on her collection. In 2003 her award-winning *Same Differences* exhibit featured photos of people with their teddy bears — many taken in Nazi Germany — alongside work by Maurizio Cattelan, Walker Evans, Gustave Le Gray and Douglas Gordon.

The Distillery District and East End Galleries

Formerly the Gooderham and Worts Distillery, this 5-hectare national historic site located at 55 Mill Street is a pedestrian-only village full of unique businesses, artisans, galleries and North America's largest collection of Victorian industrial architecture.

Steven Schwartz and Chris Knights are new transplants to the Distillery District; located in Building #37, they moved in 2009 after several years on West Queen West. Their artists include radical neoist, mixed-media/performance artist Istvan Kantor, steel sculptor Cory Fuhr and Ryan Van Der Hout, who creates photograms through manipulating non-traditional photographic processes. The Thompson Landry Gallery also expanded in 2009, opening a new site in Building #32 in addition to their original in #5.

Petroff Gallery

With their motto of "Tout Quebec, tout le temps..."
(All Quebec, all the time) they showcase the best and
brightest of Quebec's emerging artists, as well as a
collection of masters including A.Y. Jackson and Henri
Masson. Over in Building #74, Red Eye Studio Gallery
is an artist-run location featuring contemporary artists
working in painting, drawing, sculpture and mixed
media.

On the other side of the Don Valley in Riverdale a
new fledgling gallery area has been developing. Queen
Street East aims to rival its counterpart, West Queen
West. Artists needing cheaper housing and workspace
have moved here, and a community of restaurants,
stores and galleries is gradually growing. The
HangMan Gallery at 756 Queen Street East is a not-
for-profit gallery providing a location for the Artists'
Network, as well as fully juried individual and group
exhibitions from Toronto, elsewhere in Canada and
beyond. A couple of doors away is another artist-run
centre — the Eastern Front Gallery. Both galleries
feature work of new and
emerging local artists.

Throughout the City

New art areas are emerging
regularly in Toronto. Along
Roncesvalles, Dundas West
near Lansdowne,
Harbourfront, Morrow Ave,
Eglinton West and in many
other places there are
galleries to explore.

Petroff Gallery

Tucked away on a small
street near Dundas West
and Roncesvalles, there are
three interesting galleries on
Morrow Avenue. The Peak
Gallery at 23 Morrow
features new and emerging
Canadian and international artists. Next door at the
Christopher Cutts Gallery (21 Morrow Ave) there is a
focus on mid-career abstract artists. Across the
courtyard is the Olga Korper Gallery, featuring the
stunning photographs of Robert Mapplethorpe, the
sculptures of Reinhard Reitzenstein and the paintings
of Denyse Thomasos. Drive up Roncesvalles and leave
via Dundas West to find a few more scattered galleries.

A trip north to Eglinton West is worthwhile to see
the Petroff Gallery alone, although there are other
galleries nearby in Forest Hill including the Lonsdale
Gallery, featuring Philip Iverson, Sheila Gregory and
Ilan Wolff. Formerly the Show of Hands Gallery,
Petroff features a bright storefront window that draws
attention on this busy street of shops, bars and
restaurants. Petroff specializes in three-dimensional art,
including glass, ceramics and woodworking.

Theatre and Dance

Marichka Melnyk

CanStage's Dream in High Park

Toronto's theatre and performing arts scene is one of the best reasons to visit the city, and has put it on the global map as a major cultural heir to London and New York. Offerings range from a repertoire of well-known plays of various eras, to popular musicals, to groundbreaking new works that showcase both Canadian and international talents.

Listings for current productions can be found online at the artistic companies' websites, and reviews are regularly published in the mainstream press and the free independent newspapers distributed around downtown: *NOW* and *eye weekly*. Local broadcasters, including CBC Radio One (99.1 FM in Toronto), also frequently provide commentaries and overviews on what's currently playing around the city.

Theatre

Toronto's mainstream, big-name play and mega-musical offerings are dominated by the company created by David Mirvish and his late father Ed, which presents its shows in four major theatres downtown.

Two are on King Street West in the city's entertainment district. Those seeking a classic atmosphere will find it at the Royal Alexandra Theatre, a national historic monument built with a royal patent from King Edward VII, which celebrated its 100th birthday in 2007. Ed Mirvish restored it to its original elegance. It was once the place where Torontonians came to see performances by everyone from Edith Piaf and Orson Welles to the Marx Brothers and Mae West. The Edwardian influence is also apparent in the remarkably steep slope of the balcony seating, and the limitation of wheelchair and accessible seating to orchestra levels. Since its restoration, the Royal Alex, as it is known, has been home to crowd-pleasing musicals like *Rent* and *Mamma Mia!*.

A block away from the stately Royal Alex is its shiny new successor, the Princess of Wales Theatre, which opened with the blockbuster musical *Miss Saigon*. The 2000-seat theatre is roomy and contemporary, built to accommodate large crowds and the technological demands of modern blockbuster shows. As a result the "PoW" hosts some of the city's largest productions — among them *The Lion King*, the world premiere of the musical based on Tolkien's *Lord of the Rings*, and a new production of *The Sound of Music*.

Royal Alexandra Theatre

The third jewel in the Mirvish crown is the Canon Theatre, uptown from King Street near the Eaton Centre. Formerly known as the Pantages, an old vaudeville house, it was renovated to its original glamour. Best known for its ten-year reign as the home of the popular Andrew Lloyd Webber musical *The Phantom of the Opera*, the Canon has also welcomed other well-known international productions such as *The Colour Purple* and *Spamalot*.

Up Yonge Street from the Canon is the Panasonic Theatre, formerly the New Yorker, a cozy space whose shape visibly carries traces of its past as a movie theatre. Located on Yonge, just south of the major intersection at Bloor, the Panasonic features visiting shows as well as long-running popular ensemble pieces like Blue Man Group.

The Canadian Stage Company is Canada's largest contemporary English theatre company. It celebrated

Berkeley Street Theatre, Canadian Stage Company

the 20th anniversary of its emergence from a series of smaller, experimental, local theatre companies in 2007. Today it presents a full-subscription series of mostly mainstream productions each year, offering original works by Canadian writers and producers like the internationally acclaimed theatrical dance production *The Overcoat*, mixed with pieces by internationally recognized playwrights and composers like Tom Stoppard and Stephen Sondheim.

The fall-to-spring season productions are presented in either CanStage's traditional

CanStage's *Little Shop of Horrors*

CanStage's *The Elephant Man*

CanStage's *Midsummer Night's Dream*

home at the Berkeley Street Theatre, an intimate brick-lined conversion space, or at the newly renovated Bluma Appel Theatre in the St. Lawrence Centre for the Arts on Front Street near Union Station. In summer, however, the main venue is a grassy valley in High Park in the west end where CanStage presents its annual Dream in High Park — usually a family-friendly production of a Shakespearean comedy. For more than a quarter of a century now, locals and visitors alike have enjoyed the Toronto tradition of arriving in the early evening for a picnic before catching a show under the stars for the price of a pay-what-you-can ticket (although the suggested donation is $20).

The Soulpepper Theatre Company attracted attention when it appeared in 1997 because it was founded by twelve of Canada's most respected performers and artists. Their goal was to create a classical repertory company that would allow people to see Canadian interpretations of well-known plays that are often heard of, but not regularly produced, by writers ranging from Molière and Chekhov to Beckett and Pinter. In 2006 the company opened its own state-of-the-art venue called the Young Centre in Toronto's historic Distillery District, east of downtown. There it offers a full season of international classic plays, and features some of Canada's best stage actors drawn from across the country, including the Shaw and Stratford Festivals.

DanCap Productions is a new company to the Toronto scene that brings modern musicals to the city. Among their offerings are a long-running production of *Jersey Boys*, occupying the Toronto Centre for the Arts in the north end of the city, and the satirical *Toxic Avenger* musical that prompted the renovation of the Music Hall, a hundred-year-old movie theatre then concert venue on the Danforth, repurposed for stage productions.

Several smaller companies specialize in cultivating Canadian theatre, often with an alternative perspective. Three that emerged in the 1970s carved out a place as nurturers of Canadian production, and are notable for being housed in converted spaces that were once factories, stables and a bakery.

First, the Tarragon Theatre, founded in 1970, is a hothouse for original Canadian works, and considers itself a playwrights' theatre. It regularly presents new plays by established writers, including translations of works from Quebec, and acts as an incubator for rising talent.

Second, and farther from the entertainment district in the heart of downtown, the Factory Theatre — housed in a converted factory space — calls a gentrifying industrial district between King and Queen

Streets West home. Factory develops original Canadian talent as well. Its productions often echo the theatre's neighbourhood by imbuing an edgy and alternative or experimental flavour.

Third, and the oldest alternative theatre devoted to new Canadian work, is Theatre Passe Muraille, just north of Factory and Queen Street West, in a historical building on Ryerson Avenue. TPM supports fledgling companies with innovative or provocative works, and has launched many well-known Canadian actors and writers who were encouraged by the company to break new ground.

Other small theatre options include Buddies In Bad Times Theatre, located near the area commonly called the Gay Village near Church and Wellesley. Buddies is a leader in queer theatre, and features the Rhubarb Festival for new works, as well as a regular season at its Alexander Street venue.

Benevolence,
Tarragon Theatre

Several other companies around the city produce pioneering works in both conventional and unconventional venues; they range from readings to single-night events and interactive or performance art. Among the recognized names are Nightwood Theatre, Theatre Columbus, Crow's Theatre, Necessary Angel and Obsidian Theatre. There are also many small community-based companies attached to theatre spaces throughout downtown that produce interpretations of popular plays. One is the Alumnae Theatre, presenting contemporary and classical theatre; another is Canopy Theatre, which showcases young professional talent in outdoor venues like the Philosopher's Walk Stage.

Families can enjoy the child- and youth-oriented fare at the Lorraine Kimsa Theatre for Young People. The theatre both originates and imports productions, many based on popular children's books such as Mordecai Richler's *Jacob Two-Two and the Hooded Fang* or stories by Robert Munsch. The season also usually includes more serious drama for older children and new works.

Kyle Cameron in
Cranked, Lorraine
Kimsa Theatre for
Young People

One venue offering theatrical opportunities for all ages is Harbourfront Centre. As the non-profit home of various cultural and seasonal festivals, the centre brings in performers from all over the world to present theatre for various age groups and sensibilities. It also produces the World Stage festival and runs an incubator program for emerging performance projects called HATCH, to develop new talent. Theatrical performances take place all over the complex, most of them set in the York Quay Centre, which houses the Studio Theatre and Brigantine Room. Adjacent are the former ice house — now converted to the Enwave Theatre — and the award-winning Fleck Dance Theatre (formerly Premiere) on the upper floor of the Queen's Quay Terminal building, above the shops on the ground floor.

The newly renamed Sony Centre for the Performing Arts (formerly the Hummingbird Centre) on Front Street reinvented itself based on its history as a premiere venue for big productions. Opening in the 1960s as the O'Keefe Centre, it welcomed audiences

of more than 3,000 for musicals like *Camelot* and performances by internationally acclaimed performers like Harry Belafonte and Tony Bennett. It was also the long-time home for the Canadian Opera Company and National Ballet and brought performers from abroad like the Bolshoi Ballet to Toronto. Now upgrading with state-of-the-art electronic and

Sony Centre

multimedia equipment to handle the technological requirements of modern pop shows and musical performances, the theatre reopens in fall 2010 to celebrate its 50th anniversary as a contemporary popular-production space.

Dinner theatre remains a popular evening out for both locals and visitors. A favourite is the Mysteriously Yours … Mystery Theatre, where an interactive murder mystery provides a comic twist on images and genres from pop culture like *Casablanca*, Agatha Christie mystery novels and *The Sopranos* television series. Mysteriously Yours is popular for birthdays and marriage proposals, made memorable by nimble improvisation from the performers — good humour prevails to bond the viewers in a pleasant evening over an excellent meal. The theatre is located north of downtown near Yonge and Davisville, a short walk from the subway on Yonge Street, and new shows are created several times a year.

Farther afield, Stage West Mississauga offers Las Vegas-style dinner theatre on the western edges of the city, close to the airport. As part of a complex that includes hotel accommodations, a three-storey waterslide and other entertainment, Stage West offers a full season of shows ranging from musicals to performances by visiting celebrities. The theatre is an

immense space containing both table seating and plush banquettes, and guests are invited to partake in an extensive buffet before sitting back to enjoy the evening's production.

Theatre Festivals

While many theatres slow down or close for the summer, the region at large blossoms with theatre festivals that provide several weeks' worth of widely varied entertainment, including two major events, the Stratford and Shaw festivals.

Linnea Swan in *Appetite*, **Summerworks Theatre Festival**

The Fringe Festival in early July brings in over 100 productions from all over Canada and the world, all lasting ninety minutes or less and at affordable prices. The Fringe is curated by lottery, so the selection is eclectic, and several plays are presented in unconventional spaces like bars, restaurants or outdoor parks as well as regular theatres, centralized in the Annex area on Bloor Street West between Spadina and Bathurst.

The SummerWorks Festival in August is a juried festival showcasing works of varying lengths and genres, many of them original pieces being workshopped by local playwrights.

Harbourfront Centre has a dramatic spring lineup with the World Stage festival of international works, and the Milk International Children's Festival that includes other events and activities as well as theatre and musical performances. Over the summer different communities hold weekend-long ethnic festivals that incorporate music, theatre and dance into their lineups.

The internationally acclaimed Stratford and Shaw Festivals both take place outside Toronto's city limits, about two hours' drive away. Stratford has been a leader in Shakespearean theatre for more than fifty years. The season, between April and November, offers a roster of the Bard's plays mixed with works by other great playwrights and popular musicals from the twentieth century, in four theatres.

The Shaw Festival, held in Niagara-On-The-Lake, was founded in 1962 and pays tribute to the plays and the times of George Bernard Shaw. The ten-play season includes works of his peers, and contemporary pieces that reflect Shaw's era. Both festivals complement their playbills with speakers, luncheons and events linked to the performances.

Bird's Eye View, SummerWorks Theatre Festival

Dance

Fans of classical dance and ballet will be interested in the National Ballet of Canada's offerings, now presented in the brand new, long-awaited, state-of-the-art Four Seasons Centre on University Avenue in the heart of downtown Toronto. The Ballet honours the classics but, largely under the direction of former artistic director James Kudelka, has carved out a niche as a reinterpreter of traditional favourites. It has also reinvigorated many well-known works with a modern and creative new perspective, to win over new audiences and inspire traditional ballet-goers. That movement continues under artistic director, Karen Kain, who was for many years Canada's prima ballerina.

Among the National Ballet's innovations are the comic ballet *An Italian Straw Hat*, based on a nineteenth-century French farce, and *Cinderella*, in which Kudelka expanded and enhanced the beloved fairy tale into a visual spectacle of art deco and art

Stratford Theatre Stage

61

The Imperial Ice Stars, *Swan Lake on Ice*, Sony Centre

Collective of Black Artists, Next Steps Festival

Sampradaya Dance Creations, Next Steps Festival

nouveau. Every winter, the National Ballet's production of *The Nutcracker* is a seasonal favourite with families.

Several other companies focus on contemporary dance. Toronto Dance Theatre blends the contribution of the dancers under the leadership of choreographer Christopher House with modern technology, music and movement to develop original works. For thirty years, the Danny Grossman Dance Company has created pieces rooted in founder Grossman's personal philosophy, and now performs its own repertoire as well as works by other dance artists from North America.

Ballet Jorgen is the second-largest ballet dance company in Ontario and the only Canadian ballet company with a repertoire consisting exclusively of original works. The company tours across Canada and North America, performing for an annual audience of more than 50,000 people. Danceworks is the presenter of Toronto's longest running dance series, showcasing an eclectic selection of works from across Canada, including free noon performances with talkbacks. They, along with several other small companies, perform in various venues, but primarily at the stages at Harbourfront Centre — the Fleck Dance Theatre and the Enwave Theatre. Harbourfront also hosts many visiting performers and troupes who come here from all over the world.

Thanks to the city's diverse multicultural mix, Toronto is home to choreographers and performers who incorporate their heritage and traditions from around the globe into their dance creations. Local performers of note include Menaka Thakkar, William Lau, Nova Battacharya and Lata Pada, and troupes like the Arabesque Dance Company, the Esmeralda Enrique Spanish Dance Company and Quilombo do Queimado Grupo de Capoeira, among many others. The inDance company presents experimental South Asian dance under the direction of choreographer Hari Krishnan.

The city features various dance festivals that showcase local companies and performers. In July, Dufferin Grove Park in the west end hosts Dusk Dances, a showcase of short dance pieces by various choreographers inspired by the natural environment of the park. The pay-what-you-can event is designed to be accessible to new audiences and to provide a new venue in which to enjoy and appreciate dance. And the NextSteps festival at Harbourfront Centre on the waterfront focuses on what is new and emerging in the dance world in Toronto, rooted in the choreographers' cultural origins.

Symphony, Chamber Music and Opera

Michael Crabb

Toronto's musical life is rich, varied and continually evolving, from the grandest operatic, symphonic, chamber and choral masterworks to multi-disciplinary presentations and cutting-edge experimentation.

The trend is towards new formats and ways to connect artists and audiences — of every generation. Organizations are proactive in countering the lingering notion that "serious music" cannot be popular and accessible, whether through pre-performance talks, meet-the-artists events or special educational and outreach programs.

There's something for every taste, although a little digging may be needed to uncover the less-well-publicized gems. Local music lovers know to pick up a copy of the informative, free magazine *Wholenote* — also available online — with its detailed listings of just about everything there is to hear in classical, new music and jazz.

The 2,600-seat Roy Thomson Hall (RTH) is the city's major orchestral venue, but since September 2009 it has been ideally complemented by the Royal Conservatory of Music's acoustically refined 1,100-seat Koerner Hall. Under the direction of Mervon Mehta, son of famed conductor Zubin Mehta, the

Toronto Symphony Orchestra

Toronto Symphony Orchestra

architecturally stunning new venue programs a wide variety of music, from orchestral, chamber and solo concerts to jazz and world music.

RTH, meanwhile, is best known as the home of the Toronto Symphony Orchestra (TSO). Under the musical direction of dynamic maestro Peter Oundjian since 2004, the venerable TSO is experiencing a popular renaissance with programming — almost 100 annual concerts at RTH — that covers the gamut. Acclaimed international soloists such as Emanuel Ax, Lang Lang and Evgeny Kissin headline the concerto repertoire. There are the big meaty symphonies — Beethoven, Berlioz, Mahler, Schubert, Shostakovich and Tchaikovsky — but new Canadian works are also featured, and the season is enriched with visiting orchestras and guest conductors such as Charles Dutoit and former TSO music directors Andrew Davis and Jukka-Pekka Saraste.

Even when the TSO is not in residence, RTH is rarely dark. It presents its own International Vocal Series, leading foreign orchestras and smaller, specialized ensembles.

Chamber music devotees head for the renovated Jane Mallett Theatre (St. Lawrence Centre for the Arts), where Music Toronto offers a full season featuring many of the world's leading chamber ensembles.

The TSO may be the orchestral heavyweight in terms of scale but Tafelmusik, by virtue of its many recordings and extensive touring, is arguably the bigger star internationally. Tafelmusik, founded in 1979, is now one of the world's foremost period-instrument baroque orchestras. Led since 1981 by violinist Jeanne Lamon, and with a core of eighteen players and its own complementary choir, Tafelmusik has gone from strength to strength, expanding its repertoire from the era of Bach, Boccherini, Handel and Purcell to include such classical composers as Mozart and Beethoven. Audiences love the intimacy of Tafelmusik's downtown venue, the historic Trinity-St.

Roy Thompson Hall against the cityscape

Paul's Centre. The orchestra also currently offers a miniseries in the acoustically superb but underutilized George Weston Recital Hall in the former borough of North York.

Tafelmusik additionally serves — often under the expert baton of British early-music specialist Andrew Parrot — as the orchestra for another remarkable Toronto musical success story, Opera Atelier. From modest basement lecture-hall beginnings at the Royal Ontario Museum in 1985, Opera Atelier has grown to become a full-fledged company. Its productions, staged at the ornate 1,500-seat Elgin Theatre, are almost invariably sold-out. With a repertoire largely focussed on the pre-Romantic era (roughly the period 1600 to 1800), the company has won a fervent local following and international acclaim for its imaginatively realized and ravishingly designed productions.

Artistic directors Marshall Pynkoski and Jeannette Zingg blow the cobwebs from baroque and classical opera. While respecting period tradition, Pynkoski (he stage directs) and Zingg (she choreographs) breathe fresh life into such time-honoured works as Mozart's *The Magic Flute* and *Don Giovanni* as well as rarities like Gluck's *Iphigénie en Tauride* or Lully's *Armide* by re-imagining them from a contemporary sensibility. Meanwhile the dance components, once so integral to opera but often given short shrift in contemporary productions, are a dazzling highlight of almost every show.

Four Seasons Centre

A relatively new kid on the block, Toronto Masque Theatre, is also gaining a foothold with productions both historic and contemporary that celebrate the masque tradition of combining music, dance and spoken word.

As for grand opera, the major player is unquestionably the august Canadian Opera Company (COC), triumphantly ensconced since 2006 in the Four Seasons Centre for the Performing Arts, the 2,000-seat, purpose-built hall the COC's late and beloved general director, Richard Bradshaw, fought so tirelessly to realize.

The COC was already packing in the crowds at its former venue, the cavernous Hummingbird (now Sony) Centre, but the move to an elegant new opera house with superb acoustics — audaciously launched with a bold production (Canada's first) of Wagner's *Ring Cycle* — has been the most significant event in the company's artistic evolution. The COC, now lead by general director Alexander Neef and music director Johannes Debus, balances operatic warhorses, often in radical productions, with less-well-known fare.

Glen Gould Theatre

Canada, given its relatively small population, has historically produced a remarkable number of outstanding singers. Among today's generation, Ben Heppner, Isabel Bayrakdarian, Michael Schade, Richard Margison, Measha Brueggergosman and others are high flyers on the global vocal scene. Patrons of Toronto's Opera in Concert were able to hear many of them on the way up, thanks to the company's tradition, begun in 1974, of showcasing rising homegrown

Atrium, CBC

talent. Sunday afternoon presentations at the renovated Jane Mallett Theatre (St. Lawrence Centre for the Arts) also provide aficionados with the opportunity to hear a varied range of works beyond the popular operatic mainstream. Recent seasons have included such gems as Vivaldi's *La Griselda*, Mozart's *Zaide* and Korngold's *Die Tote Stadt*.

As for new opera works, Wayne Strongman's Tapestry, three decades strong and based in the Toronto's mixed-use Distillery District, is a crucible of adventurous creativity. Its annual studio showing of aptly named Opera Briefs and its fully produced showcase of short works, Opera to Go, are often complemented by multi-disciplinary collaborations with other local arts groups.

Toronto is proof that Canada also has a strong choral tradition. Whether it's the great — in every sense — Toronto Mendelssohn Choir, a smaller group such as the Nathaniel Dett Chorale that specializes in Afrocentric music or a youth group like the Toronto Children's Chorus, the city has plenty to offer vocal ensemble fans. Worthy of note, although by no means exclusively, are the Amadeus, Orpheus and Tallis Choirs and the Elmer Isler and Jubilate Singers. From Renaissance music to modern choral compositions — with naturally a generous crop of the seasonal stalwart, *Messiah* — Toronto's choral groups just about cover the field.

Fall through spring provides the highest concentration of concert activity, but summer also offers tempting attractions. Conductor Agnes Grossman's Toronto Summer Music Festival showcases top-ranked artists, both local and international, from such Canadian stars as pianists André Laplante and Anton Kuerti to the Leipzig String Quartet. Concerts, depending on scale, are held at various University of Toronto venues including the acoustically refined 490-seat Walter Hall and the 800-seat MacMillan Theatre.

Summer in the city, however, is very much about the outdoors, and the Toronto Music Garden, located right by the water at the west end of the harbour, provides a delightful way to indulge a love of live music in an open-air setting.

In the late 1990s Toronto-based Rhombus Media produced an acclaimed TV series called *Inspired by Bach*. The first film brought together the genius of cellist Yo-Yo Ma with that of Boston landscape artist Julie Moir Messervy to interpret Bach's numinous *Suite No. 1 in G major* in a natural setting. Rhombus, Ma and Messervy subsequently almost persuaded the City of Boston to translate the film into a permanent music garden. When that deal fell through, Toronto stepped up to the plate and Boston's loss became Toronto's gain. Like the Bach suite, the Toronto Music Garden — worth a visit for its own sake — is designed in six parts.

From late June to mid-September this enchanting park features an eclectic range of free concerts, usually on Thursday evenings and Sunday afternoons, programmed by artistic director Tamara Bernstein. It could be early music, a string quartet, a vocal group, a Korean drum ensemble or even dance. And J. S. Bach is almost invariably included in the mix, for obvious reasons.

Refreshing programming that ignores the traditional distinctions of old and new, "serious" and popular, is a feature of several smaller Toronto music groups.

Andrew Burashko's Art of Time series extends this open-minded approach through fascinating multimedia collaborations with other genres such as dance and film. Burashko, an acclaimed Canadian pianist who made his concert debut with the TSO at age sixteen, formed Art of Time in 1998 as a collective of musicians with a shared interest in mixing things up and exploring new connections. Whether it's improvised Ashkenazi Jewish music, Shostakovich in jazz mode or an innovative take on The Beatles, Art of Time concerts, generally presented in Harbourfront Centre's intimate Enwave Theatre, consistently delight and surprise.

Jettisoning conventional notions of music presentation is the hallmark of another enterprising

Esmerelda Enrique, Toronto Music Garden

Top: Glen Gould
Studio, CBC;
Bottom: Glen Gould
statue, CBC

Toronto organization, renowned oboist Lawrence Cherney's Soundstreams. Its official mantra is "Music Beyond Boundaries," and as a catalyst and curatorial organization Soundstreams certainly lives up to that principle. Spanning cultures and eras from Byzantium to First Nations lore, and from twelfth-century chant to brand-new works, Soundstreams is always delightfully unpredictable. Where "new" music is concerned — art music, international and Canadian that's freshly scored or composed in recent times — there is plenty to choose from.

For more than thirty-five years, under the artistic direction of flutist and composer Robert Aitken, New Music Concerts (NMC) has nurtured performers and audiences with presentations featuring leading musicians and ensembles in work that embraces a broad range of contemporary composers. Venues vary through the NMC season but concerts are often held in the Music Gallery at Saint George the Martyr, close by the trendy stores and bistros of Queen Street West.

Arraymusic is another respected local proponent of contemporary music, with a particular emphasis on experimentation and risk taking. Formed in the early 1970s as a university-student-composer collective, Arraymusic likes to push traditional boundaries and find new ways to engage. With its eight-member ensemble — itself an ear-catching instrumental grouping of woodwind, brass, percussion, piano and strings — Arraymusic's annual activities range from regular concerts to unusual interdisciplinary collaborations with dance, visual and theatre artists.

Esprit Orchestra has earned itself a leading position on the Toronto new music scene. Formed by conductor Alex Pauk more than a quarter of a century ago, Esprit offers a fall-through-spring series at the Jane Mallett Theatre, but also ventures out to explore unusual concert settings. Its multi-day New Wave Composers Festival in early May spreads out across the GTA. Whether it is commissioned work from such Canadian composers as Brian Current, Rose Bolton and Alice Ping Yee Ho or the Canadian premiere of pieces by such international luminaries as Ligeti, Penderecki, Schnittke and Takemitsu, Esprit explodes the once prevalent prejudice against new music by demonstrating just how varied and exciting it can be.

Even Toronto's popular Hannaford Street Silver Band follows the category-busting trend by playing the old and the new, from traditional marches to commissioned works from leading Canadian composers.

Toronto, with its musical variety, offers a great many opportunities for music lovers.

Nightlife

Melissa Brazier

Toronto has a wide variety of locales for high rollers. If you're flush with cash and sporting your best threads, this city has a lot to offer for an upscale evening.

The Black Bull Pub

Queen Street West

This area, comparable to New York's Soho, has been dubbed a haven for hipsters, who flock to grungy pubs and small bars to hear live music from local bands. But there are a few posh resto-lounges too. Fairly new and very trendy, the Tattoo Rock Parlour offers a rock themed evening (think Guns N' Roses and Bon Jovi) that features a long list for bottle service. A little farther down Queen is the Melody Bar of the Gladstone Hotel. This pub-like scene has a wide variety of entertainment, including karaoke night every weekend. Both venues are a little out of the way on the fringe of the city.

An oldie but a goodie, the Drake Hotel — a lounge/rooftop patio/dining room/raw bar/live music venue — is a

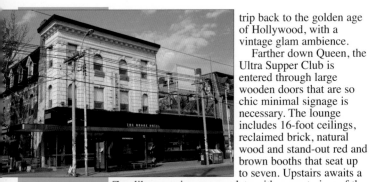

Top and bottom:
The Drake Hotel

trip back to the golden age of Hollywood, with a vintage glam ambience.

Farther down Queen, the Ultra Supper Club is entered through large wooden doors that are so chic minimal signage is necessary. The lounge includes 16-foot ceilings, reclaimed brick, natural wood and stand-out red and brown booths that seat up to seven. Upstairs awaits a Zen-like experience, complete with a great view of the skyline and fresh frozen cocktails.

Czehoski has tasty desserts such as crème brûlée and chocolate mousse cake, served by candlelight. Depending on the season, upstairs there's a cozy fireplace or an outdoor garden oasis. Strong cocktails made seasonally are also top patron picks. For jazz aficionados there's the Opal Jazz Lounge. Designed by architect/designer/jazz musician Harvey Cowan, this spot boasts a 20-foot photo collage, a Heintzman grand piano and an impressive Maurer chandelier autographed by performers.

King Street West

One of Toronto's hottest neighbourhoods, this entertainment district (between Spadina Avenue and Bathurst Street) boasts some of the city's most sophisticated bars. The open-concept Crush Wine Bar offers twenty-five to thirty-five wines per month to please even the pickiest palette in an intimate setting, including a feature of the month. Atelier and the Spoke Club are "need to know someone" kind of places. These private clubs are exclusive for local, as well as visiting A-listers. The Century Room, with fourteen private areas available for reservation, is for those who want bottle service. A night here can be a gathering of friends sipping on Grey Goose, or a dance revolution on the spacious floor near the back.

Cheval, Schmooze, Brant House and West Lounge are also sleek bars that combine the comfort and closeness of a lounge with the dance room of a club. All offer bottle service and VIP areas. Joe Mamas is a smaller venue with a red motif that hosts live Motown/R & B music, and its late-night menu features delicious soul food.

There are also some swanky venues just off King. Elegant resto-lounge Marben on Wellington has a delicious signature black-cherry-rum cocktail called "Lost My Cherry Blossom," served only before 11:00 p.m. After that, exclusive fruity shots include the "Pinup Girl" or "Hypnotizer." The atmosphere here is friendly yet chic. Also on Wellington is C Lounge, a one-of-a-kind in Toronto. Spa meets lounge at this haven for downtown professionals. This venue is water-themed with several indoor waterfalls and a candlelit pool on the back patio that's surrounded by VIP cabanas and couches. The loos have masseuses and makeup artists.

Boasting a sexy colour palette of deep purples, greys and blacks, with down lighting, State Theatre at King and Bathurst offers a night of majesty. Depending on the night, there might even be a lone violinist to set the mood for grandeur. Besides lounges and clubs, farther down King is the theatre district.

The Wheat Sheaf on King West

Financial District and Area

Home of Toronto's financial professionals, this area also offers some fabulous after work resto-lounges. Friday nights the crowd consists of men and women in power suits relaxing over cocktails and appetizers after a day of stocks, bonds and trades. Canoe and Jump are two world-class locales of the Oliver Bonacini Restaurants. Canoe, located on the 54th floor of the Toronto–Dominion Centre and open till 10:30 p.m., Monday to Friday, is a great place for happy hour. Jump is the next stop for the office crowd. A luxurious New York-style bar with a high glass ceiling, it's open till midnight.

The Sultan's Tent & Cafe Moroc is a Moroccan-themed resto-lounge where dining meets entertainment fit for royalty. Designed as a traditional "diffa" (lavish banquet), this venue features belly-dance performances seven nights a week that run late into the night on weekends. Turf Lounge describes itself as "where Bay Street comes to play." This bar shows live simulcasts of international horse races on plasma screens. Turf brings the fun of betting on the ponies to downtown.

The Sultan's Tent & Cafe Moroc

Ki (pure, undiluted, raw) is a modern Japanese bar where people meet for premium sake. Signature sake cocktails include Kyushu Cosmo, Ginger Sake, Plum Sake. . . and the list goes on.

Speaking of specialty drinks, Vertical has some of the most creative cocktails in the city, complemented by a bar menu of delicious Mediterranean munchies. The bar has a 40-foot-long sandstone top where

Ultra Supper Club

patrons can sip on a Caipirinha, which features sagatiba pura cachaca, crushed lime and organic sugar. In the hotter months crowds sit outside, bellini in hand, on the mezzanine patio overlooking the parkette and waterfall of First Canadian Place. Bymark, primarily known for its restaurant on the concourse level, has a bar located in the courtyard. Featuring dark woods, black leather

box chairs and very modern sharp lines, this is a great place to sit and relax, martini or scotch in hand.

Yorkville and Area
Located between Charles Street West and Davenport Road, and Avenue Road and Yonge Street, Yorkville used to be all hippies and bohemians. Now, this area of Toronto is the poshest in the city, home to shopping for D&G and Gucci, fine dining and upscale nightlife. Celebs aplenty can be spotted in this area during Toronto's yearly International Film Festival in September. Club V was designed with A-list jet-setters in mind. With four glamorous rooms (dance room, main room, VIP room and patio) this hotspot makes the classic martini new with original Grey Goose-based concoctions such as the "V" and "French Kiss."

Located at the four-star Four Seasons Hotel, Avenue overlooks Yorkville Avenue and includes a golden staircase, more than 100 candles, Italian/French handmade furniture, marble floors and a 20-foot onyx bar that's the centre of the action. At the three-floor resto-lounge Flow, the theme is stripes. The extensive drink menu features three options: straight up, over cubes or crushed, and there are bar-menu tasters from thin-crust pizza to Iranian caviar.

At the centre of the shopping district, Remy's is restaurant by day, hopping club scene by night, a place for those who are truly cool. After a tragic fire, Sassafraz returns renovated and raring to please, reclaiming its status as the "it" place in Toronto. Amber is the basement place to be Tuesday to Saturday all evening until 2:00 a.m. The small capacity of this bourgeois destination means an extremely strict door policy: faux Chanel and rip-off Prada definitely not allowed.

Richmond and Adelaide
This area is stereotypically known as the place to find teenage clubsters in risqué outfits, punch drunk after a night of tequila body shots and other such antics. But, it does have some class.

In the Mood Supper Club and Jazz Lounge does

exactly what it says. Velvet curtains and soft lighting combined with live jazz, neo-soul and R & B make this a place to relax and unwind. Another upscale place with the city's best live music is Live@Courthouse. This historical venue features everything from bebop, swing and Latin to blues and jazz. Balcony seats are also available for a great view of the performance, and there's a black velvet rope that guarantees VIP exclusivity.

The Devil's Martini and the Fifth Social Club (pre-reno Easy & the Fifth) are two of Toronto's more spacious clubs that still give the warm feel of a loft, as plush seating meets large dance floors. Refreshingly, both play an eclectic variety of music (Top 40, hip hop, '80s retro, house and more) to suit a variety of tastes. Suite 106 is known for not being too loud, allowing patrons to actually speak to each other without bursting any eardrums. This Is London, just as the name says, is English-inspired and often hosts fun theme nights: fancy attire only as bouncers are known to turn away people who don't fit the criteria.

Runway 224 is for fashion fans, as it hosts regular catwalk shows. This venue occupies three floors and has Toronto's only swinging dance platform complete with sexy go-go dancers. The romantic year-round patio, complete with fire pit and waterfalls, has a killer view of the skyline.

College Street

Known as Toronto's "Little Italy," between Bathurst and Dufferin Streets, this area is a place for the cool and chic, with an eclectic mix of bars. The age group is generally mid-twenties to mid-thirties. A College original, Souz Dal, has been on the strip longer than

Cafe Diplomatico, College Street

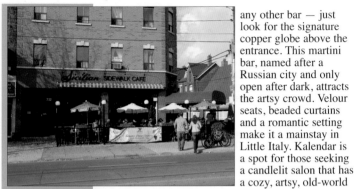

Sicillian Sidewalk Cafe, College Street

any other bar — just look for the signature copper globe above the entrance. This martini bar, named after a Russian city and only open after dark, attracts the artsy crowd. Velour seats, beaded curtains and a romantic setting make it a mainstay in Little Italy. Kalendar is a spot for those seeking a candlelit salon that has a cozy, artsy, old-world feel. Flight 55 is where dark wood meets vibrant yellow and red furniture, crystal chandeliers and a subtle background DJ.

In contrast, Li'ly combines the intimacy of dining with the bumping and grinding of a club. Upstairs diners sit in a mahogany space lit by candles — downstairs the party's at a sleek steel bar, with mirror-lined walls, DJ and a small dance floor. When it gets busy it can get really hot down there. The pink and black decor and open concept isn't what makes Chinadoll Lounge unique. It's the all-female staff and long list of cocktails. Although this may sound like a girls'-night-out place, generally guys go where the girls are. Dining meets entertainment meets dancing at Plaza Flamingo, a unique Spanish experience with tapas, flamenco shows, lessons and dancing all night long.

Bloor Street West

Although this strip is commonly known as the "Annex" and is mostly home to University of Toronto students, farther east but still on Bloor West there are two stops for modish nightlife. Lobby has been said to bring style back to Toronto with its upscale modern design. A thin rectangular venue, on one side is a long bar with several bartenders guaranteeing fast service. On the other side are VIP booths for bottle service. Modern art covers the walls of this haven for

Panorama Restaurant

fashionistas and metrosexuals. Farther up Bloor Street is Panorama on the 51st floor of the Manulife Centre. This lounge boasts the best view of uptown/downtown Toronto. A floor-to-ceiling window gives a panoramic view of the city, while crystal chandeliers, Barcelona furniture and a signature frozen cocktail, "Panorama," makes this spot a hotbed of elegance and class.

Dining

Shaun Smith

Canoe Restaurant

When it comes to fine dining, there has never been a better time to visit Toronto. The city is experiencing a golden age in the culinary arts, led by a generation of master chefs and restaurateurs who have come into their own over the past decade. Add a host of rising young stars to that mix and the result is nothing less than a gourmet's paradise. A visitor could dine in Toronto for weeks, experiencing the creations of a different top chef each night, and not once be disappointed.

Below are some of Toronto's finest dinner spots, where visitors can expect to discover exquisite food, stellar wines, sophisticated ambience and impeccable service. Many of these spots also serve lunch. Some are closed Sunday and Monday, so be sure to phone for reservations.

Downtown Central
With its spectacular view from the 54th floor of the TD Centre, Canoe has been pleasing well-heeled gourmets for more than ten years. Chef Tony Walsh's refined Canadian cuisine receives critical raves, drawing as it does on top-quality domestic ingredients such as Springbank bison tenderloin, Yarmouth lobster and Quebec suckling pig. The wine list features an

extensive collection from Ontario's Niagara region. Farther downtown, Harbour Sixty Steakhouse is for serious carnivores. In this opulent room across from the Air Canada Centre, home of the Toronto Maple Leafs and the Toronto Raptors, pro athletes often enjoy post-game protein fixes. A full range of steaks is available, from a 14-oz filet mignon to daily Kobe beef selections, as well as seafood. Wines show outstanding depth from California.

Kitty-corner from Toronto's new opera house, you'll find chef David Lee manning the stoves at Nota Bene, on Queen Street West. One of Toronto's hottest reservations, Nota Bene opened in 2008 and was named best new restaurant by *Toronto Life* and *enRoute* magazines. Chef Lee cooks an eclectic menu of daring sophistication, with influences from as far afield as Spain, Nova Scotia and Hong Kong. Elegant service complements a modern dining room.

Canoe Restaurant

No Toronto visit is complete without a trip to the new Frank Gehry-designed Art Gallery of Ontario, inside of which you can dine in the appropriately named restaurant, Frank. Chef Anne Yarymowich draws ingredients from Ontario-based farmers and artisanal producers to create a menu of bistro fare such as roasted duck magret with Niagara sour cherry compote, or grilled lamb ribs with minted pea pesto. Frank boasts one of the best selections of Ontario wines in town.

Tucked behind the King Edward Hotel, Colborne Lane is an edgy, chic spot where wunderkind chef Claudio Aprile marries art and science in a cuisine influenced by molecular gastronomy. Tiny portions with complex flavours, such as lamb rib-eye crusted in dry olives and pumpernickel, served with caramelized eggplant, toasted cumin rosti and green tea-infused yogourt, arrive in multiple courses. Through special arrangement, guests can even sit at an exclusive table inside the kitchen.

Behind City Hall, chefs at Lai Wah Heen in the Metropolitan Hotel, display the most recent trends in

The Wine Bar

pan-Chinese cuisine, producing dishes of exquisite refinement, in styles from spicy Szechuan to aromatic Guangdong. Favourites include oolong tea-smoked duck breast, and braised Yoshihama abalone. Dim sum is also served daily at lunchtime.

Downtown East

Famous for his prix fixe tasting menus (multicourse meals of small plates at a set price) is chef Lorenzo Loseto at George, on Queen Street East. He prepares menus of six or eight courses using only the freshest market ingredients. His light and vibrant dishes, such as sesame-glazed wild salmon with basil custard, or twice-baked vanilla soufflé, perfectly match the restaurant's airy, ornate style.

Don't be put off by the slightly shop-worn quality of the tiny Hiro Sushi restaurant on King Street East. Sushi aficionados know that what the room lacks in ambiance is more than made up for by the brilliant food of Chef Hiro Yoshida. Sit at the bar and eat Omakase ("trust me") style, enjoying impeccable sushi, sashimi and maki, as well as dishes like lemon-infused roasted tilefish, or unctuous tamari-marinated black cod. Excellent saki selection.

Downtown West

Chef Susur Lee has two restaurants, side-by-side, on King Street West. Madeline's offers continental dishes such as crispy Cornish hen with gorgonzola cheese sauce, or spinach ricotta gnocchi with garlic, chili and pine nuts. The room is opulent yet casual with Victorian, Moorish and Asian design elements. Next door, Lee is this chef's ode to his Chinese roots, with dishes such as coconut lime soup or roast scallops with duck confit and black bean sauce. The feel at Lee is sleek, modern and hip.

A few doors west of Lee, Conviction is chef Marc Thuet's latest creation. As seen on the reality-TV series *Conviction Kitchen*, Thuet has staffed his restaurant with ex-convicts, yet maintains his exacting high

Madeline's Restaurant

standards, serving bistro-influenced fare such as wild Scottish pheasant and foie gras terrine, or whey-fed Mennonite pork with crab-apple coulis. Farther west, at Tecumseth Avenue, Amuse-Bouche offers an intimate setting, where chefs Jason Inniss and Bertrand Alépée serve contemporary French cuisine of exceptional quality. Their refined palates and exquisite presentations — for dishes such as coffee-cardamom glazed duck breast or fennel consommé with chipotle ice cream — have drawn critical raves. Alépée's desserts are brilliant.

A number of exceptional restaurants can also be found on the streets north and south of King West. Brothers Guy and Michael Rubino are known internationally from their Food Network television show, *Made to Order*. AME, on Mercer Street, is their Toronto home, where Guy helms the kitchen and Michael runs front of house. Open late, this newly re-designed spot is home to the city's high-fashion crowd and boasts a modern Japanese menu featuring exquisite sushi, sashimi and hot dishes such as grilled sea bream on cedar. Also south of

Cowbell Restaurant

King Street West, in the old warehouse district of Liberty Village, is Mildred's Temple Kitchen. Chef-owner Donna Dooher applies a refined sensibility — especially with vegetables — to bistro-style cooking, taking advantage of the best seasonal ingredients in dishes like cucumber and fennel ribbons with salt cod, or curried cauliflower with Niagara grapes. The minimalist, concrete and white-leather room buzzes with life and energy.

To the north, two restaurants add hearty culinary sophistication to the funky neighbourhood of Queen Street West. The Rosebud resembles a classic 1940s chophouse, with its wood panelling and ceramic floors. Chef-owner Rodney Bowers serves up satisfying fare such as Shiraz-braised beef short ribs, and orecchiette pasta with sweet Italian sausage. Ten doors west is Czehoski. Once a Polish/Czech deli, it has been renovated into a hip, retro space offering such comfort food as organic beef burgers, and chestnut flour and cheddar pierogies.

Mildred's Temple Kitchen

Also in the Queen West district, Jacobs & Co. Steakhouse, on Brandt Street, feels like something out of *Mad Men*, boasting a dining room that is pure early-1960s formal elegance, with slate walls and leather banquettes. Steak is taken very seriously here, so expect to see Kobe, Wagyu and Angus cuts (all aged in-house) that run over $100 per plate. If that's too pricey, head farther west on Queen to the

neigbourhood of Parkdale to visit Cowbell, where chef Mark Cutrara is a devotee of locavore cooking, using almost exclusively ingredients found in Southern Ontario. The menu morphs according to what local organic farmers have available. Carnivores will delight in the specialty cuts and house-made charcuterie served in this cozy room, furnished with old church pews.

Farther north, on College Street, Chef Dustin Gallagher, at Grace, serves up simple, yet superbly prepared bistro fare, such as tomato braised monkfish or lamb pot pie with sweet peas, in a chic yet homey atmosphere. Also on College, Chiado offers formal old-world dining, with a menu by renowned chef-owner Albino Silva, specializing in Portuguese seafood such as grilled squid with fresh coriander, and grilled and roasted salt cod. Chiado's wine list overflows with Portuguese labels, including thirty ports.

Midtown

Splendido Bar & Grill, on Harbord Street, is one of Canada's top restaurants. Chef Victor Barry's menu routinely names the local organic farms where he procures artisanal meat, produce and cheese. The stately elegance of the dining room, flawless service and a cellar of more than 1,000 bottles make Splendido a serious gourmet destination. Those who take Japanese cuisine seriously will enjoy Kaiseki Sakura on Church Street, a stylish spot done in pink and black where traditional multicourse Omakase tasting menus are artfully prepared by chef-owner Daisuke Izutsu. Amongst the eight courses might be treasures like black tiger-shrimp tempura in spicy yuzu sauce, or boiled beef tongue with miso sauce. Drinks include numerous saketinis.

Inside Nota Bene restaurant

Above: Jamie
Kennedy at the
Gardiner

There are a number of superb restaurants in the highly fashionable Yorkville neighbourhood. On the fifth floor of the Michael Lee-Chin Crystal addition of the Royal Ontario Museum (ROM) on Queen's Park Crescent, C5 (Crystal Five) affords diners the opportunity to eat inside a veritable sculpture. Decorated in white leather and glass, C5 serves lunch daily and dinner Thursday, Friday and Saturday, with an Asian-fusion menu built around locally raised ingredients, such as Quebec squab and Niagara wild boar.

At Pangaea, on Bay Street, chef-owner Martin Kouprie's menu is inspired by world cuisines, offering dishes such as caribou with wild mushroom jus, and tuna tartar with ginger sesame dressing. The decor is elemental, with patinas evoking the rain forest. An award-winning wine cellar shows more than 450 labels. Opus Restaurant, on Prince Arthur Avenue, is where serious oenophiles swoon over a ninety-page wine list showing more than 2,500 wines. *Wine Spectator* magazine has given this cellar its Grand Award for five years running. In this dark and seductive dining room, chef Jason Cox serves fine continental dishes, such as roast lamb with parsley risotto, and Atlantic lobster with fava beans. Opus also offers numerous caviars.

At the edge of Yorkville, on Davenport Road, Mistura is home to the contemporary pan-Italian cooking of chef Massimo Capra, seen on TV's *Restaurant Makeover*. In this effervescent room, locals enjoy such delights as wild boar ravioli, and veal scaloppine with porcini mushrooms. Mistura's chic upstairs lounge, Soppra, is a great nightspot for live jazz and blues.

Uptown

The well-heeled neighbourhoods of North Toronto support a thriving gourmet restaurant community. Perched atop the Toronto escarpment, Scaramouche's elegant dining room offers a spectacular view of downtown. Chef-owner Keith Froggett's cooking receives critical raves, with dishes like roasted loin of rabbit with chanterelle mushrooms, and fricassee of lobster. East of Scaramouche, chef-owner Didier Leroy's Didier, at Yonge Street and St. Clair Avenue, is perhaps the city's best classic French restaurant, serving such delights as foie gras, arctic char and black truffle bisque, and steak tartare. This dignified room feels transplanted straight from Paris. A bit north of Didier, and tucked off Yonge Street inside Delisle Court, is Cava, where chef-owner Chris McDonald serves a tapas-inspired menu of dishes like grilled octopus, braised pork belly, salt cod cakes and house-made chorizo. More than twenty wines are offered by the glass, with seventeen sherries and a broad variety of Spanish cheeses.

Farther north, there are three outstanding restaurants. Célestin's pretty and bright room, in a vintage 1920s bank building on Mount Pleasant Road, plays host to superb contemporary French cuisine by chef-owner Pascal Ribreau. The critical raves received for dishes like roasted sweet-garlic and almond soup, rabbit ravioli, and smoked monkfish are all the more amazing considering Ribreau is a paraplegic, cooking from a wheelchair. Opened by the legendary Toronto restaurateur Franco Prevedello in 1987, Centro, on Yonge Street, has changed ownership numerous times, but never lost its cachet. Current chef and co-owner Bruce Woods serves a menu with Italian foundations and Asian and Spanish accents. The plush dining room

AME Restaurant

bustles with glamorous energy, while a huge cellar shows remarkable depth in old-world vintages. Across the road from Centro, chef-owner Mark McEwan's North 44, named for the city's latitude, is an equally glamorous destination. Eclectic flashes of Italian, French, Asian and North American cuisines influence the cooking. Serious steaks are a specialty. Expect flawless service in this buzzingly lively room. North 44's cellar includes more than thirty champagnes and sparkling wines, and thirty dessert wines.

Shopping

Melissa Brazier

Shopping along Bloor Street

Toronto Eaton Centre

Shopping in Toronto is unlike shopping in any other city. With a mix of chains and independent Canadian-owned stores, it has a unique vibe. Toronto is a haven for shoppers, no matter what they are looking for.

Main Shopping Areas

Eaton Centre

Located downtown between Queen and Dundas on Yonge Street, this mall has more than 230 stores spread over three storeys. It has something for everyone, from clothing to electronics and everything in between, which makes it a one-stop-shopping destination. As shoppers ascend to the top floor, the stores tend to become more expensive. The bottom floor has chains such as Old Navy and H&M, the middle level is home to Jacob and Esprit, while the upper level features Harry Rosen, Lacoste, and so on. Newer stores include A/X Armani Exchange, Bath & Body Works and Hollister. No wonder it was voted the number one most visited tourist attractions in Toronto: it can take half a day to check out all that this huge complex has to offer.

Bloor Street West

Appropriately nicknamed the "Mink

Mile," Bloor Street between Yonge and Avenue Road is a hotbed of high-end shopping, including fashion heavy-hitters like Gucci, Hermès, Christian Dior, Chanel, Louis Vuitton and Prada. For shoppers who don't have a money tree in their backyard but still demand style, there are more affordable chain stores like FCUK, BCBG, Club Monaco, Gap and Banana Republic. As Canada's high–end department store, Holt Renfrew features international designers like Armani and Burberry, as well as scads of fabulous Canadian lines like Pink Tartan, Lida Baday, Greta Constantine and more. Or to add a little cultural flavour, the Indian-inspired fashions of Indiva — think lots of beaded detailing and bright colours — is also found on Bloor. Noir is good for the glitz and glam of rock 'n' roll fashion circa David Bowie. For those who like their bling, jewellery and accessory locales include Birks, Tiffany & Co., Cartier, Royal de Versailles and La Difference. Bloor also has top-of-the-line men's fashion, which can be spotted at Marc Laurent, Harry Rosen and Ermenegildo Zegna, to name just a few.

Holt Renfrew, Bloor Street West

Redecorating? Pavillon Christofle carries fine tableware, flatware and crystal while Le Caprice de Marie-Claude has excellent bath lines and bed linens. William Ashley China (located in the Manulife Centre) offers great china, crystal, flatware, silverware and children's gifts. The Manulife Centre shopping complex also includes stores that specialize in everything from books and stationery to ladies' and men's fashions. For shoe-aholics, Davids is two floors of yummy selections the likes of Christian Louboutin and Salvatore Ferregamo. More affordable options are available next door at Capezio or down the street at Nine West. For beauty products the places are the Body Shop, MAC Cosmetics, L'Occitane en Provençe and Aveda Boutique.

Yorkville

North of Bloor, Yorkville is another haven for high-rolling shoppers. This area is a gallery of small courtyards, alleys, chic cafés and funky fashion boutiques. Yorkville offers exclusive stores that are not only stylish, but also original. Canadian designers have made this area home and their boutiques include such well-known names as Philippe Dubuc, Marilyn Brooks and Linda Lundstrom. Designs by Naomi, run by a sister team, includes a changing room complete with candy and a small gallery of fashion art for sale. Over

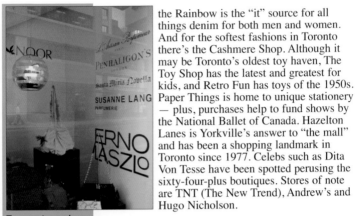

the Rainbow is the "it" source for all things denim for both men and women. And for the softest fashions in Toronto there's the Cashmere Shop. Although it may be Toronto's oldest toy haven, The Toy Shop has the latest and greatest for kids, and Retro Fun has toys of the 1950s. Paper Things is home to unique stationery — plus, purchases help to fund shows by the National Ballet of Canada. Hazelton Lanes is Yorkville's answer to "the mall" and has been a shopping landmark in Toronto since 1977. Celebs such as Dita Von Tesse have been spotted perusing the sixty-four-plus boutiques. Stores of note are TNT (The New Trend), Andrew's and Hugo Nicholson.

Top, centre and bottom: window shopping, Yorkville and Queen Street West

Queen Street West

From University Avenue all the way to Shaw Street, Queen West offers some of the most unusual stores in the city, from fashion to home decor. For those seeking unmatched style there are Lilith and Peach Berserk. For those craving designer labels The Showroom always stocks well-known lines, with new ones added each season. Fairly new additions to this uber-chic area include Next Door, Jacflash, Change and Moda. For innovative men's and women's shoe designs the day can start at Fluevog Shoe. For unique Canadian west coast fashion there is the Vancouver-based chain Aritzia. Or, for retro designs, there is Pink Cobra and Fashion Crimes. And Pages Books & Magazines is one of the oldest indie book stores in Toronto.

For visitors with kids, one block farther along is the trendy children's store Kol Kid. Past here, shoe addicts will run into Heel Boy, home to some of the cutest shoes in the city. Delphic specializes in high-end men's street fashion, and Klaxon Howl has a mix of vintage pieces and the latest labels. In between these two is Kama Kazi Kids and Kama Kazi Style Boutique. Both feature hard-to-find international labels. The Paper Place (also known as the Japanese Paper Place) has hand-crafted papers, boxes, albums, cards and more. Boutique Le Trou is where owner Marlene Shiff hand picks all the pieces, including those by Canadian fashion sensations Carrie Hayes, Lucian Matis, Zoran Dobric, and so on. Another designer duo is composed of sisters Melanie Talbot and Kristina Bozzo of Common Cloth. For home decor some stores of note are Pavilion, Commute Home, Quasi Modo, Queen West Antique Centre and Simone Interiors.

College Street

From Borden to Grace, College

Street ("Little Italy") has a wide range of distinct independent shops, where shoppers can find everything from a retro table to a funky dress. She Said Boom is a great place to pick up some vinyls and the latest indie concert tickets. Sim & Jones, Touched By Angels, Ewanika, Tessi and Girl Friday are all women's fashion hot spots guaranteed to dress you from head to toe. Having a bad hair day? Lilliput Hats features an array of coif covers from casual, couture and classic to cocktail, vintage and romantic. Zing Home's, on Palmerston Avenue just off College, has retro and contemporary furnishings and accessories. Mink, at College and Euclid Avenue, features all-handmade accessories, many of them one-of-a-kind. Each piece is carefully crafted by owner and designer Christine Papadakos. Nothing is cooler than a Vespa, and Motoretta is a scooter-lifestyle store that has everything fans need. The place to be for music enthusiasts is Soundscapes, which stocks CDs, DVDs, books and magazines. GMB suits men who want fashionable yet comfortable and boasts labels like Boss Orange and Lacoste. Run by graduate art students, Organic Metal Gallery promotes young designers, offering custom jewellery as well as classes teaching others to create their own bijoux. The best place to get gifts for those back home is definitely Red Pegasus.

Kensington Market

Near the College Street shopping district, Kensington Market is where shoppers flock on the hunt for a deal. Hidden gems can be found throughout the area in between butchers' shops, fish markets and cheese shops. This area is mostly known for its vintage finds, and some great stores to hit are Vintage Depot and Bungalow. For second-hand clothing (not quite vintage) there is Urban Catwalk. Usoto is not for the faint of style — be

Balzacs, Distillery District

warned, the designs are different and funky. Reasonably priced men's clothes are available at Tom's Place. For those whose inner decorator is eclectic yet classic, the home decor shops available are New World Furniture, Orbital Arts, the Royal Trade Company of Canada and the Economy Store. Jewellery that will make any outfit pop can always be found at Butterfly.

Distillery District

This historic neighbourhood, located at Parliament and Mill, has been dubbed by *Toronto Life* magazine "the Hippest Address in Town," and for good reason: it covers all shopping needs from A to Z. Toronto's first pedestrian-only village, this area is for shoppers and art lovers alike. Sound Designs offers truly high-end electronics from the latest plasma TVs to pricey stereo systems. For hand-crafted bling, peruse the designs of Leif Benner. For those who still know the

thoughtfulness of a mailed letter, Jonesy Charismatic Stationary provides an environmentally friendly option. Photography enthusiasts will find themselves at home at Pikto, which carries the latest in image tools and a photo lab available for customers' use.

Queen's Quay and Front Street

This area in the south end of the city is also host to a wide range of shops, hence the tagline "it's a quay

Gooderham and Worts, Distillery District

thing." Queen's Quay is along Toronto's harbourfront on Lake Ontario. The Queen's Quay Terminal is a luxurious shopping mall that's home to the fashions of Canadian designer Tanya Lam and the keepsakes of Tilley Endurables. Shops of note farther along the harbourfront also include Bounty for Canadian works of art, the outdoor International Market in the summer and the Harbourfront Antique Centre for knick-knacks and collectibles. Harbourfront Centre always has shopping activities on the go. North of the harbourfront is Front Street, another locale for great shopping. Nicholas Hoare is an elegant space where readers can peruse the mix of mostly British books. Just a skip from here is Europe Bound, the store for outdoors enthusiasts, with everything from the perfect pair of hiking shoes to backpacks and space savers. Lastly there is the St. Lawrence Market for the small craft stations throughout the two-storey venue.

Uptown

A little north of downtown, but still just a subway ride away, is Yonge and Eglinton, also known as "young and eligible." This neighbourhood's trendy shops, cafés and restaurants attract uber-hip single professionals in their mid-twenties to mid-thirties. At the pinnacle of Yonge and Eglinton shopping is Pure + Simple Spa, which offers fabulous facials, and the best array of organic beauty products in the city, featuring its own signature line. The staff are super-knowledgeable and helpful. Delineation Hair & Skin Essentials is great for hair expertise. The stylists know their stuff and carry exclusive products such as Bumble & Bumble, Philip B and Chantecaille.

Restoration Hardware has everything that a home could wish for, from furniture to bed and bath. For women's fashions, Just For You Fashions carries a lot of Canadian designers, and Kaliyana Artwear offers "the kit" — six essential pieces that create twenty different outfits. A few blocks along Gowans, The

Shop has excellent scented candles, cards and gifts. Fashionable men will find the latest in cool threads at David Findlay's Boutique. For plus-size women, The Answer has beautiful designer fashions available in sizes 6 to 22. Lastly, a store that can actually make swimsuit and lingerie shopping fun for all women is Melmira, but an advance appointment is needed.

Shopping by Category

Antiques and Collectibles
Antique and collectibles stores are spread all over Toronto, but Mount Pleasant, a little north of downtown from Millwood to Eglinton Avenue East, is a hub. Some antique stores of note include Horsefeathers, Susan's Antiques, Nadia's, Bernardi's, Whimsy Antiques, Sharon O'Dowd Antiques, The Antique Collection and Lorenz Antiques. This area also offers collectibles at stores such as Little Dollhouse Company, George's Trains, Quilter's Quarters, Alexandre Antique Prints, Maps & Books and more.

Another area with a high concentration of antique and collectibles stores is Yorkville. The antique stores include C.C. Lai Chinese Antiques, David Gilles Antiques, Elisabeth Legge, Antique Prints, Eurotiques, Fifty-One Antiques Ltd., Hung's Antiques, Kamimura Gallery, Louis Wine Antique Dealers Ltd. and Mark McLaine Collection, to name a few. Toronto Antiques on King is also home to many fine knick-knacks.

Indigo Bookstore

Bookstores
The World's Biggest Book Store on Edward Street occupies two floors, has 27 km of shelves and more than 140,000 book titles. With sixty-five departments it's close to impossible not to find what one wants. Chapters and Indigo are two other large havens for bookworms, with three floors and a Starbucks. For smaller independent bookstores there are Nicholas Hoare, Pages Books & Magazines, Book City, Eliot Bookshop and This Ain't the Rosedale Library. There is also Mable's Fables for children's books and The Cookbook Store for culinary enthusiasts.

Chain Stores
Toronto is home to many chain stores. Some to keep an eye out for include Club Monaco, Gap, H&M, Banana Republic, Roots,

the Bay, Holt Renfrew, Pottery Barn, French Connection, Holt Renfrew, Winners and Forever 21.

Canadian Clothing Designers
Canadian designers are making more and more of a splash on the international fashion scene. Some labels to look for are: Comrags, Lida Baday, Ross Mayer, David Dixon, Carrie Hayes, Arthur Mendonça, Nada, Vawk by Sunny Fong, Bustle, Linda Lundstrom, Pink Tartan, Jeremy Laing, Common Cloth and Lucian Matis. These names can be found at several boutiques around the city or at the designers' own showrooms or stores.

China and Crystal
For the best china, crystal and flatware all in one place Ashley's or Birks are two great places to start. For just china there's also Teatro Verde and Norsud Home, both located in Yorkville.

Children's Stores
Really cool kids clothes can be found at Roots, GapKids and at department stores Sears and the Bay. Simon Says and Le Petit Pois on Mount Pleasant are great independent stores that stock clothes, piggy banks and more. Misdemeanours on Queen is another fab place for stylish girls' clothes, and Olly's on Yonge has the perfect shoes to match. The Spotted Zebra and The Toy Shop are two fun toy stores.

Designer Boutiques
For Canadian labels the best places are Price Roman, Psyche, Pho Pa, Boutique Le Trou, Fashion Crimes and Georgie Bolesworth. International design labels can be found at Holt Renfrew and at many independent shops across the city, including Freda's on Bathurst at King.

Home Furnishings
There are one-of-a-kind furnishing stores all over the city. But for a mix of contemporary and traditional furnishings there are many unique places along Queen West. Look for Dexterity, Du Verre, Industrial Storm, JP Purveyors Home, Pavilion, Rumah, Eco Italy Interiors, Commute Home, Haven, Quasi Modo Modern Furniture, Urban Mode, Era, Passion For The Past Antiques & Collectibles, Pickwick's Choice, Roseland Gallery and others.

Banana Republic, Bloor Street West

Pottery Barn on Bloor St. West

Jewellery

For really high-end there is Fabrice or Tous in Yorkville, or Birks. Other stores to watch out for include 18 Carat Jewels, Ann Sportun Experimental Jewellery, Bijoux Village Fine Jewellers, Bleu Comme Le Ciel, Bulgari, Citi Chic, Classic Creations, Colette Harmon, Corktown Designs, Eko, H. Williams & Co., Jewellery by Varouj, La Boutique Del Gioiello, Made You Look, Richard Booth and more.

Leather

Danier is a leather chain with several locations across the city. Independent stores include Rudsak, Acton, m0851, The Leather Ranch, The Olde Hide House, Phil Leather, T.O. Leather Fashions Ltd., Northbound Leather and taschen!

Malls

Malls of note downtown include the Eaton Centre and Hazelton Lanes. In the Greater Toronto Area (GTA) there are Yorkdale, Square One, Bayview Village and Pacific Mall.

Birks, Yorkville

Music

A selection of old-school vinyl stores includes Open City, Second Vinyl, Sonic Temple, Vortex and Rotate This. Other than HMV, independent music stores include Flash and Crash Music, Penguin Music, Refried Beats, Second Spin, She Said Boom and Sonic Boom.

Men's Clothing

For work clothes there are Tom's Place, Boomer, Great Stuff, Korry's, Le Club Menswear, Off The Cuff, Stagioni and Vassi. For casual wear other than the usual Gap, Banana Republic and Eddie Bauer, independent stores include Anti Hero, Decibel, Delphic, Gotstyle, Klaxon Howl, Lounge Retail, Noise, Nomad, Overkill and Uncle Otis. Lastly, for fancy evening occasions there are Harry Rosen, Nicolas Men and Perry's Yorkville.

Second-hand Clothing

Gently used and vintage clothing can be found at Act Two on Mount Pleasant, Antiques at the St. Lawrence Market North, Brava, Cabaret, House of Vintage, Preloved, I Miss You, Salvador Darling and 69 Vintage, all on Queen Street West. In Kensington Market there's also Courage My Love, Dancing Days and Exile. Other stores of note include Divine Decadence Originals, Gadabout, The Paper Bag Princess, Print Fine Vintage, Sticks and Stones Antiques and, of course, Value Village.

Parklands

Christine Beevis

Toronto waterfront walkway

In addition to its world-renowned entertainment, museums and shopping, Toronto is also known for its great green spaces, a large urban forest and excellent cycling. The city's tree-lined streets account for much of this greenery, but the most significant contributors are the wooded ravines that line the city's major rivers, the creeks and tributaries that feed them, the string of islands just to the south of Toronto Harbour and the long shore-based spit on the eastern lakeshore.

Visitors will discover an entirely different side of Toronto by exploring its parks and recreation trails. Many of them owe their existence to the destruction caused in 1954 by Hurricane Hazel, one of southern Ontario's worst natural disasters. Following the hurricane's massive destruction, the city developed a plan to disallow residential development along its ravines. Today, most of the ravines adjacent to Toronto's three rivers (the Humber, Don and Rouge) and three largest creeks (Etobicoke, Mimico and Highland) are parks, accounting for some twelve per cent of the city's area and covering more than 8,000 hectares. Portions of these parks are still undeveloped and are home not only to squirrels, chipmunks, raccoons and skunks, but also to groundhogs, opossums, porcupines, cottontail rabbits, red foxes, eastern coyotes and hundreds of birds, including waterfowl.

These parks offer numerous recreational opportunities, from riding stables, golf courses and quiet formal gardens, to a nineteenth-century town, farm and former brickworks. On many trails (often marked by the distinctive "Discovery Walks" symbol) the city has erected signs with maps and information on the history of each area, as well as the local flora and fauna. Brochures for many walks are available at City Hall, on the City of Toronto website and at all library branches.

Most parks are easily accessible by TTC and feature washroom facilities and picnic areas, as well as trails suitable for walking, biking or in-line skating. For visitors with limited time available, the best way to explore these parks and trails is to focus on the Toronto Islands, the Waterfront Trail or the Don Valley Trail.

Toronto Islands Park

The Toronto Islands are actually a collection of sandbars interrupted by lagoons and rivulets rather than truly separate entities. Originally a peninsula, the narrow neck connecting the Islands to the Toronto shoreline was destroyed by a series of storms in the 1850s. By the turn of the twentieth century, the Islands had been enlarged with landfill to three times their original size, and accommodated summer resorts, fancy homes and makeshift cottages.

Today the Islands house an airport, a small community of permanent homes (on Ward and Algonquin Islands), the Centreville amusement park, beaches, several yacht clubs and a school. They are also dotted with clean washrooms, drinking fountains and playgrounds. Bikes can be brought from the mainland or rented at Toronto Island Bicycle Rentals.

Spectacular views of the city are to be had from many points on the Islands.

The Islands can be reached by one of the ferries located at Bay Street and Queen's Quay, behind the Westin Harbour Castle Hotel.

Toronto Island with view of downtown

Walking tour of Toronto's Lakeshore (20 km)

The Martin Goodman Trail, which now runs the length of Toronto's waterfront, is a segment of the award-winning Waterfront Trail — an uninterrupted trail that stretches 325 kilometres from Stoney Creek near Hamilton in the west all the way to Trenton in the east. By following the trail east or west of Yonge Street, visitors will discover a number of the city's best parks and recreation areas.

East on the Martin Goodman Trail

From the foot of Yonge Street, follow the trail eastward along Queens Quay past the Redpath Sugar Refinery Museum, which celebrates one of Canada's first factories, founded in 1854. Continue south along Cherry Street through the Port Lands. Turn south (right) at Leslie Street, to reach the Leslie Street Spit (see below). A turn to the north (left) at Cherry Street

Cherry Beach

leads up the Don Valley (see below).

By continuing along the rest of the Martin Goodman Trail, walkers will discover the neighbourhood known as "the Beaches." Here the path runs beside a lovely tree-shaded boardwalk, past numerous playgrounds, snack bars and washroom facilities, and is only a block from the Beaches' fine restaurants, boutiques and shops. Farther east, the trail passes the R. C. Harris Filtration Plant. Built in the 1930s, the building is a good example of art deco style. The trail eventually reaches the Scarborough Bluffs (see page 93).

Leslie Street Spit

Officially called Tommy Thompson Park, the Spit is entirely man-made and may be the world's only "Important Bird Area" located in a major city. Since the 1950s, millions of tons of hard-packed clay, shale, construction debris and concrete have been deposited here to create an irregularly shaped series of peninsulas and coves with names like Rubble Beach.

Often referred to as an urban wilderness, the Spit has now become a refuge for more than 290 species of shore and water birds and about 300 plant species. The ponds, forests and wetlands are home to a variety of turtles, toads, frogs and snakes, and more than forty species of fish occupy the surrounding waters.

It is another excellent vantage point from which to see the city, as well as a great spot for biking and in-line skating on its 10-km two-lane paved surface, ideal for novice cyclists or skaters. Do note that it is windy here even on a summer day and blustery the rest of the time.

No private cars are allowed in the park, but a free shuttle van runs hourly from the main gate at the corner of Leslie and Commissioners streets. From about May to October dog owners are asked to leave their pets outside the park.

Don River at Riverdale Park

Don Valley

The lower reaches of the Don River once meandered gently through a large wetland before draining into Ashbridges Marsh at the edge of Lake Ontario. Gradually, as development in the area increased in the 1950s, the wetland was filled in and the river forced to flow between concrete walls to create more land for industry and the Don Valley Parkway. Today, the 38-km river is one of the most urbanized watersheds in Canada and enters Lake Ontario through the Keating Channel at the western end of the Port Lands.

Despite these changes, the Don Valley has remained a major refuge for local flora and fauna and is rich in recreational opportunities. Local residents have rehabilitated the river and its banks and planted more than 60,000 trees and shrubs, as well as swaths of wildflowers and grasses. A marsh has been created just south of Bloor Street to help filter the water and attract wildlife.

Three remnants of nineteenth-century life are of particular interest on the Don Trail:

Farther north along the valley is the Brick Works, the last of Toronto's brickyards to close in 1989, 100 years after it opened its doors. Now part of the park system, its 16.5 hectares have been restored into a magical setting of wetlands, marshes, meadows and forest. The former quarry face is internationally acclaimed by geologists for clearly displaying successive waves of prehistoric glaciation. The site is accessible from the Bayview Extension north of the Danforth.

Todmorden Mills and Art Centre houses the Eastwood-Skinner paper mill — reputed to have been continuously occupied longer than any other building in Toronto. Also on the site are a rustic cottage built in 1797 and a mid-nineteenth-century house. Nearby, a wildflower preserve has been created. Todmorden offers a range of arts and craft activities and is accessible from the Don Trail or Pottery Road (off Broadview or Bayview).

Toronto Brick Works Factory

As it continues north from Pottery Road, the Don Trail becomes hillier and leads to E. T. Seton Park, named after the nineteenth-century naturalist and chronicler of the Don Valley. Here, at "the Forks of the Don," there is a choice. The westerly Wilket Creek route leads to Edwards Gardens. A pleasant place to walk, the gardens have both formal and natural areas, including a large rose garden and an immense collection of rhododendrons. The on-site Civic Garden Centre is the headquarters for gardeners throughout the city. It houses an excellent gift shop and offers annual sales of plants, bulbs and seeds and numerous lectures and tours.

The easterly route at the Forks leads to Taylor Creek Park and Dentonia Park Golf Course. Farther north, in the Central Don region, are Sunnybrook Park's sports fields, a Vita Parcours exercise trail and the Central Don Stables near Eglinton Avenue and Leslie Street, with two indoor arenas and some 15 km of trails.

The Don River Trail is ideal for cyclists, hikers, joggers and in-line skaters. The main route can be reached by taking the Martin Goodman Trail east along Queen's Quay and turning north at Cherry Street.

Scarborough Bluffs and Bluffers Park

Stretching for about 14 km along the Lake Ontario shore at the easternmost point of the Martin Goodman Trail, the Scarborough Bluffs and Bluffers Park rise from the Eastern Beaches of Toronto in the west to West Hill in the east. At their highest point at Cliffside, the cliffs (also known as "Cathedral Bluffs" to local

The Scarborough Bluffs

residents) rise as high as 100 m above the water.
Primarily formed by the erosion of packed clay soil, in
some places the clay has been shaped into interesting
sculpture-like shapes.

Sunnyside Pavillion

The best place to view the Bluffs is from
the shore, and the only road access is from
Bellamy Road at Cliffside, which leads down
to Bluffers Park. A popular point for
picnickers and boating enthusiasts, the Park
does not offer separate pedestrian or biking
trails. To get there, take Brimley Road south
from Kingston Road until its end point.

West on the Martin Goodman Trail

Westward from Yonge the Martin Goodman
Trail leads past some of Toronto's most
renowned landmarks — the CN Tower,
Rogers Centre and Harbourfront. At Bathurst
Street, the trail passes Little Norway Park,
which commemorates the Norwegian aviators
who trained at the nearby City Centre Airport
during the Second World War. Next comes
Coronation Park, named in memory of the crowning of
King George VI in 1937. Farther along, the trail is
flanked by the impressive archways of Exhibition
Place to the north (the site of North America's first
urban wind turbine), and Ontario Place to the south.
The trail then heads on towards Marilyn Bell Park,
named for the sixteen-year-old girl who was the first
person to swim across Lake Ontario in 1954.

The area from this point to the Humber River is
known as the "Western Beaches." Central to this area
is Sunnyside Park, whose 1922 bathing pavilion
remains intact. To the north, and easily accessible, is
High Park (see below). Just before the trail crosses the
suspension bridge spanning the Humber River (see
below), it passes the Lion Monument — a majestic
limestone sculpture marking King George VI's visit to
Canada in 1939.

Of special interest in this area are: the Humber Bay
Butterfly Habitat; a series of ponds used to filter storm
water runoff; the meditative Sheldon Lookout; the
mouth of Mimico Creek; and just 1 km past the
suspension bridge, a delightful footbridge designed by
Santiago Calatrara, the architect of BCE Place. The
Waterfront Trail continues farther into the former City
of Etobicoke, sometimes as a dedicated off-street path,
at other times an on-street but clearly marked route.

High Park

High Park, situated in Toronto's west end, is one of the
city's largest recreation areas and welcomes more than
one million visitors annually. The 161-hectare park
was formerly the estate of architect and city surveyor
John Howard, whose home, Colborne Lodge, sits on
high land overlooking the lake. Ecologically, the park
is unique for its rare savannah habitat treed with black
oak. In addition to bike and hiking trails, the park

contains the full-service Grenadier Restaurant, snack bars, a small zoo, the Jamie Bell Adventure Playground (designed by local children, parents and teachers), numerous ponds and streams, a motorized tram, an outdoor skating rink in the winter and a sculpture collection.

High Park is accessible by subway (at High Park station) or by car (enter via Bloor Street just west of Keele Street). Note that the park's roadways are closed to cars on summer weekends.

Humber River Trail (18 km)
The Humber River was an important transportation route for the area's First Nations inhabitants and for subsequent explorers and missionaries. Although heavily developed throughout the first half of the twentieth century, the Humber now has much of the pastoral feel it must have had in earlier times, thanks largely to the impact of Hurricane Hazel in 1954. Since then, the shore has been reforested and naturalized to prevent future flooding.

Top and bottom: Humber River Pedestrian Bridge

The Humber Trail is a pleasant 13 km ride or walk from the Lakeshore to Scarlett Mills Park at Eglinton. An additional 5 km leads all the way to Dixon Road. The route travels in a gently winding northerly direction past the Old Mill (at Bloor Street) and on through Etienne Brûlé Park. It then passes through Home Smith Park to James Gardens, a former family estate with spring-fed pools and rare trees. Also nearby are Black Creek Pioneer Village and Lambton Woods, site of a large wildflower preserve.

To reach the Humber from the Martin Goodman Trail, head north at Windermere Avenue, pass beneath the Gardiner Expressway, around the back of the Humber Treatment Plant and through South Humber Park. From here, a short on-street jog up Stephen Drive is required before rejoining the off-street path opposite the Humber Marshes.

Organized Activities, Special Events
A number of organizations offer guided tours of parks and recreation areas. Among these are the Parks Department of the City of Toronto, the Green Tourism Association and Heritage Toronto. The Toronto Field Naturalists and LEAF (Local Enhancement and Appreciation of Forests) offer customized guided walks. There are numerous opportunities for cyclists to take part in guided tours; information is available from the Toronto Cycling Committee. Access Toronto has current information about a variety of cultural events hosted in the parks.

Sports

Jean Paul Pelosi

Toronto Maple Leafs banner, Air Canada Centre

Toronto is a premier sports town where there is never a shortage of action. Hockey, football, baseball, lacrosse, soccer or motor racing — the city has something to suit every type of fan. Ticket prices are reasonable for most events and all of the major venues are close to public transportation routes. And even if fixtures are sold out, Toronto offers plenty of sports bars and restaurants screening live games day and night.

Hockey

From October through to April, Toronto embraces hockey the same way Londoners revel in soccer and Mumbaites celebrate cricket. To be in the city during this time is a treat for sports lovers and casual observers alike.

The pre-game buzz is as much a part of the Toronto hockey experience as the contest itself. Crowds gather outside the 18,000 seat Air Canada Centre (ACC), where the city's beloved Toronto Maple Leafs play their hockey. The Front Street bars near the ACC are usually packed and Union Station swarms with raucous fans grabbing a burger or hot dog. During hockey season, there is no event more eagerly anticipated by locals than a Maple Leafs game — other than a Maple Leafs playoff game that is!

As a member of the "Original Six" National Hockey League (NHL) clubs, the Toronto Maple Leafs are one of the most storied franchises in all of professional sports. They have won thirteen Stanley Cup championships since their inception in 1917 and have been a part of Canadian folklore for generations. Legendary names like Don Metz, Tim Horton, Frank Mahovlich and Darryl Sittler still inspire fans today. And while the number of Leafs all-stars has declined over the years, the popularity of the team has not. Fuelled by a rich history and unwavering in spirit, Toronto's hockey fans seem to multiply when fall comes around. And they are as expertly critical of their players as they are blindly devoted to them.

Ricoh Coliseum, at Exhibition Place

Though it's been more than forty years since the Maple Leafs last won the Cup, there have been signs of a renaissance in recent seasons. The team continues to take a more physical style under head coach Ron Wilson, and has shown that they can compete with the best clubs in the NHL. And the locals are believers — willing the team on every year, no matter the results of the previous season. Talking about the ups and downs of the Maple Leafs is a favourite pastime of Torontonians.

The Toronto Marlies of the American Hockey League (AHL) provide another hockey option when Leafs tickets are hard to come by — and they often are. The Marlies play at Ricoh Coliseum, and they are the Leafs' farm club. A number of great NHL players first made their name playing for the Marlies. A more intimate hockey fixture can be found at the Hershey Centre outside the downtown area in nearby Mississauga, home of the Ontario Hockey League's (OHL) Mississauga St. Michael's Majors.

Baseball

Perhaps the most recognizable venue in Toronto is the giant, white-domed Rogers Centre, still known by locals as the SkyDome. Built in 1989, the Dome is a hallmark of 1980s ballpark architecture — futuristic and grand. It also houses two-time Major League Baseball (MLB) World Series winners the Toronto Blue Jays, who won the series in 1992 and 1993. The SkyDome was the first covered park in North America with a fully retractable roof. Like most baseball stadiums across the continent, the Dome has its own charm and provides a thrilling setting for nine innings of "hardball."

Rogers Centre, home of the Toronto Blue Jays

From April to October, Jays supporters soak up the hot summer air, sip on cold beer and watch the team's sluggers make a few dents in the stadium panelling. On game days, early birds gather for breakfast or a snack along John Street. Fans hustle down Blue Jays Way toward the Dome's main entrance, eager for tickets behind home plate. The sidewalks along Front Street near the Rogers Centre are typically filled with street painters, rowdy scalpers, kids with big novelty baseball gloves and hotdog vendors.

And the Rogers Centre is a great place for the Mexican wave, which comes around on a slow scoring day. The championship banners hanging from the ceiling are a reminder of the standard of baseball once played in the stadium. And judging by the ever-increasing attendance, today's big budget Jays are close to tasting similar success.

Basketball

With the likes of Canadian-born Steve Nash lighting-up the National Basketball Association (NBA) at present, both Canada's and Toronto's basketball cultures are stronger than ever. But like most NBA expansion teams, the Toronto Raptors struggled to make noise in the competitive Atlantic Division for many years. After trading away the franchise's most prolific scorer, Vince Carter, in 2004, many felt bewildered about the team's future. Following a couple of transition years and a playbook redesign, however, things are starting to look brighter for Toronto's professional basketball team.

The Raptors are fast becoming one of the powerhouse clubs of the NBA's Eastern Conference. They play a fast brand of basketball and dazzle fans with an athletic squad that shoots a high percentage. And they even lure the occasional celebrity fan to home games at the Air Canada Centre. (Samuel L. Jackson, amongst others, has been known to drop in and show his support.)

The Raptors were division champions in the 2006–2007 season, earning them a playoff berth and a significant chunk of respect around the league. Repeating that success has proven difficult since then, but there are hopes for another run at the NBA finals under new coach Jay Triano. And while keeping all-star power forward Chris Bosh signed on with Toronto may prove to be a difficult task, the team continues to develop and there is plenty of reason for Raptor fans to be excited about the future of basketball in the city.

Raptors' tickets can be expensive, especially those located courtside. A better selection of seats is generally available a week or two ahead of game day.

Rogers Centre baseball field

Leafs and Raptors banners

**Toronto Argonauts
Quarterback
Michael Bishop**

Canadian Football

The Toronto Argonauts of the Canadian Football
League (CFL) is the city's oldest sports organization,
dating back to 1873. The "Argos" have a loyal fan base
that appreciates the intricacies of Canadian football.
Like the American equivalent, Canadian football has
large padding, clashing helmets and forward passing.
With the exception of a few rule differences, it is
essentially the same game. The Canadian game,
however, prides itself on high scoring. With less
running from the backfield and more emphasis on the
quarterback, football north of the border tends to be
faster and more spontaneous.

One of the more high profile and successful squads
in the Canadian Football League, the Argonauts last
won the Grey Cup in 2004, and finished strongly in
2006 before losing the East Division final to rivals, the
Montreal Alouettes. Since then, success has been hard
to come by, and the team has gone through a number
of head coaches, in addition to numerous roster
changes. But a club with this much championship
experience (fifteen Grey Cups in all) won't be out of
the winners' circle for long.

Argos tickets are usually available for home games,
but the best seats go quickly.

Soccer

Major League Soccer (MLS) arrived in Toronto in
2007 in the shape of Toronto FC. And the newest MLS
team — Canada's first — has been a rousing success
so far. The club enjoyed strong fan support in its first
season at BMO Field, buoyed by the city's
multicultural population, which tends to appreciate the

"beautiful game." The stadium, located at Exhibition Place, also hosted games for the 2007 FIFA U-20 World Cup.

Though results have been mixed since the "Reds'" inaugural season, the club plays before full houses and as set MLS attendance records. With its popularity at the grassroots level and now in the professional game, soccer is destined to be a Toronto staple for years to come.

Other Toronto Sports

Toronto also provides elite level lacrosse, one of North America's best hard-court tennis tournaments, a great day at the horses and the high-octane world of motor racing. Amongst many other first-class sporting events the mix also includes squash, rugby and cricket.

The Toronto Rock shares the Air Canada Centre with the Leafs and Raptors and has won an astonishing five National Lacrosse League championships over the last ten years. And because the team has never failed to make the playoffs since the league began in 1987, the red, white and blue are a hot ticket between January and April.

The world's best tennis players converge on Toronto every second year for the Canadian Open, better known as the Rogers Cup these days (the city alternates hosting the men's and women's tournaments with Montreal). The likes of Roger Federer and Rafael Nadal headline the men's draw, while Amelie Mauresmo and Ana Ivanovic were recent champions in

Top and bottom:
BMO field

the women's tournament. The event is held at the Rexall Centre, on the campus of York University, just north of the city.

The Woodbine Racetrack, northwest of the downtown area, provides racing of the four-legged variety. Big money has been spent to turn the venue into a first-class entertainment complex but the main draw card is the thoroughbred and harness racing. Interestingly, the legendary Secretariat ran his last race at Woodbine. North America's oldest thoroughbred event, the Queen's Plate, has been run at Woodbine since 1860. The race is 2 km (1.25 mi.) long and is exclusively for three-year-old thoroughbred horses foaled in Canada. Every July, seventeen starters fill the gates for a chance at the million-dollar purse. The 2009 winner was Eye of the Leopard, ridden by Eurico Rosa Da Silva, a Brazilian jockey based in Canada.

A day at the Woodbine Racetracks

Those with a need for speed can enjoy Champ Car motor racing at Exhibition Place each year. Formerly the Molson Grand Prix, the Honda Indy of Toronto is fast, furious and well worth the price of admission. Champ cars are single-seat open wheel racing vehicles, similar to Formula One cars. The main difference, however, is that they are heavier and possess sculpted undersides that enable easier overtaking. Champ cars also use treadless tires to enhance their performance. Scottish driver Dario Franchitti won the 2009 race, the second time he has won in Toronto.

Squash is also a crowd pleaser in Toronto, which is home to the PACE Canadian Classic at the John Bassett Theatre in the Metro Toronto Convention Centre every January. Lightning quick Egyptian teenager Ramy Ashour has been a consistent winner in recent years and is likely to star in the competition for years to come.

Toronto is also no stranger to high-level rugby, playing co-host to the Churchill Cup, which features Canada, the United States, England and three other invited sides. Ireland A won the 2009 tournament, which was held in the United States.

Highlighting its diversity, Toronto is known as the mecca of cricket in the Americas as well. There are more than 200 cricket teams and fifty grounds around town. Various international fixtures have also been played in Toronto over the years, and just north of the city lies the highly regarded Maple Leaf Cricket Club, which is only one of two grounds in Canada to be approved for one-day internationals.

Gay Toronto

Danny Glenwright

Toronto Pride
Parade

Toronto takes pride in being gay and fantastic, and this secret has been out of the closet for years. Canada's largest city is one of the only places in the world where it's commonplace to see same-sex couples strolling hand-in-hand along city streets, both in and out of its gay neighbourhoods. It's also one of the few places where those same hands might be sporting wedding rings, thanks to recent legislation legalizing gay marriage. But for those who are not the domestic type, Toronto also has plenty to offer for single travellers looking for a little debauchery. Toronto's annual pride celebrations are one of the world's largest, and the city is also home to North America's biggest gay and lesbian theatre company and Canada's leading queer film festival. Toronto will also play host to the international World Pride Festival in 2014. And with the recent emergence of a new gay neighbourhood, Toronto is one of the few international cities that can claim more than one gay village.

The Nucleus

Church Street, between Bloor and Dundas, is the historic heart of Toronto's gay world and the go-to place for all things pink. Located in the centre of the city, it is recognized by most locals as the true queer village and is within walking distance of most of the city's major sights and many hotels. Even though it has lost a bit of its original lustre over the years, it is still an important stop for any gay traveller. Within a few city blocks can be found most of Toronto's gay bars, restaurants, bathhouses and shops. Most windows display a rainbow sticker, the pedestrians are fabulous and there is a party to be had behind nearly every door.

Many of Toronto's gay institutions can be found on the strip between Bloor and Carlton. Woody's and its twin-sister bar Sailor (the two are connected) are Church's most recognizable nightspots, having gained notoriety on gay television as the setting for many scenes in the popular American series *Queer as Folk*, which was filmed in Toronto. Shoulder to bare shoulder most nights of the week, Woody's is known for its theme nights — which include a best chest contest — often hosted by Toronto's most popular drag queens. Zipperz-Cell Block, at the south end of the strip at Carlton Street, is another gay scene mainstay, known not only for boisterous cabaret-themed drag shows, but also for a popular piano bar and busy weekend dance nights. Further north are two newer nightspots: Voglié and Straight Lounge. Voglié boasts some of Toronto's hottest lesbian events and Straight is the place to be seen for the trendy, polished young gay set. It's also the best spot for yummy martinis, which come in every colour of the rainbow.

Church & Wellesley

If you prefer rougher men, head to the Black Eagle, which caters to the leather-and-denim crowd, and check out their popular underwear, wrestling and fetish theme nights. Although women are welcome in most gay bars in Toronto, ladies might want to visit Slack's restaurant and bar, the most well-known lesbian hangout and another gay-scene perennial. And those in the mood for more dancing usually head to Fly, Toronto's premier gay dance club, on Gloucester Street, or The Barn and Stables, a legendary bar and dance complex dominating the corner of Church and McGill streets. The Barn, which was closed for several

Zelda's

Pride Flag

The Gladstone

years following the murder of its owner, was recently restored and reopened, yet it's still sporting the notorious mural of two cowboys with their arms around one another and its dance nights are busier than ever.

After a wild Toronto night, comfort food and maybe a stiff Bloody Mary can be found at the aptly named Hair of the Dog, south on the Church strip. It offers gay Toronto's best brunch. Or there's Bulldog Cafe, which has the city's tastiest lattes. The Churchmouse and Firkin at Maitland is the strip's best pub with two floors, a cozy interior and Toronto's friendliest staff. For outdoor drinking in the summer season, directly across the street is O'Grady's pumping patio, the best place to scan the street for cute boys and sassy girls.

Fuzion is an upscale restaurant featuring a delectable contemporary menu designed by one of Oprah Winfrey's personal chefs. Located in a gorgeous 120-year-old Victorian house, the fashionable eatery on Church morphs into a swank lounge after the dinner hours and its garden and suitably named outdoor "Flirt Bar" is just private enough to sneak a late-night smooch.

And for up-to-date advice on all things gay in Toronto, visit Church Street's newly expanded and renovated 519 Community Centre. It offers courses, support groups, counselling and the latest Toronto information on HIV/AIDS and safe sex. Those interested in Canada's queer past may also want to spend a few hours sifting through the collections in the Canadian Lesbian and Gay Archives at its new location on Isabella Street.

Go West

Considering Toronto's multicultural flavour, it is only natural that its ever-growing gay community would also diversify and branch out. A fresh queer vibe has sprung up in the city's west end — nicknamed "Queer West Toronto" or QWT — and the area is now a mandatory stop on any Toronto tour. The Queen West strip and Parkdale areas are the hub of queer activity in the west, with most of Toronto's newest gay and lesbian venues situated here. Gentrification has turned what was once a rundown strip into a colourful centre for artsy types and local hipsters, and it is also home to some of the city's best restaurants and trendiest accommodations.

The Drake and Gladstone are the most chic hotels on Queen Street and the site of several of the area's popular mixed nights. The

Gladstone (or "Gaystone" as locals call it) is the oldest hotel in Toronto and has recently undergone extensive renovations that saw each room individually designed by a local artist.

The Beaver Cafe is a Queen West eatery with a classic Canadian name but typical kitschy American diner decor. Known in the daytime for its tasty paninis and at night for its vibrant queer nights, it is the newest staple of Toronto's gay scene. Monthly lesbian, transsexual, gay mixer and bear-and-cub nights are all well attended and the employees (like the clientele), are eclectic and friendly.

Gay-owned Mitzi's Sister is another stylish west-end restaurant and nightspot, as are its Parkdale neighbours Stone's Place and Mezzrow's. Another popular hangout, Rhino, boasts local artwork and The Cadillac Lounge has a large, busy patio that caters to the local queer crowd. Queen West's Come As You Are is Canada's first co-operatively run sex store and with its flawless selection of books and toys, it is a definite gay hangout.

Statue of Alexander Wood

The newest Toronto gaybourhood is not only confined to Queen Street; visiting queens can seek out other fashionable venues on nearby College and Dundas, including Andy Poolhall, El Convento Rico and the Mod Club. And Toronto's newest gay neighbourhood is also hosting the now annual Queer West Fest in mid-June, the latest celebration on the city's gay calendar, just a week before the main gay pride festivities.

Mark Your Calendar

Every year, during the last week of June, Toronto is transformed into a gay wonderland. The annual Pride Day is one of only eight City of Toronto "Signature Events" and the rainbow flag is raised at City Hall. Heralded as one of the world's largest gay events, Toronto Pride annually records up to one million spectators at its frenzied and flamboyant Pride Parade and almost as many at the myriad events on Church Street and throughout the city.

Buddies In Bad Times Theatre

The Church Street area sparkles again in October for the annual Halloween street party when the strip is decorated with the best tricks and treats in the city. For those who like it a bit kinkier, there is Toronto's version of San Francisco's Folsom Street Fair, an annual fetish event. Now called the Church Street Fetish Fair, the growing event is held annually in mid-

August and Church Street is closed to traffic in order to host a large marketplace and dance area. And for those who are into runway fashion, Toronto's annual Fashion Cares benefit for the AIDS Committee of Toronto (ACT) is the city's glitziest event. Brush elbows with international and local celebrities (Patti LaBelle, Erasure, Shirley Bassey and Pamela Anderson have appeared in past years), sip champagne and gawk at the gorgeous, half-naked entertainment, all while supporting a good cause.

Inside Out, Toronto's annual lesbian and gay film festival, is held for eleven days at the end of May and is the largest queer film festival in Canada. It regularly averages crowds of more than 30,000 so it's best to get tickets ahead of time for the many screenings, panel discussions and artist talks. Alternatively, for live queer drama, Buddies in Bad Times Theatre on Alexander Street is the largest gay and lesbian theatre company in North America and regularly presents the country's best talent in queer drama, comedy, burlesque and cabaret.

Knowing Me, Knowing You

To experience the steamier side of Toronto, there are eight bathhouses in the city, most of which are located in the gay ghetto near Church Street (seven of them are open 24 hours). Spa Excess on Carlton Street is well-known and has been voted one of the world's best saunas by several international gay magazines. Steamworks on Church is also popular. New, clean and busy most nights of the week, it has a pool, hot tub, private rooms where you can view more than fifteen porn channels, a gym and monthly theme nights with local DJs. For strippers, Remington's on Yonge Street is a Toronto institution with two floors, a wide range of male flesh and plenty of side rooms for those who want their very own private dancer. For a public display of flesh, take a ferry to Toronto Island and soak up the rays and gays at Hanlan's Point, Toronto's nude beach. And for that perfect swimsuit, Canada's largest gay retailer, Priape, sells the latest trunks as well as leather gear, DVDs, sex toys and circuit-party tickets from its Church Street location.

Woody's

For the most up-to-date information on queer Toronto events, pick up a copy of one of the city's two gay mags — Xtra or Fab — or tune into Proud FM, Toronto's gay and lesbian radio station at 103.9 on the dial. This Ain't the Rosedale Library is a quaint gay-friendly bookstore in Kensington Market with a great selection of local and international gay magazines and literature. As well, gay-owned Glad Day Bookshop on Yonge Street has been operating since the 1970s and has a friendly and knowledgeable staff.

Annual Events

Lonny Knapp

Thousands of people from all over the world descend on Toronto all year round. Some come to take part in conferences and trade shows at the Metro Toronto Convention Centre and Exhibition Place in the heart of downtown, or at the International Centre near Pearson Airport. Others come to be a part of cultural celebrations in one of Toronto's many eclectic neighbourhoods, or to join the thousands at one of Toronto's infamous street parties. Some are enticed by the world-class cuisine served up in the city's restaurants and cafés, others by Toronto's vibrant arts scene.

Word on the Street Festival

With literally hundreds of annual events happening throughout the year, ranging from the expected to the eclectic, and with more events added every year, there is always something going on in Toronto.

Described below are just a few of these eagerly anticipated events. The latest issues of *NOW* magazine, *eye weekly* and *Toronto Life* publish updated event listings.

Skating, Nathan Phillips Square

Winter

Despite the cold, Torontonians don't hibernate in the winter — in Toronto, winter is a time of celebration.

The Royal Agricultural Winter Fair, a Toronto tradition since 1922, is the largest indoor agricultural, horticultural, equestrian and canine event in the world. This ten-day fair brings the sights, sounds and even the smells of the country to the city every November, providing Torontonians with the opportunity to watch

Floats: Santa Claus Parade

One of a Kind Show wares: Frederique Bonmatin, top, Tara Marsh, bottom

horses jump, trot and dance in competition for the blue ribbon. Other attractions include a livestock auction and the "Biggest Vegetable Competition," in which farmers from across Ontario show off their prize (and sometimes freakishly large) pumpkins, tomatoes and zucchinis to the amazement of the audience. The fair is educational, entertaining and fun for the whole family.

The Christmas season gets under way in mid-November with the arrival of the annual Santa Claus Parade, a Toronto institution for more than a century. Every year thousands line up along the parade route to catch a glimpse of jolly old St. Nick. What began as a one-float parade in 1905 is now an impressive display: animated floats accompanied by literally hundreds of clowns and at least a dozen marching bands parade through downtown to the delight of cocoa-sipping children of all ages.

On December 31, thousands of revellers descend on Nathan Phillips Square to rock in the New Year as part of Citytv's annual New Year's Eve Bash. The outdoor event is televised across the nation and features performances by Canada's hottest recording acts — in recent years, sizzling performances by the likes of Nelly Furtado kept parka-wearing partygoers warm despite frosty temperatures. The family-friendly event is billed as the biggest party in town, and it is definitely the cheapest: admission is always free.

The TorontoWinter City Festival arrives to heat up Toronto in late January. This fourteen-day event, showcasing Toronto's hospitality industry, is really three festivals in one: Winterlicious celebrates Toronto's culinary diversity by offering discounted dinners at the city's finest restaurants; Wild on Winter (WOW) treats the city to free outdoor performances by Canadian musicians and world-renowned theatre troupes on festival weekends at Nathan Phillips Square; and the Warm Up Series invites everyone indoors at the city's top tourist attractions with discounted admissions and special events scheduled.

Spring

Plenty of rain, at least one unexpected snowstorm and two massive gardening shows regularly herald the arrival of spring in Toronto. The International Home and Garden Show at the International Centre, and Canada Blooms at the Metro Toronto Convention Centre are two events designed for all those with green thumbs. A stunning display of local and exotic flowers in full bloom in March is a sure way to shake off the winter blues.

Twice annually the One of a Kind Show rolls into town. This ten-day event appears first in November and then again in March, bringing innovative artists, jewellers, clothing designers and the plain crafty together under one roof to show off and sell their hand-made and one-of-a-kind wares. Considered by many to be Canada's top arts and crafts show, One of a Kind is a great place to find distinctive and unique gifts.

Festival season begins in April with Hot Docs — North America's largest documentary film festival. This highly anticipated event features more than 100 cutting-edge documentaries from Canada and around the world and offers Torontonians the opportunity to

Hot Docs film festival

see many of the year's award-winning documentary films long before their theatrical releases. The rise in the popularity of documentary films suggests that movie goers crave substance over style, but although the Hot Docs festival has expanded, it maintains its intimate feel; many of the films' directors appear at the screenings to answer questions and to stimulate discussions after the credits roll.

Since 2000, Doors Open Toronto has been allowing visitors to bypass those pesky security guards and employee-only signs to view more than 150 of Toronto's historical and landmark buildings. Banks, breweries, courthouses, cemeteries, factories and office buildings offer free access and guided tours of areas ordinarily off limits to the public for two days in May.

Summer

Despite high temperatures and the sometimes intense humidity, Toronto is truly an exciting place to be in the summer when every park, neighbourhood and public space is busy with celebrations both big and small.

Toronto Jazz Festival

In June, the sound of saxophones floats on the summer air, signalling the kickoff of the Toronto Jazz Festival. Since its inception in 1987, this renowned event has featured legendary jazz artists like Sonny Rollins, Oscar Peterson and Peter Appleyard in a series of ticketed and free indoor and outdoor concerts.

Launched in 2007, Luminato adds yet another not-to-be missed event to the already jam-packed summer calendar. This ten-day multidisciplinary arts festival aims to provoke thought and encourage participation with hundreds of free event, performance and art installations throughout the city. As part of the 2009 festival, exactly 1,623 guitar-toting Torontonians gathered in Yonge-Dundas Square to strum Neil Young's "Helpless." The event set a new Canadian record for largest guitar ensemble, but narrowly missed a mention in the *Guinness World Book of Records*.

Drowsy Chaperone, Toronto Fringe Festival

In an explosion of vibrant colour and booty-shaking sounds, Toronto celebrates its lesbian, gay, bisexual, transsexual, transgender, intersex, queer, questioning and two-spirited communities with Pride Week, held annually in the last week of June.

Every July, the Fringe Festival, Toronto's largest theatre festival, commandeers every imaginable (and some unimaginable) theatre space in the city as more than 100 independent productions take to the stage at almost thirty venues across town. The Fringe Festival offers up both classic and alternative stage productions that typically range from the truly great to the gloriously disastrous and has notoriously made fans of those who claim to despise the theatre.

Musician, Toronto Jazz Festival

Toronto's other theatre festival kicks off in the first week of August — SummerWorks hosts more than forty independent performances at a handful of venues across town, as well as offsite performances, workshops and a host of free activities. It is the largest juried theatre festival in Canada.

In mid-July, the Beaches Jazz Festival arrives, offering more great music by local and international jazz musicians. And every weekend during the summer, eclectic performers from around the world (and just around the corner) take the stage as part of the Harbourfront Music Series.

Opa! In early August, vendors serve up flaming cheese (saganaki) and seasoned meat skewers (souvlaki) by the truckload at the Taste of the Danforth festival. Each year huge crowds attend this multicultural street party on Danforth Avenue, home of North America's largest Greek community, to celebrate Greek culture and to sample mouth-watering Greek cuisine.

Then, just when you thought summer in Toronto couldn't get any hotter, the Toronto Caribbean Carnival (Caribana) arrives to turn up the heat. During this two-week party, the smell of spicy jerk chicken and the sound of reggae music fill the air. The festival culminates on the August long weekend with a parade featuring thousands of brilliantly costumed men, women and children, and dozens of floats carrying calypso, steel drum and reggae bands that keep onlookers along the parade route grooving all day long.

Every Labour Day Weekend the skies above Toronto become a playground for fearless pilots who take to the air in state-of-the-art military jets, restored relics and souped-up stunt planes to thrill and astound the fans on the ground as part of the Canadian International Air Show. Among the regular participants at the Air Show are Canada's iconic Snowbirds, a precision aerobatic team that flies over Toronto's skyline in impossibly tight formation.

Caribana Street Parade

A Toronto tradition for more than 100 years, the Canadian National Exhibition (the "Ex") heralds the end of summer. A trip to the Ex is bittersweet for children who know that after they've finished eating their fill of cotton candy, corn dogs and popcorn, and after they have played all the games in the midway and spun themselves silly on amusement park rides, it's time for the new school year to begin.

Word on the Street Festival

Fall

In a display of glitz and glamour, a galaxy of stars comes out to shine every September as part of the Toronto International Film Festival (TIFF). Since its inception in 1976, the TIFF has grown exponentially and is now considered the premier film festival in North America, and second only to the Cannes Film Festival globally. During the ten-day festival, megastars — in town to promote their latest flicks — can be spotted shopping, dining and partying in Toronto's tony Yorkville. Their appearance inevitably turns normally polite and mild-mannered Torontonians into digital-camera-wielding paparazzi.

Word on the Street

Scotiabank Nuit Blanche, *Night of St. John*

Scotiabank Nuit Blanche, *Balloonscape*

The Word on the Street Book and Magazine Festival transforms Queen's Park into a book-lover's paradise on the last Sunday in September. This one-day free festival features workshops for aspiring authors, readings and signings by hundreds of authors and poets and performances and storytellers for the kids. Book lovers can have their favourite books signed by Canada's best-selling authors or discover the season's hottest titles while purchasing discounted books and magazine subscriptions at the huge market place. Word on the Street is held annually to unite publishers, authors and book lovers in a celebration of the written word and is always fun for the whole family.

Wacky, weird and wonderful, Nuit Blanche, the newest of Toronto's annual events, showcases our city's vibrant arts scene and gives Torontonians yet another excuse to stay up all night. This sunset-to-sunrise celebration, held at the beginning of October, is a celebration of contemporary art and culture and a huge hit with insomniacs, sleepwalkers and kids hoping to stay up past their bedtime. The inaugural celebration in 2006 attracted more than 400,000 attendees to free, family-friendly and adult-oriented events throughout the city. This unique festival features all-night exhibits at typical venues for the arts such as museums and art galleries; performances at non-typical venues such as libraries, churches, nightclubs and car washes; and massive art installations that hijack entire parks or spill out into the city streets.

The International Festival of Authors rounds off Toronto's annual event calendar at the end of October. This ten-day event attracts the best writers of contemporary world literature to Toronto for readings, interviews, lectures and book signings at the Harbourfront Centre. Highlights include readings by Giller Prize- and Governor General's Literary Award-winning authors. At the closing-night gala, the Harbourfront Festival Prize is awarded to an individual deemed to have made a substantial contribution to the world of books and writing.

Central Toronto Neighbourhoods

St. Lawrence Neighbourhood

Bruce Bell

St. James'
Cathedral

On the morning of April 7, 1849 a massive fire swept through the downtown core of Toronto. In its aftermath an opportunity arose to replace an old colonial town that was mostly built of wood and sticks with a new city built of stone and brick. With only a few exceptions, the structures of the St. Lawrence neighbourhood — once the centre of the old town of Toronto — were built after the Great Fire of 1849, and at its centre was the magnificent St. Lawrence Hall. The neighbourhood that over the years has spread out around the hall and adjacent market has been called the heart of Toronto and today offers visitors a great mix of historic architecture, first-rate theatres, unique museums and cozy restaurants.

St. Lawrence Hall and the Farmers' Market

Built in the classical style at the corner of King Street East and Jarvis Streets, St. Lawrence Hall looks much the same as it did when first opened in 1851. With its intricately carved stonework and massive Corinthian columns rising up from the street, this brilliant structure, topped off with a cupola dome inset with a clock, ranked as the pre-eminent concert hall in Toronto for the first twenty-five years of its life.

But in 1874 a spectacular new venue, the Grand Opera House, opened in Toronto, and it immediately stole the crown from St. Lawrence Hall. The latter never recovered and began a long decline that would last well into the twentieth century. The restoration of St. Lawrence Hall and the building of a new North Market became part of Toronto's official centennial project, celebrating 100 years of Canada's Confederation. On the evening of December 28, 1967, Governor General Roland Michener, along with architect Eric Arthur, officially reopened the Hall by igniting the gas fireplace in the Great Hall in front of a glittering crowd. On that night St. Lawrence Hall was rightfully declared a national historic site. Today, after 150 years, the Hall is still a much sought-after location for wedding receptions, graduation balls and musical recitals.

Top and bottom: Farmer's Market (North Building)

The Farmers' Market — also known as the North Market — is attached to the south end of St. Lawrence Hall, and although the utilitarian structure in which it is housed was built much later, it shares in the Hall's venerable history. In fact, every Saturday for more than 200 years, farmers from the outlining areas have come to this spot to sell their goods. The market is busiest before noon on Saturdays, when it is filled with stalls selling fresh fruits and vegetables, baked goods and choice cuts of meat. On Sundays the North Market is turned into one of Toronto's largest flea markets; and during the week it is rented out for various functions, including an annual swearing-in ceremony held every November 3 (the

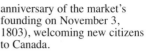

anniversary of the market's founding on November 3, 1803), welcoming new citizens to Canada.

St. Lawrence Market

Across the street, the St. Lawrence Market — also known as the South Market — is the cornerstone and historic heart of Toronto. The massive building, standing on the southwest corner of Jarvis and Front Streets, survived the Great Fire of 1849 and faced the wrecker's ball twice in the twentieth century. Over its life, the St. Lawrence Market has been, in one form or another, home to a fisherman's wharf, Toronto's second City Hall, a police station and a jailhouse.

With its powerful steel arches, graceful yet intricate brickwork, hidden alcoves and the great fan window that looms over the inside, the vast St. Lawrence Market today ranks among the world's best food markets. Unique foods, fresh fish, poultry and meats, together with fruits and vegetables, are all sold in one historic location. Its centre block is now the Market Gallery — an exhibit space for historical documents and art. Like the North Market, the building comes alive on Saturday mornings with early morning shoppers. Many of those shoppers take breakfast in the form of a peameal bacon sandwich at the Carousel Bakery on the west side of the market's upper level. A Toronto favourite for more than thirty years, the bakery is renowned for this sandwich, although its breakfast-on-a-bun, a generous mix of peameal bacon, cheese and an egg, rates a close second. A broader selection of baked goods, including organic and wholegrain bread, is available downstairs in the market's lower level at Stonemill Bakehouse Ltd. Visitors looking for cuts of meat or cheeses will find them on the upper level, at merchants such as Brown Brothers Meats and Alex Farm Products. The offerings on the lower level are more diverse and include mainly specialty items such as coffee at Everyday Gourmet, jams and condiments at A Bisket in a Basket and even honey at Honey World.

Top: St. Lawrence Market (South Building)

Flatiron Building on Front Street

Gooderham (Flatiron) Building, Berczy Park and Front Street Shops

To the west of St. Lawrence Market, at the apex of Church, Wellington and Front Streets, stands arguably the most photographed building in Toronto, the Gooderham (Flatiron) Building. Built in 1891 by George Gooderham, the multi-millionaire owner of the prosperous Gooderham and Worts distillery, it pre-dates New York's more famous Flatiron building by ten years. Fortunately the Flatiron was spared when an army of bulldozers swept through the old downtown core during the urban renewal of the late 1950s and early 1960s, and was finally designated an historic site in November 1975. Today it is a much-sought-after business address.

Behind the Flatiron building can be found Berczy Park, which opened in 1975. Pronounced bear-tzee, this tiny inner-city park is a splendid monument to the enormous contributions of William von Moll Berczy (1748–1813), who along with a group of German settlers built the first bridge across the Don River and helped to construct Yonge Street. A monument dedicated to Berczy and the German pioneers is located at the west end of the park. Across the street from the Berczy Park are a number of great little shops, located on the south side of Front Street. Perhaps the most famous of these is the Nicholas Hoare bookshop, which has been in the neighbourhood for more than thirty years. An intimate, privately owned bookshop, it is a haven for booklovers. Two doors down from Nicholas Hoare is Europe Bound, which offers anything and everything for the adventure and travel minded, including travel books, high-end outdoor clothing, bicycle gear and climbing gear.

Hockey Hall of Fame

The Sony Centre and the Hockey Hall of Fame

Farther west along Front Street, towards Yonge Street, is the Sony Centre. Formerly home to the Canadian Opera Company and the National Ballet of Canada, the Sony Centre opened its doors on October 1, 1960 and was originally known as the O'Keefe Centre.

The whimsical yet powerful mural, *The Seven Lively Arts* by York Wilson, was installed here at a time when theatre lobbies were dominated either by landscape or portrait paintings from a bygone era. Located on the north wall in the main lobby of the Sony Centre, the mural is 30 m long and 4.5 m high and depicts painting, sculpture, architecture, music, literature, dance and drama — hence its name. When he died in 1984, York Wilson was acclaimed as Canada's greatest muralist and the O'Keefe mural is considered his best work. Still very much in demand as a concert venue, ground was broken on a massive renovation of the Sony Centre in October 2009.

Across the street, on the northwest corner of Front and Yonge Streets, is the Hockey Hall of Fame. Set in the historic Bank of Montreal building, which dates from the nineteenth century, the ground floor of this shrine to hockey is chock full of memorabilia — everything from the heroic Jacques Plante's first goalie mask to a re-creation of a Montreal Canadien's dressing room to what seems to be every puck, every stick and every coin that was ever used in one extraordinary game or another. But as cherished as these icons of the sport may be, they pale in comparison to what lies at the centre of the complex — a striking former banking hall that houses the sanctuary of hockey's incredible history. Around the walls of this Valhalla to hockey, double sheets of etched glass announce each of the Hall of Fame's honoured members. And at the heart of this entire complex stands the icon that people come from all over the world to see: the Stanley Cup, hockey's most famous and desired prize.

The King Edward Hotel

A walk northward on Yonge Street and then east on King leads to another of Toronto's iconic buildings. When the King Edward Hotel opened on May 11, 1903, the city had never seen anything like it, with its sweeping parlours for men to enjoy their port and cigars as their wives whiled away the afternoon sipping tea in elegantly appointed lounges. The "King Eddy,"

Le Royal Meridien
King Edward

as it is known locally, has over the years attracted its fair share of attention. In 1964, angry protestors picketed the hotel when they discovered that the world's greatest movie star, Elizabeth Taylor, was staying there with her lover Richard Burton, both being married to others at the time. Shocking and scandalous! That event was followed by 3,000 teenagers invading the lobby when news got out that the Beatles were staying at the hotel. And in 1969 John Lennon and Yoko Ono spent the night at the King Eddy before going on to Montreal, where they staged their famous bed-in for world peace and an end to war.

In 1980, the hotel underwent a major retrofit that brought back some of the glamour for which it was celebrated during its opulent Edwardian days. A traditional English high tea is available at Le Royal Méridien King Edward every afternoon.

St. James' Cathedral and St. James' Park

Farther east along King Street stands the magnificent English Gothic-inspired St. James' Cathedral.

For most of the nineteenth century, St. James' was under the influence of Bishop John Strachan, one of the most powerful men who ever lived in Toronto. A hero to the people of York when, as legend has it, he drove the Americans away after their week-long occupation in 1813, Bishop Strachan was fiercely anti-Catholic and very much at the helm of the Orange Order that dominated City politics well into the 1950s. Today, St. James' Cathedral is a document in stone and glass of Toronto's more than 200-year history. Its spire, constructed after the Great Fire of 1849 and completed in 1875, was once the tallest in Canada. And inside, the cathedral's magnificent stained-glass windows (including one inlayed with Tiffany glass), along with bronze and marble monuments that line the cathedral walls, help tell the story of the people who built Toronto.

The Cathedral Church of St. James, as it's officially is known, is the centre of the Anglican Diocese of Toronto and when in town, the Queen and other members of the Royal Family often attend Sunday services here. Behind the cathedral is St. James' Park, a wonderful inner-city park with rolling hills, winding footpaths, spreading maple trees and Victorian garden. The peaceful setting belies a more gruesome past, as the park is still home to the great cholera pits of Toronto. It's estimated that more than 5,000 bodies are buried beneath the grassy slopes at the park's northern end.

St. James' Cathedral

King Street East

This historic neighbourhood blends seamlessly into the present day along King Street between Jarvis and Parliament, as modern condos, furniture stores, antique shops and restaurants all vie for space.

This stretch of King Street could in fact be called Toronto's own "decor row." Several great furniture stores are situated here, including Harvest House Furniture and the internationally renowned Roche Bobois, which is located just north of King Street on Parliament Street. When they aren't buying furniture, the neighbourhood's condo dwellers are probably frequenting the local restaurants, which range from the very high-end Biagio Ristorante and La Maquette to traditional, hearty diners like the Patrician Grill. The Hot House Café, located at the corner of Front and Church, just south of King, is a Toronto favourite for its generous Sunday brunch. And a number of antique shops are located on the south side of King Street.

Enoch Turner Schoolhouse

Just east of Parliament Street, and set in the old Irish neighbourhood known as Corktown (after County Cork in Ireland), the Enoch Turner Schoolhouse was Toronto's first school building and is the oldest still standing in the city. In the days before free public education, the school offered education to mostly poor immigrants. A true philanthropist, brewer Enoch Turner knew that only the sons of the very wealthy could attend school at the prestigious St. James' Church down the road and so he built his own schoolhouse for the less well-to-do in 1848, on the grounds of the Little Trinity Anglican Church. Today the Enoch Turner Schoolhouse is a living museum, giving students a taste of what it was like to be in class 150 years ago.

Financial and Theatre District

Regan Ray

Bay and Front Street

In 1983 the Toronto Stock Exchange moved out of its original location at 234 Bay Street, the symbolic centre of the city's financial district. Eleven years later the new tenants re-opened the building to the public as the Design Exchange, a museum and research centre devoted to design. This creative use of an historic space in the financial district is indicative of the unique proximity of culture and finance in Toronto's downtown core.

King Street is the heart of the city's theatre area, while Bay Street is its financial hub. And in Toronto, these two districts sit side by side. The unique juxtaposition of commerce and culture keeps Toronto's

King St. West at Spadina

core attractive to visitors and breathes life into the glass and steel towers dominated by Canada's big

banks. A walk through the area from Front Street in the south to Dundas in the north, or from Bay Street west to Peter Street, passes everything from the tallest skyscraper in the country to the oldest theatre in the city.

The Royal Alexandra has been operating for more than 100 years, making it one of the oldest theatres in North America. Along with the newer Princess of

Wales, it is owned and operated by the Mirvish family, Toronto's premier theatre patrons. These two venues are the main locations for large-scale productions such as *Miss Saigon* and *Lord of the Rings* and are the focal point of the district. Roy Thomson Hall, the circular glass concert hall that is home to the Toronto

The Royal Alexandra Theatre

Symphony Orchestra, is directly across the street from the Royal Alex. When the first stars on Canada's Walk of Fame were laid down in 1998, there was no better location than King and Simcoe streets, which surround these three prominent buildings, to honour Canadian arts figures such as Jim Carrey and Margaret Atwood. And the King Street strip between Simcoe and Peter streets offers an abundance of dining options from around the world, as well as being just a stone's throw from some of Toronto's other main attractions.

One of those attractions is undoubtedly the CN Tower. A cruise up the elevator is certainly a thrill, but it's nothing compared with standing on a glass floor 342 metres above the street. They'll tell you the 24 square metres of glass can withstand the weight of fourteen large hippos, but somehow that doesn't help alleviate sweaty palms. Just below the tower sits the Rogers Centre, home of the Toronto Blue Jays baseball

Air Canada Centre

team and the Toronto Argonauts CFL football team. If hotdogs and peanuts don't appeal, the stadium features restaurants such as the Hard Rock Café and Sightlines, with prime views of centre field plus buffet or à la carte menu options. In 1999 the Air Canada Centre (ACC) replaced the old Maple Leaf Gardens as the home of the Toronto Maple Leafs hockey team. The NBA basketball team, the Toronto Raptors, also moved into the newer stadium.

Just north of the ACC, at the foot of Bay Street, is the city's transportation hub, Union Station. Since Britain's Prince of Wales cut the ribbon on opening day in 1927, Union has grown into the main artery for trans-Canada trains, the commuter GO

CBC building

Train and the TTC urban subway system. Toronto's intricate underground walkway system, PATH, also links with Union. PATH is a network of indoor pathways lined with shops and restaurants that weaves through the downtown core from the ACC in the south, through all the financial district towers and as far north as Dundas Street and the Eaton Centre.

The Sony Centre sits next door to Union and was the home of both the National Ballet of Canada and the Canadian Opera Company until 2006, when the new Four Seasons Centre for the Arts on Queen Street was completed. Theatre, culture and the arts spread out from the King Street core and mingle with the financial centre north of Union. For instance, Brookfield Place at Yonge and Front Streets is a 240,000 square metre tower complex designed to maximize the number of corner offices the building can accommodate. It houses some of the world's most prestigious financial and legal firms. But Brookfield also boasts the Hockey Hall of Fame and the Allen Lambert Galleria, a six-storey glass thoroughfare that often houses art installations or other exhibitions. It is truly a magnificent work of architecture, as are so many of the behemoths that make up the financial district. First Canadian Place is the tallest of the bunch

First Canadian Place, Royal Bank Plaza

at 300 metres, while the golden Royal Bank Plaza is said to have 24-karat gold cooked into the window panes at a cost of $70 per pane.

On the north side of all these grand towers is another cluster of theatre venues. The world's last operating double-decker theatre, the Elgin and Winter Garden Theatre, is at 189 Yonge. In 1989 the original vaudeville pair were treated to major restorations. Since then the two separate theatres have presented major productions such as *Cats* and *Rent*, as well as providing a major screening venue for the annual Toronto International Film Festival. Another production space managed by the Mirvish family is the Canon Theatre at 244 Victoria Street. Originally a vaudeville and movie theatre, the Canon didn't become a live theatre space until 1989, when a Famous Players and Cineplex Odeon rivalry halted any showings of motion pictures. The 2,200-seat theatre opened with *The Phantom of the Opera* and since then shows ranging from Monty Python's *Spamalot* to Broadway's *Wicked* have graced the stage. Just down the street is the marvellous Massey Hall, easily visible with its vibrant red doors and hanging neon sign. Massey Hall is well known for its fantastic acoustics and has attracted acts as diverse as Luciano Pavarotti and Bob Dylan.

TD Centre Cows, courtyard off Wellington Street

There is, however, more to Toronto than the big-name theatres. A whole host of smaller performance spaces, art galleries, restaurants and cafés can be found in the area and adds to its eclectic feel. Second City is a mainstay of Toronto comedy, which produced such stars as John Candy and Eugene Levy through its television offshoot, SCTV. The company moved into a new space at Mercer Street and Blue Jays Way in 2005. Right around the corner from Second City is the Diesel Playhouse, a 408-seat space that houses alternative theatre and cabaret. The coloured cube on Front Street that houses the Canadian Broadcasting Corporation (CBC) is also a great option for viewing live television tapings, concerts or strolling through the CBC museum.

Below and inset: Massey Hall

During the summer months, double-decker bus tours cover the major attractions and allow passengers to get on and off at their leisure, which is a good way to explore. A couple of companies even use amphibious vehicles that tour the city by bus and head out onto the harbour for a view from the water. But as with any city, the best way to scour Toronto's financial and theatre district is with a good pair of walking shoes and a whole lot of time.

Queen Street West

Todd Aalgaard

Trinity Bellwoods Park

Queen Street West begins at the intersection of King Street, Roncesvalles Avenue and The Queensway in Toronto's west end. From there, Queen West extends eastward to Yonge Street, becoming Queen Street East at the intersection. The original baseline for Toronto's east-west grid of intersecting streets, the area of Queen West is an ethnically and culturally diverse group of neighbourhoods and districts. After more than twenty years of continuous transformation and development, it has become a major international centre for the arts and one of Toronto's most recognized tourist destinations.

Such development has utterly transformed what was historically a largely industrial and commercial strip in Old Toronto into a part of the city reflecting the Soho districts of London and New York, a distinction that has inspired campaigns to have the area renamed. A cosmopolitan yet bohemian flair remains, with even the most upscale boutiques between Yonge Street and Spadina retaining an inspired sense of design to reflect the energy, diversity and colour of the surrounding neighbourhood. While some may see the character of other cities in Queen West, its atmosphere remains undeniably and distinctly Toronto.

Parkdale East and the Gallery District

Parkdale East, otherwise known as the Gallery District, ranges from Dufferin Street in the west to Trinity Bellwoods Park. Reflecting the energy that changed this part of Toronto, the north side of Queen West is replete with nightclubs and galleries occupying nearly every storefront, while the south side is largely dominated by the environs of the Queen Street Mental Health Centre.

The Stephen Bulger Gallery, opened in March of 1995, showcases one of the city's largest collections of photography, featuring more than 15,000 photographs by international artists. Gallery 1313 is an example of how the city has used older buildings to further the arts community, transforming previously abandoned space into a not-for-profit gallery, which, with the ample room provided, allows a diversity of artists to exhibit their work at minimal cost.

Given the explosion of interest in Parkdale East by realtors and other commercial interests, escalating property prices have driven smaller galleries, bars and residents to less expensive parts of the city. Much of this can be attributed to the revitalization and renewal of the Drake Hotel. Opened in 1890 under the name "Small's Hotel," it was purchased and renamed in 1949. As a lodging house and nexus for the punk and rave scenes of the 1970s and 1980s, the Drake suffered the economic decline of the surrounding community prior to its present incarnation. Following its sale in 2001, the Drake became one of the city's most widely reputed nightclubs and arts venues, with the goal of becoming a focal point for the burgeoning Gallery District. Today, the Drake's success has attracted public institutions like the Museum of Contemporary Canadian Art and draws events such as Nuit Blanche, an annual, all-night, city-wide arts festival.

The Drake Hotel

The social concerns and artistic energy of the neighbourhood are evident throughout Parkdale, where many of the city's top-rated natural foods, crafts and clothing stores are situated. The Knit Café, at 1050 Queen Street West, is an excellent location for both the experienced and uninitiated craftster, a relaxing, inviting environment for knitters of all skill levels. The Stylegarage at the intersection of Queen Street West and Shaw is a focal point of Toronto's art and design district, a showcase for some of the city's best aesthetic furniture designs and a gallery for the artisans and designers of West Queen West. And for film buffs, nearby Black Dog

Trinity Bellwoods Park

After the 2008 fire on Queen Street West

Video carries a wide selection of hard-to-find titles in film and video, both old and new.

Trinity Bellwoods Park

Part of Trinity Bellwoods Park was once the Garrison Creek ravine, and this creek still exists beneath the park. The current parkland was purchased in 1851 by Bishop John Strachan, an Anglican Deacon whose intent was to build a private school in response to the University of Toronto's recent secularization. The result was Trinity College, constructed a year later in 1852. The original Trinity College campus left this location in 1925, and was amalgamated into the U of T at its present site. Today, the Queen Street campus's lone remnant is the wrought iron and stone gate at the south entrance to what is now Trinity Bellwoods Park.

Trinity Bellwoods celebrates Toronto's preservation of natural green space. A stunning example of modern urban biodiversity, the park is a lush, expansive home to the park's ubiquitous white squirrels, along with many species of both native and imported trees. A network of pedestrian and bicycle paths weaves through the parkland, lined by black Victorian lamps that lend soft light and unmistakable charm. Colloquially known as the "bowl," the former site of the ravine itself is an off-leash dog park, attracting drumming circles and performers in the summer and tobogganers in winter. Spurred by the cultural and aesthetic revitalization of nearby Queen West, the park is also the site of events such as Portugal Day and AlleyHaunt, a series of installations, performances and art exhibitions in nearby alleys and garages, themselves a showcase of the community's diverse artistry.

Trinity Bellwoods Park to Spadina

Eastward from Trinity Bellwoods Park to where Queen Street intersects with Spadina is one of Toronto's most colourful districts. A variety of nightclubs and bars, including the Bovine Sex Club, the Velvet Underground, Catacombs, Freakshow and the Abyss, occupies a 5 km stretch of Queen Street revolutionized by the goth culture of the early to mid-1990s. Many of the neighbouring businesses are likewise eclectic, including cannabis culture shops such as Jupiter and Come As You Are, a co-operatively run erotic boutique.

The shopping here is diverse, for those with a creative flair. Much of the independent, do-it-yourself attitude that fostered the ambience and culture of this neighbourhood is reflected by numerous beading and arts and crafts stores, supporting a strong community of artisans. In February 2008, a six-alarm fire destroyed a number of historic buildings, indeed an entire city block, on the south side of Queen Street at Bathurst Street. The plans for revitalizing the area, which include a condo development, may change the neighbourhood's culture in the future.

CityTV building

Spadina to University

Prior to the 1980s, Queen Street between Spadina and University had the same artsy feel for which Queen west of Trinity Bellwoods is known today. In the 1960s and 1970s, arrayed with aging storefronts and diners, unique terra cotta architecture and affordable housing, Queen West attracted Toronto's bohemian culture. Spearheaded by this influx, which included many students from the nearby Ontario College of Art & Design, Toronto's music scene evolved at bars such as the Horseshoe Tavern, the Cameron House and the Rivoli, eventually reaching the rest of Canada. In 1985, CHUM-TV followed the trend to its epicentre and opened its doors at 299 Queen West, the neo-Gothic former home of the Methodist Church of Canada, the United Church of Canada and Ryerson Press. Today, housing CTVglobemedia, 299 is iconic nationwide as the very visible headquarters for MuchMusic, Canada's first music television channel.

A watershed moment in Toronto's cultural history, this sudden exposure permanently changed Queen

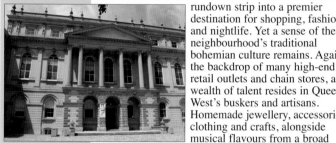

Osgoode Hall

West, raising its profile nationwide. Before long, larger audiences and wealthier investment had transformed a rundown strip into a premier destination for shopping, fashion and nightlife. Yet a sense of the neighbourhood's traditional bohemian culture remains. Against the backdrop of many high-end retail outlets and chain stores, a wealth of talent resides in Queen West's buskers and artisans. Homemade jewellery, accessories, clothing and crafts, alongside musical flavours from a broad cultural spectrum, create a festival atmosphere in this already vibrant area.

Toronto's music scene continues to thrive, particularly near the corner of Queen and Spadina at bars like the Horseshoe Tavern and Gorilla Monsoon. Locally these establishments carry an air of prestige, especially among musicians, as they are reputed to have launched the careers of Canadian acts like the Tragically Hip, Blue Rodeo, Jane Siberry and Jeff Healey.

Osgoode Hall
cow gates

University to Yonge

Queen West from University Avenue to Yonge Street is the site of some of Toronto's oldest, most well-known landmarks, including Osgoode Hall, Nathan Phillips Square, both the Old and New City Halls and the Eaton Centre. Recent developments have also brought the Four Seasons Centre for the Performing Arts, the home of the Canadian Opera Company and the National Ballet, to the southeast corner of Queen West and University Avenue. Historically, this stretch of Queen West is also the site of Canada's oldest retail outlets.

Osgoode Hall

In 1829, the Law Society of Upper Canada acquired a 2.4-hectare site at 130 Queen Street West, the northeast corner of Queen Street and University Avenue. In 1832, construction of Osgoode Hall was completed. An ornate example of Palladian architecture, the building remains a radiant reminder of early Toronto. Even the wrought-iron fencing captivates. Today, Osgoode Hall is the home of the Law Society of Upper Canada, the Ontario Court of Appeal and the Superior Court of Justice. Osgoode Hall Law School, presently located at York University, moved from this location in 1969.

Nathan Phillips Square and City Hall

Nathan Phillips Square, an open area directly in front of City Hall on the south side, is an open meeting place reminiscent of New York's Washington Square, attracting visitors and events year round. The large reflecting pool in summer becomes a festively lit skating rink in winter, a romantic fixture at the foot of city hall's distinctive modernist presence. Construction of City Hall commenced in 1961, the result of a citywide call for a new centre of government at what was once the site of Toronto's first Chinatown. It replaced Old City Hall at the corner of Queen and Bay, constructed in 1899. An impressive Romanesque building, the Old City Hall was, during its time, the largest of its kind in North America. Its clock tower remains a focal point on Bay Street, visible from Queen Street to Front Street in the south.

The Eaton Centre

At the corner of Queen Street West and Yonge Street is the Toronto Eaton Centre, one of the largest shopping malls and office complexes in the city. With 330 stores, and drawing more visitors than anywhere else in the city, the Eaton Centre is the busiest tourist attraction in the city. It retains its original name despite the demise of the shopping chain itself in 1999. It rests on the site of the original Eaton's store, neighbouring Old City Hall and the Church of the Holy Trinity, among the only parcels of land at the intersection of Queen and Yonge not previously owned by Eaton's. Another notable exception is the Bay (formerly Simpson's) on Queen West's south side, one of the first retail branches of the rival Hudson's Bay Company.

Nathan Phillips Square

Yorkville and Bloor Street

Niara Modi

Yorkville

For the hunter-gatherer turned shopper-browser, Yorkville-Bloor is where a decreasingly coy and conservative Toronto displays its fondness for luxury, pleasure and consumer-driven indulgences of every imaginable kind.

Once a suburb of Toronto, Yorkville today consists of a small cross-section of streets that feature historic and contemporary architecture along with a high-end mix of art and commerce. A walk through tiny York Lane, for instance, leads past the storefront of Giorgio and Hugo Boss. Farther up on Hazelton Avenue, sculptures of Canadian wildlife guard the sidewalk and window of a contemporary art gallery. A wooden sign for Sotheby's, the legendary English auctioneer, hangs unobtrusively from a second storey, while treasures from the Far East are promised below at C.C. Lai's antique store. With its high density of boutiques, art galleries, restaurants, salons and cafés, the discovery of hidden delights tucked away in its narrow streets is part of Yorkville's charm. Yorkville is also a fun place to promenade — to see and be seen — where shoppers and window-shoppers can get an eyeful of each other, along with the residents and tourists who rub shoulders within the neighbourhood.

Yorkville Laneway

Modern Yorkville is bordered by four major roadways. Bloor Street and a stretch dubbed the "mink mile" marks the southern boundary. Here, flagship stores for brands like Roots, lululemon, Nike and Pottery Barn can be found alongside deluxe international retailers like Royale de Versailles, Louis Vuitton, Hermès, Chanel, Davids and Prada, to name a few. Avenue Road forms the western boundary, with the Park Hyatt hotel and the unmissable ROM Crystal marking the southwestern corner. To the north, Yorkville is bordered by Davenport Road, a First Nations trail that dates back 12,000 years and is one of the few Toronto streets that, unlike the rest of the city's perpendicular grid, retains its original winding pathway. Davenport was an important part of the early fur-trading circuit and links now, as it did then, directly to Yonge Street. The northwest corner of Avenue and Davenport, nicknamed "Ave and Dav," is a favourite for flower shops, stores focused on all things to do with interior decoration, as well as a few pleasant eateries. To the east, Yorkville is bordered by Yonge Street, one of Toronto's first roads built under the order of Lieutenant Colonel (and later Governor) John Simcoe.

Pottery Barn, Yorkville

Some History

Yorkville's early colonial history is rooted in alcohol. Between 1808 and 1810, a far-sighted entrepreneur built the Red Lion Inn at the corner of Bloor and Yonge, near the tollgate entrance to the city core. The inn was frequented by rural farmers travelling Yonge Street to sell their wares at St. Lawrence Market and became a popular and important social and political gathering place. Slightly north of the Red Lion Inn, Joseph Bloor (after whom Bloor Street is named) opened a brewery in the Rosedale Ravine. The brewery brought industry to Yorkville and soon the village began flourishing and growing. Yorkville became home to merchants, craftsmen, artisans and workers and was officially incorporated as a village in 1853.

Bloor and Bellair

Of course, for thousands of years prior to the arrival and occupation of the Europeans, settlements of the Iroquois, Seneca and Mississauga people had been

Shops, Yorkville

scattered throughout the area. But the newly incorporated village of Yorkville prospered enough to build its own landmark Town Hall, designed by architect William Hay. The hall housed a police station and library and was meant to include an arcade of shops. The arcade was never built and was eventually redesigned for use as stables and barns for the horses that served the Toronto Street Railway, which began running in 1861. During the Second World War the hall was used as a club for servicemen but burned to the ground in 1941. Fortunately the original Yorkville coat of arms was saved and can be seen today hanging at Fire Station 312, a building with a strong resemblance to the old city hall. By 1883 Yorkville was annexed by Toronto.

Yorkville Branch, Toronto Public Library

Not all of Yorkville's history is mild and industrious. The site of today's Park Hyatt hotel once housed the Tecumseh Wigwam, a log cabin pub, complete with hitching posts. The Wigwam achieved notoriety when the owner's son was hanged for the murder of a coachman.

Yorkville itself became notorious as the centre of the hippie movement in the sixties. In the 1960s the area was a hotbed of creativity, particularly in the music world. On any given night you could have heard Joni Mitchell, Neil Young, Ian and Silvia, Zal Yanovski or Gordon Lightfoot. Some, like author Nicholas Jennings in his book Before the Gold Rush, argue that Yorkville is really the birthplace of Canadian pop music.

A Walking Tour of Yorkville

The best way to start a tour of Yorkville is to head north on Yonge Street, like many diligent students, to the Metropolitan Reference Library, designed in the 1970s by Raymond Moriyama, who was also the architect of the Ontario Science Centre. Though the library is inconspicuous from the outside, the interior atrium is striking, and Moriyama's design allows the building to function both as a public monument and a greatly enjoyed community space.

Past the Cookbook Store (once the site of a bakery) culinary treats can be had at Crêpes à Gogo at the corner of Yorkville Avenue. Farther west is the urban garden that commemorates the site of the old Town Hall, and two old civic institutions. The Yorkville Library, built with an endowment from Andrew Carnegie, celebrated 100 years of service in 2007 and is Toronto's oldest standing public library. Farther west, Fire Hall 312, built in 1876, has been restored in several stages and remains Toronto's oldest functioning fire station. The station's exterior is noteworthy for its polychrome orange and yellow brickwork, popularly known as "streaky bacon." Also of note is the Yorkville coat of arms, salvaged from the destroyed city hall, which hangs on the front exterior.

Above and below:
Yorkville Shopping

On Yorkville Avenue there is a wide range of stores for shopping or browsing. Muti (88) sells fine Italian ceramics. L'Atelier Grigorian (70) specializes in jazz and classical music on CD and DVD. For the mystically or spiritually inclined, a new resident is the International Kabbalah Centre (101). Comfort can also be found in homemade ice cream at Summer's Sweet Memories (101). Over the Rainbow (101) is a famous hub for designer denim and all things jeanswear-related, and the Arctic Bear (125) specializes in Inuit sculpture, prints and artwork.

Farther north at Hazelton Avenue is a row of art galleries. The critical mass of galleries in Yorkville has made it an art destination. Yorkville galleries are also recognized for nurturing and launching numerous

Canadian artists into the national and international art world. Perhaps the most noteworthy contribution to Canadian art made by a gallery that continues to operate can be found at Mira Godard (22). Information on monthly neighbourhood art walks can also be found in a number of participating galleries.

Also on Hazelton Avenue is one of two beautiful, surviving board and batten churches. It was built in 1876 and bought by the Heliconian Club, an association of women in the arts, in 1923 (the club itself was established in 1907).

On nearby Scollard Street more art can be found at Gallery One (121), and at impresario Drabinsky's Gallery, now back on Yorkville Street (114). For a food break or more shopping the upscale Hazelton Lanes mall offers boutiques, fashion retailers, jewellers and furnishing stores along with foodie delights. Natural and organic food retailer Whole Foods Market has its only Toronto store here. Famed chef Greg Couillard has also launched two restaurants, the Spice Room and Chutney Bar and the African-themed Manyata Courtyard Café, in the lower level of Hazelton Lanes. A fast and economic option can also be found at the Hero Certified Burger.

For coffee there is Lettieri or MBCO Boulangerie de Montréal on Cumberland Street, and a good place to digest lunch is the controversial, award-winning and popular Yorkville Park. The result of an international design competition, the park had many critics in its early days. It is intended to provide a sense of Ontario's topography, hence the large 650-tonne rock thrusting out beside the exit of the TTC, along with wildflowers, a conifer garden and birch grove. A steel-framed waterfall slices the open space in half, while the narrow pathway alongside it has become a popular place to perch for a rest, a look around or a lover's

Cumberland Street

embrace. At night the park features dramatic lighting, and on weekends live music adds to the atmosphere.

Like the rest of Yorkville, Cumberland Street is filled with restaurants, bars and cafés, as well as a small independent movie theatre, the Cumberland. At the eastern end of the street is the unassuming but historic Pilot Tavern, Restaurant & Bar (22) established in 1944. The Pilot has always been actively involved in the arts community and is particularly popular for its rooftop deck. Also at the eastern end of Cumberland is a popular toy store, Kidding Awound (91), a favourite with adults and kids, featuring puppets called the Axis of Evil Dolls and Great Psychotherapist Dolls, along with more traditional amusements.

Walking Bloor Street

The corner of Bloor and Avenue Road, where the Park Hyatt hotel, built in the 1920s, eventually took the place of the notorious Tecumseh Wigwam, is a good place to start the tour. First named the Queen's Park Plaza, the rooftop garden bar and restaurant was a popular haunt of the literati and remains a romantic spot with a great view of the city.

Above and below: Park Hyatt Hotel, corner of Bloor and Avenue

Along with the Park Hyatt, neighbouring hotels such as the InterContinental, the Four Seasons and the elegant Windsor Arms Hotel all offer highly praised restaurants.

Kitty-corner to the Hyatt is the neo-classical revival, porticoed L. M. Treble building, which today houses a large Club Monaco store. The northern portion of Bloor Street along mink mile once contained Toronto's Potter's Field, with a cemetery called The Stranger's Burial Ground. The cemetery was closed in 1854, and the land emptied and sold. Today instead of

unmarked graves, Bloor Street rings out with names like Bang & Olufsen, Starbucks, Pottery Barn, Williams–Sonoma, Nike, lululemon, Banana Republic, Escada and the Gap.

East of Bay Street is Holt Renfrew (5), Canada's swankiest department store. This is the company's flagship store, with a long-serving, gracious doorman at the entrance. Underground in Holt Renfrew Plaza awaits another treasure for children. The Science Shop has every manner of toy, puzzle and gizmo related to things scientific. Retail favourites at street level include William Ashley (55), Birks (55), Stollery's (1), and Harry Rosen (82). H&M, Guess, Zara, FCUK, Coach, Cole Haan and Prada can also be found on Bloor Street.

In the nearby Manulife Centre (55) are two more flagship Canadian stores: Indigo Books and Music and Bay Bloor Radio, which specializes in hi-fi and quality audiovisual equipment. From here a walk down St. Thomas Street leads to Tiffany, or for high tea at the Windsor Arms Hotel. Theatre Books (11) serves fans and members of the performing arts communities, including theatre, music, opera, dance and film. The store even sells screenwriting software.

The Yorkville-Bloor experience can be brought to a close at a number of excellent, even romantic, restaurants in the area. To dine with a view, there's the Manulife Centre's Panorama Lounge. A good view of the street can also be had at Dynasty, the elegant second-floor Chinese restaurant in the Colonnade complex. Those with energy and a desire for something new can make their way out of Yorkville down and across to the historic University of Toronto area. Harbord Street near the university is also growing a reputation for its excellent restaurants.

If Yorkville has emptied wallet or soul, a wander north up Avenue Road, past Davenport to Roxborough leads to an old limestone church on Avenue at Roxborough. This is the home of the Hare Krishna Temple. On weekends, the temple serves free multi-course meals at certain times of the day, and lunch with a charitable contribution.

Indigo, Manulife Centre

Neighbourhoods Further Afield

Miles Baker

Little Italy

The College streetcar (Route 506) from either the College or Queen's Park subway stations, takes visitors to a neighbourhood that was once home to the majority of Toronto's Italian community and is today a real gem in the city's nightlife. Little Italy, which is located roughly between Bathurst Street and Ossington Avenue along College Street, can be explored in two parts: the Italian section and the university section. The two do overlap, but College east of Clinton (and therefore closer to the University of Toronto) is a collection of hip, younger-oriented bars, while College west of Clinton is the more traditional Italian neighbourhood.

Dining is the main attraction in Little Italy, with late-night entertainment a close second. Live venues like the Mod Club (722 College) or Revival (783 College) showcase international talent and host Toronto's thriving music scene. Both are also popular dance clubs. Café Diplomatico (594 College) is

Cucina, College Street

Café Diplomatico, College Street

137

Shops and Café, Little Italy

one of three established neighbourhood restaurants with large outdoor patios that are usually filled during the summer — the other two are Bar Italia (582 College) and Grappa Ristorante (797 College). There is also a patio at the Sicilian Sidewalk Café (710 College), a family-owned café that dates back to the 1950s. Its owners, the Galipo family, were among the many Italian immigrants who arrived in Canada in the twentieth century and settled in the neighbourhood. For non-Italian food, Sushi Island (571 College) has some of the best sushi in the city and an excellent all-you-can-eat maki special.

It's common to see couples and small groups of friends walking from one establishment to another along College Street. The strip of restaurants, clubs and shops is distinctly calmer than that of the city's entertainment district, and it doesn't have the density of other Toronto neighbourhoods such as the Annex on Bloor Street. But it is still lively. During the summer, the Big Chill (367 Manning St.), a cute outdoor ice cream stand with a unique selection of flavours, is usually surrounded by locals buying a cone.

Shopping isn't the focus of life in Little Italy, but what is available in the neighbourhood is fantastic. It's easy to spend hours in Balfour Books (601 College), which is known for rare finds and good deals on used books. Ever been curious to find a copy of *Time* magazine from 1954? Dragon Lady Comics & Paper Nostalgia (609 College)

offers exciting retro pulp magazines and periodicals and is popular with comic-book collectors and bibliophiles alike. At Motoretta's (554 College St.) showroom, shoppers will be hard pressed not to find the Vespa they always wanted in just the right colour! And Soundscapes (572 College) has developed a reputation in recent years as being Toronto's best record store and the place to go for contemporary rock and roll or a rare reissue of a jazz classic.

Kensington Market and Chinatown
Exiting the same College streetcar (506) before Bathurst Street near Spadina Avenue, visitors will wander into two of the city's unique areas: Kensington Market and Chinatown. Kensington Market stretches between Bellevue Avenue, College Street, Spadina Avenue and Dundas Street. Once a Jewish ghetto, the market now houses dozens of specialty food and clothing stores that have been converted from residential houses.

Restaurant, Little Italy

Most of the clothing stores offer vintage or second-hand clothing at several price points. Stores such as Courage My Love (14 Kensington Avenue) and Exile (20 Kensington Avenue) are established venues. On the Kensington Avenue stretch of the market, in between all the clothing stores, there are some precious accessory stores, many of which sell original homemade crafts. Stores like Clickclack (38 Kensington Street) and Butterfly (42 Kensington Street) are popular for their unique items.

The food in Kensington Market is known for being cheap and fresh. Restaurants in Kensington are typically small, but different. The Hungary Thai (196 Augusta Avenue), for example, offers a combination of Hungarian and Thai food. King's Café (192 Augusta Avenue) is one of Toronto's better spots for vegetarian food. La Palette (256 Augusta Avenue), a tiny French restaurant with an authentic bistro menu, offers prix fixe meals. And the neighbourhood's largest butcher, European Meats on Baldwin Street, also serves up what they sell.

In the summer, the streets in Kensington Market are alive with pedestrians moving from shop to shop, getting what they need for the day or enjoying one of the independently run coffee shops, like Moonbeam Coffee (30 St. Andrew Street) or Ideal

Chinese restaurant, Chinatown

Kensington Market

Coffee (84 Nassau Street), where it's common to watch young people debate philosophy or politics, or play backgammon on a patio. Cars are generally unwelcome in the market, especially on Pedestrian Sundays, when the streets are blocked off to traffic. Some nights communal drum circles will collect on the streets of the market, sharing their music with the community — and spectators are sometimes asked to join in.

Kensington also houses the best dance spot in Toronto — Goin' Steady. On the first Saturday of almost every month, the nautically themed Boat (158 Augusta Avenue) — former family restaurant — hosts a truly retro dance party where the pop, girl groups, R & B and doo-wop of the 1950s and 1960s gets everyone in the room bopping. For a more contemporary booty shaking there's Supermarket (268 August Avenue), with its mix of live bands and DJs spinning funk and rock.

Chinatown, which borders Kensington Market on Spadina Avenue and Dundas Street, is a neighbourhood made up mostly of fruit stands, novelty shops and a wide selection of Chinese restaurants. Each restaurant offers authentic Chinese cuisine along with the North American version of Chinese food. An all-day dim sum

Kensington houses

restaurant makes for a nice afternoon snack, and a welcome break after walking through Kensington. On the streets, visitors will also find nuts, berries, dried food, bulk candy and — a local favourite — coconut milk straight out of the shell. A large number of souvenir stores are located in the area, as well as Internet cafés and software stores. The Art Gallery of Ontario (317 Dundas Street) is nearby.

Chinatown is a crowded area, especially on weekends, but that shouldn't dissuade visitors who are prepared for a slow walk from enjoying the area.

The Danforth

Visitors who take the Bloor-Danforth subway line east of Yonge Street to stations from Broadview through Donland will find themselves in Toronto's own Greektown neighbourhood. The white and blue street signs are written in Greek in "the Danforth," as the area is commonly called, and it's a lot like Little Italy: both neighbourhoods have retained their ethnic identity while becoming more cosmopolitan. Expect to eat and drink well in little Italy, but on the Danforth there are a lot more shops.

Restaurants along the strip range from somewhat hokey — but still tasty — establishments to younger, hipper places with exotic Greek names. Restaurants like Kokkino (414 Danforth Avenue) serve the kind of food that one would expect to see in Greece today: traditional meals with world-flavour infusions. The very spacious Christina's (492 Danforth Avenue) has a large, heated patio and the occasional live performance to accompany a meal. And the two-storey Myth (417 Danforth Avenue) has both dinner and dance spaces with a good-sized stage.

The Danforth offers a varied experience for a whole day. Some of the finest tailors in the city can be found on these streets, from The Dressroom (269 Danforth Avenue) to Korry's Clothiers (569 Danforth Avenue), which is where many of Toronto's sport stars get their suits made. There are also many franchise stores on the Danforth for anyone looking for the distinct taste of Starbucks or McDonald's.

The coolest place on the Danforth at the moment is the Carrot Common (328 Danforth Avenue) — a mini-mall for alternative lifestyles. The building is owned

Greek salad

by a small collective of companies, including the Big Carrot, a worker co-operative grocery store that specializes in organic food, and the Cooperative Resource Pool of Ontario, a co-operative venture capital group. It houses seventeen unique stores as well as office and studio space. The whole building operates on the principle of clean, organic living.

At the corner of Logan and Danforth Avenues there is a small courtyard where locals meet and families gather to watch a small fountain, greet each other and gossip in their mother tongue. As far as public spaces go, the Alexander the Great Parkette is probably the best meeting place in Greektown. Greektown on the Danforth also offers independent theatre in the form of Bad Dog Theatre (138 Danforth Avenue). The Music Hall (147 Danforth Ave.) is the city's best music venue after Massey Hall.

This is definitely an area to get out of the car and walk around. It's not the kind of place to hastily pull out a camera and take pictures of the landmarks or attractions — plan to

Harold Night at the Bad Dog Theatre

spend the afternoon, have a seat and relax.

Unless you're visiting in August, that is. The annual Taste of the Danforth Festival is one of the city's largest and best-known festivals, with more than a million people attending each year. Restaurants open their doors and their kitchens, offering small samples of their best dishes while traditional Greek musicians play on each of several stages. During the day there is

Taste of the Danforth Summer Festival

face painting and other activities to keep youngsters happy. At night festivities become more of an over-19 affair.

Niagara

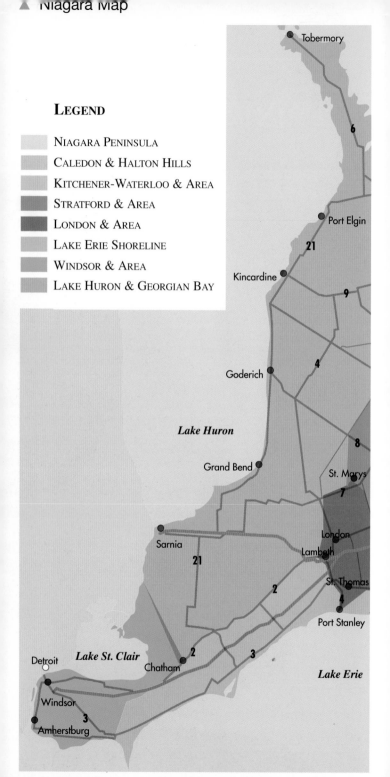

LEGEND

- NIAGARA PENINSULA
- CALEDON & HALTON HILLS
- KITCHENER-WATERLOO & AREA
- STRATFORD & AREA
- LONDON & AREA
- LAKE ERIE SHORELINE
- WINDSOR & AREA
- LAKE HURON & GEORGIAN BAY

Tobermory

Port Elgin

Kincardine

Goderich

Lake Huron

Grand Bend

St. Marys

Sarnia

London

Lambeth

St. Thomas

Port Stanley

Detroit

Lake St. Clair

Chatham

Windsor

Amherstburg

Lake Erie

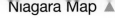

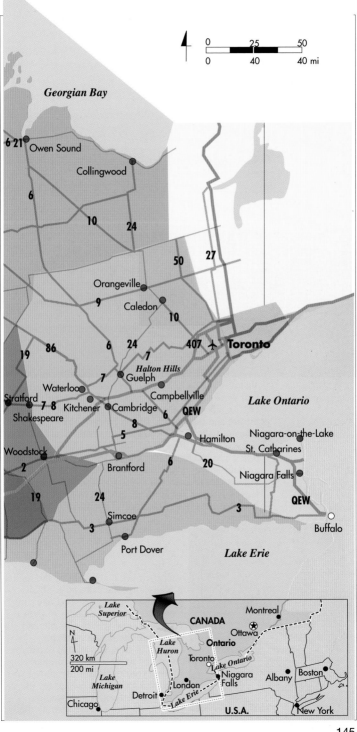

145

Exploring Niagara

The Niagara Escarpment

Visitors staying in Toronto for more than a day or two will want to venture to the Niagara region west of the city. In addition to its rich offerings of wine, food, art, theatre and history, the region around the city of Niagara Falls is also known for its natural beauty. The scenic 130-km drive along the Queen Elizabeth Way (QEW) to Niagara Falls, which typically takes about an hour-and-a-half, is bordered on one side by the deep blue waters of Lake Ontario, and on the other by the jagged Niagara Escarpment, a rough ridge of elevated land that runs from Niagara to Tobermory in northern Ontario.

Boardwalk

The best option for travelling to the Niagara region from Toronto is by car. Car rental services abound in Toronto, and the freedom afforded by having your own vehicle to explore the region is well worth the extra cost. Small towns like Niagara-on-the-Lake recognize that the majority of their visitors will be arriving by car, and parking in the region is neither difficult to find, nor all that expensive compared to the rates in Toronto. Having your own car truly allows you to get the most from the variety of attractions offered in the Niagara region, whether you are visiting the falls themselves, browsing boutique shops in Niagara-on-the-Lake or exploring Canada's early history at Fort George.

But the trip to Niagara from Toronto can also be accomplished by bus or train. Greyhound Bus offers daily departures from Toronto's main bus terminal at 610 Bay Street, near the Eaton Centre. The cost of a round trip to Niagara Falls with Greyhound is around $50, and represents a relatively inexpensive and convenient option for those without their own vehicle. Niagara Falls Tours operates a bus service from Toronto to the falls that picks up travellers directly from their hotel. VIA Rail also offers transportation to Niagara Falls from Toronto's downtown core. Trains depart from Union Station and drop travellers off near the Whirlpool Bridge, a few blocks from Niagara Falls' downtown. Keep in mind, however, that train service to Niagara Falls is less frequent and is more expensive than taking the bus.

Once visitors have arrived in the Niagara Region, the means of exploring (whether by car, bike or foot) really depends on what they want see, so planning the trip beforehand is a must. If your destination is the city of Niagara Falls or a small town like Niagara-on-the-Lake or even St. Catharines, then once you have arrived, there really is no reason to use the car. All of these destinations can be explored on foot, and a car is only needed for travelling between them. It is also worth noting that most — if not all — of these communities offer walking tours to visitors. The easiest way to obtain information is via the Internet or by picking up a brochure at the local tourist office.

Niagara vineyard

Bicycling in the Niagara region is an option in the warmer months, and one that has become increasingly popular in recent years. There is nothing like the warm summer's air breezing past as you take in the sights and smells of the escarpment and Lake Ontario. A number of recreational trails are available in the area around Niagara-on-the-Lake, and bicycling the various wineries in the region is also a possibility. Companies such as Zoom Leisure in Niagara-on-the-Lake offer inexpensive bicycle rentals, and information is also available from the Niagara-on-the-Lake Chamber of Commerce.

Top Attractions

Brian Heard, Adam Paul Bourret, Julia Browne, Grant Gaspari, Deirdre Hanna

Maid of the Mist

Niagara Falls

Niagara Falls is Ontario's most famous attraction. Each year, an estimated twenty million tourists visit the falls to marvel at the natural spectacle and enjoy the local attractions.

The falls actually consist of two separate cascades, known as the American and Horseshoe Falls. Both are 52 m high, but the Horseshoe Falls — with a brink stretching 790 m — is much larger. Almost two million litres of water (and the occasional daredevil fool in a barrel) plummets over the Horseshoe Falls every second.

Local attractions are a delightfully motley bunch. Various views of the falls can be enjoyed from beside, below, above or even behind the mighty flow, but they can be best viewed by strolling along acres of pedestrian walkways. Most of these follow the Niagara Parkway, which runs parallel to the river and encompasses an area known as Clifton Hill. Another option is the SkyWheel, a 53 m Ferris wheel with enclosed gondolas. Two viewing towers, the Konica-Minolta Tower and Skylon Tower, also offer views from above. Both have restaurants and gift shops. Viewing the falls from below is possible via the *Maid of the Mist*, which offers boat rides to the base of the falls. Upstream from the falls, the Whirlpool Aero Car takes passengers by cable car over the Niagara River. And for those not content with a cable-car ride, two companies offer helicopter flights: Niagara Helicopters and National Helicopters. Journey Behind the falls offers walking tours through a short network of caves and a viewing area behind Horseshoe Falls. Every evening from dusk, the falls are illuminated by a lightshow. Twice weekly (Fridays and Sundays) — between May and September — there is also a fireworks show.

Whirlpool Aero Car over the Niagara River

Away from the falls themselves, there are a number of eccentric amusements for visitors, such as the Daredevil Museum, Ripley's Believe It or Not, Nightmares Fear Factory (a "haunted house"), walking tours to see the 29 Welland murals, public tours of a hydroelectric generating station and a giant-screened IMAX movie theatre. There is also an aquarium (with attached amusement park) and a zoo. For gamblers, and those who might enjoy catching one of the occasional musical performances, there is Casino Niagara.

For quieter moments, visitors can choose between the Botanical Gardens and the Butterfly Conservatory, both run by Niagara Parks. Perhaps a little less quiet, Bird Kingdom boasts that it is the world's largest free-flying aviary.

Niagara Parkway

The Niagara Region offers more than 200 km of paved and unpaved multi-use trails, including three long-distance ones: the Greater Niagara Circle Route, Lake Ontario Waterfront Trail and the TransCanada Trail. However, for visitors with only a few hours to spare, the Niagara River Recreation Trail and the Welland Canals Trail both provide a great taste of the region.

Cycling the Niagara Parkway trails

Niagara River Recreation Trail

The Niagara River Recreation Trail extends for 56 km alongside the Niagara River and Niagara Falls, from Fort Erie to Niagara-on-the-Lake. Used by cyclists, pedestrians and rollerbladers, it runs past a number of historic sites, restaurants, parks and picnic areas, and is a great way to explore the Niagara district. Note that traffic is generally higher on weekends and holidays, and on-road cycling on the Niagara Parkway is occasionally required. Rollerblading may not be ideal at all points along the trail.

Atop the Niagara
Gorge

Niagara Gorge

Fort Erie to Niagara Falls

Beginning at Bowen Road, about 5 km from historic Fort Erie, the trail is less travelled, since this area is primarily residential and offers fewer points of interest. From here to the falls the route is quiet and runs almost level through Niagara's distinctive savannah countryside to the Niagara River, with convenient picnic stops, boat launches and campgrounds along the way.

The first historic point of interest along this stretch is Chippawa Battlefield Park, which offers a self-guided walking tour commemorating the Niagara campaign of 1814. At this point, about 3 km from the Niagara Falls entertainment district, the mist from the falls is evident. The area becomes more industrialized near the falls, with the trail flanking the Niagara Tunnel Project and the International Niagara Control Works.

Where the trail enters the entertainment district, the pedestrian traffic is often so dense and the path so narrow that cyclists will likely need to leave the trail and travel on the road, which is also densely packed with automobile traffic. There are, however, a number of vantage points from which to see the falls, including a raised platform near the *Maid of the Mist* landing.

Niagara Glen

Niagara Falls to Niagara-on-the-Lake

The route from the falls to Niagara-on-the-Lake is more well-travelled, and includes stunning glimpses of Niagara Falls and the river, access to several historic sites, the Butterfly Conservatory, gardens, wooded parks, picnic stops and access points to Ontario's wine routes.

About 4 km from the falls, the trail passes the White Water Walk at the Great Gorge, as well as the Spanish Aero Car and helicopter rides. At 7 km from the falls, it passes the Niagara Parks Golf Course, Whirlpool Restaurant, a scenic lookout over the Whirlpool and jet boat tours. Nearby are the Totem Pole Wood-Carving Park and the entrance to Niagara Glen — a nature reserve set deep in the Great Gorge. After descending into the Glen down a steep flight of metal stairs, pedestrians can hike along 4 km of paths that wind through Carolinian forest and huge boulders that were left behind thousands of years ago as the falls eroded the cliffs. Hikers should be aware that the trail is rough and proper footwear is recommended.

Below and bottom:
Butterfly
Conservatory,.

As the Niagara Recreation Trail continues, it leads to the School of Horticulture Gardens and Butterfly Conservatory, which features more than 2,000 species of butterflies in an indoor rainforest. At this point, the trail opens up again and wanders through a shady, wooded area, with the river now visible through the trees. Queenston Heights Park is situated about 12 km past the falls and offers a self-guided walk commemorating the Battle of Queenston Heights. The Queenston Heights Restaurant also offers spectacular views of the Niagara River and Escarpment.

Approximately 20 km from

the falls, the landscape opens up once more and the trail enters Niagara Grape and Wine Country. Several renowned Ontario vineyards and wineries are easily accessible from this point, as well as restaurants, picnic shelters and fruit stands. Just over 24 km from the falls, the trail eventually reaches Niagara-on-the-Lake, with its many boutiques, theatres, hotels and restaurants.

The Welland Canals Trail

The Welland Canals Trail is a well-developed path that follows the new and old canals from Saint Catharines to Port Colborne for 42 km. The Welland Canals are a major shipping link between Lake Ontario and Lake Erie. The trail is paved, generally flat, except for a 1 km stretch near Thorold, where it climbs the Niagara Escarpment. Heading south, the trail passes through downtown Welland, and close to the water to downtown Port Colborne, passing through a number of parks, the Welland Canal locks and historic districts.

Butterfly Conservatory

Along the scenic Niagara Parkway and the Great Gorge, located on the grounds of the Niagara Parks Botanical Gardens, the Butterfly Conservatory is truly an inspiring and magical place that fills visitors with a childlike sense of awe and wonder.

Observing species from the Butterfly Conservatory

The conservatory celebrated its tenth year in 2007. The 1,022-square-metre building is the world's largest glass-enclosed butterfly conservatory and home to more than 2,000 tropical butterflies belonging to approximately forty-five species, fluttering freely among the lush greenery, colourful flowers and wide-eyed visitors. Colourful clothing can attract a miniature winged explorer, who just might set down for a rest before moving on to delicately land on an actual blossom or fruit feeding station — if you're fortunate!

A leisurely stroll along the 180 m pathway takes visitors through a misty rainforest surrounding a man-made waterfall, where they can observe these gentle creatures. The plant life is labelled for easy identification, and you may encounter some of the butterflies' neighbours such as Eurasian quails, turtles, goldfish, toads and beetles, all of which play a role in this ecosystem, such as clearing dead butterflies, controlling parasitic pests and keeping populations of other insects balanced.

One of the most fascinating parts of the Conservatory is the Emergence Area. Here visitors can embrace the entire butterfly lifecycle by observing the insects in their chrysalis form, and with luck, catch sight of one emerging and unfurling its wings to dry before it flies away to begin the next stage of its life. The exhibit hall features interactive displays, live caterpillars and information on the life of butterflies.

As with most popular attractions, crowds are common, especially in summer. So plan to arrive early in the morning to avoid the heaviest of the crowds. A gift shop, café, snack bar and washrooms are all on site, and the Conservatory is fully wheelchair accessible — it won the 2007 AccessibleNiagara.com "Breaking the Barrier" Award.

Niagara-on-the-Lake

Niagara-on-the-Lake, often called "the loveliest town in Canada," was once the capital of Upper Canada. The town is home to many historic sites as well as a host of shops and restaurants.

Below: Queen Street; Bottom: actively exploring Niagara-on-the-Lake

Most of the attractions and activities in Niagara-on-the-Lake are located along Queen Street, though there is plenty to see and do in the surrounding area. Visitors travelling by car should note that the drive from St. Catharines along Lakeshore Road, and from Niagara Falls along the Niagara Parkway, make for lovely tours through local fruit and wine country.

Accommodations range widely in terms of size and price. Although there are many hotels in the town — Niagara-on-the-Lake boasts more than 100 bed and breakfasts — the "big three" stand out: the Pillar and Post, Queen's

The Prince of Wales Hotel

The Pillar and Post Inn

Landing and the Prince of Wales. These hotels reflect a European style of service, and the afternoon tea at the Prince of Wales is considered the finest in the region. Despite the number of hotels and bed and breakfasts, it's a good idea to make room reservations a few months in advance.

When wandering in Niagara-on-the-Lake, visitors are never more than five minutes from a good meal. The restaurants along Queen range from charming burger-and-fries joints like the Stagecoach to elegant fine dining at The Shaw Café & Wine Bar. For picnic supplies to take down to the waterside, which is only two blocks from the downtown core, visitors can also stop by venues like the Valu-Mart and the Theatre Deli & Gourmet Shoppe.

Shopping in the historic town centre is another favourite activity in Niagara-on-the-Lake. The town is known for its high concentration of specialty shops and small galleries, a bountiful source of antiques, home accents, upscale clothing, fine chocolates and works of art.

Visitors interested in a more cultural experience will want to check out the Shaw Festival, a local theatre company that operates three venues in town. Shows take place at 2:00 p.m. and 8:00 p.m., with the occasional lunchtime performance at 12:30 p.m. Like the hotels, it's a good idea to book Shaw tickets in advance, though experienced theatre-goers often arrive half-an-hour before the performance in the hopes of acquiring last-minute seats at a lower cost.

The Niagara Apothecary

Fort George, a key battle site during the War of 1812, is a favourite with history buffs. It is the largest of the Niagara National Historic Sites, a collection that also includes Navy Hall on Ricardo Street and Butler's Barracks on King Street. Museum lovers will want to check out the Niagara Historical Society Museum on Castlereagh Street, which features permanent exhibitions of the region's history, and the Niagara Apothecary on Queen Street, an historic recreation of an 1869 pharmacy.

For wine lovers, Niagara-on-the-Lake is the perfect starting and finishing point for a bicycle tour of the local wineries. Residents and visitors alike enjoy mapping out a route, packing a picnic lunch and travelling from winery to winery. Most of the wineries in the area offer samples for free or for a modest price, enabling guests to try before they buy.

Shaw Festival

From its humble beginnings in 1962, the Shaw Festival has become a world-class theatre company, presenting ten to twelve shows annually in three theatres, as well as hosting concerts, radio plays, tours, seminars, lectures and community events.

After its first successful year, the Festival appointed Andrew Allan as its professional artistic director and converted the assembly hall in Niagara-on-the-Lake's courthouse into the Court House Theatre. By 1973 the company had built a second venue, the Festival Theatre. The Festival can seat 861 and features unique reverse wood panelling to perfectly amplify the human voice without the use of microphones. It was later expanded to include a parking lot, an English garden and, most recently, a production centre.

The Shaw Festival

In 1980, with Christopher Newton now at the helm, the Shaw acquired a third theatre, the Royal George, an historic 1920s "road house," which was gradually converted into an elegant venue for the Festival's mysteries and musicals. Newton enjoyed the longest run of any artistic director to date, occupying the position until 2002. When he retired, Newton named his successor, Jackie Maxwell, who is, in 2010, planning her eighth season with the Shaw.

As the Festival has expanded, its mandate has changed. It was originally created to showcase the plays of the great Irish playwright George Bernard Shaw. In 1964 the mandate was widened to include any play written during Shaw's lifetime, 1856–1950. The Festival could now produce works by Shaw's contemporaries such as Noel Coward, Arthur

Miller, Anton Chekov and Oscar Wilde. In 2000, the mandate was expanded again to include plays written about this period. This shift has enabled the Festival to mount more modern and challenging plays, including works by Canadian playwrights.

Tickets to the Shaw Festival can be ordered by phone or online. The Festival's website also has information on how to become a member. Members receive special privileges, ranging from free refreshments to access to exclusive events and tours.

Above and top:
Fort George

Interpreters re-
enacting The War
of 1812

Fort George

Of Niagara's many military fort sites, the Parks Canada reproduction of Fort George is perhaps the one most worth visiting. Hastily built between 1796 and 1799 to protect British interests in Upper Canada, Fort George's location was also strategically calculated to supply forts farther west. As visitors pass under the massive timber main gates that are secured with iron

spikes, costumed interpreters and performers stage dramatic re-enactments, musket drills and lively military marches that bring to life the pivotal moment of the War of 1812 that kept the Niagara region in Canadian hands.

Fort George was eventually destroyed by American artillery fire in May 1813, and then repossessed by the British. In October 1813, one of Canada's greatest military heroes, Major General Sir Isaac Brock, Commander-in-

Chief of British Forces in Upper Canada, led a charge from Fort George against the assailing American troops, saving the colonies when all seemed hopeless. A self-guided tour of Brock's activities starts at his commemorative monument at Queenston Park and passes the small cairn at the base of the Niagara Escarpment that marks the location where he was shot.

Going through the locks

Abandoned in 1828, Fort George was reconstructed in 1930 and earned itself National Historic Site designation. Visitors can tour the officers' elegant quarters and enlisted soldiers' quarters (which housed aboriginal forces and Runchey's corps of former slaves) and see where the artificers made and repaired tools and artifacts. Scarred cannons still face Old Fort Niagara across the river and are fired at noon during the summer season.

St. Catharines and the Welland Canal
Located on the shore of Lake Ontario, St. Catharines is the largest city on the eastern end of the Niagara Peninsula. The city is a perfect base for touring as it is only a thirty minute drive from Niagara Falls, Niagara-on-the-Lake (home of the Shaw Festival and Fort George) and countless wineries (the Niagara Winery Guide website lists fifty-nine wineries in the region). Toronto and Buffalo are both just over an hour's drive away.

Although less famous than the natural wonder that is Niagara Falls, it is here at St. Catharines where the region's man-made wonder — the Welland Canal — connects Lake Ontario to Lake Erie, allowing some

The Welland Canal

▲ Niagara

Locks, Welland Canal

3,000 lake and ocean-going vessels to bypass Niagara Falls and traverse the Niagara Escarpment annually. These ships transport 40 million metric tonnes of cargo through the Great Lakes, and their passage is critical to the economies of Canada and the United States.

The canal has experienced four separate manifestations, with the first three starting in Port Dalhousie (now part of the city of St. Catharines). The first Welland Canal opened in 1829 with forty locks, then was redesigned twice over the next sixty years with course variations and fewer locks before the final eight-lock version began construction in 1913 and was completed in 1932. Since 1932 there have been changes to the canal and locks, but the current course running south to Port Colborne on Lake Erie has remained the same.

Locks 1, 2 and 3 are in St. Catharines; locks 4, 5, 6 and 7 are south in the town of Thorold; and the final lock, number 8, is located at Port Colborne. Lock 4 in Thorold is a "twin-flight" lock that allows ships to travel in both directions at the same time. There is scenic viewing at all of the locks, and Lock 3 has an elevated viewing platform that is also home to the St. Catharines Museum, which features diverse exhibits on the Welland Canal, the history of the city of St. Catharines and the city's significance as a final terminus for the Underground Railroad in the early 1800s. The Lock 3 site also hosts the Ontario Lacrosse Hall of Fame & Museum.

In addition to its place in local history as the starting site of the first three Welland Canals, the neighbourhood of Port Dalhousie also has a rich history of rowing. The Henley rowing course is one of the most perfect natural rowing courses in North America and hosts many world-class events. Annual events include the Canadian Secondary School Rowing Association Championships and the Royal Canadian Henley Regatta (which celebrated its 125th year in 2007). It was the site of the 1999 World Championships and will host the 2010 FISA World Rowing Masters Regatta. Port Dalhousie is also home to many quaint shops, an abundance of restaurants, patios and wine bars, the Lakeside Park beach and the Port Dalhousie Pier Marina.

St. Catharines' largest and most popular event is the annual Niagara Wine Festival in late September, which celebrates the region's internationally acclaimed grape and wine industry. Festival events include winery tours, tastings, seminars, outdoor concerts, artisan exhibits, family entertainment and one of Canada's largest parades. It was selected as Ontario's Cultural Event of the Year for three years in a row and as one of North America's Top 100 Events by the American Bus Association in 2005. Other popular festivals include the Niagara Icewine Festival in January and the Niagara Folk Arts Festival in May.

There are countless other attractions, festivals, scenic views and picturesque towns in the region. Travellers can visit the St. Catharines area many times and enjoy a unique experience each time.

The Albright-Knox Art Gallery in Buffalo
A legacy of Buffalo's glory days, before the St.

Port Dalhousie

Albright-Knox Art Gallery

Painting from the Ingrid Calame exhibition at Albright-Knox

Lawrence Seaway replaced the Erie Canal as a major inland shipping artery, the Albright-Knox Art Gallery houses a wealth of important art unexpected in America's third-poorest city.

The gallery was named for two major donors: John J. Albright, who funded the gallery's initial construction in 1905 and Seymour H. Knox Jr., who made possible a significant expansion in 1964. But the Albright-Knox owes as great a debt to the philanthropist who shaped its collecting mandate to become one of the first museums to collect twentieth-century Modernist art — Buffalo-born industrialist A. Conger Goodyear, who served as the first president of the Museum of Modern Art in New York City from 1929 to 1939. It was the Albright, not the MoMA, that acquired Goodyear's substantial personal collection, and it was this core that put, and keeps, the Albright on the international art map, even in the face of Buffalo's economic decline.

Collection highlights include works by Impressionists such as Monet and Degas; major Post-Impressionists including van Gogh, Cézanne and Gauguin; key Modernists including Picasso and Matisse; an impressive selection of early Soviet artists such as Malevich and Popova, acquired fifty years after their heyday in the 1920s; and major post-war figures such as Jackson Pollock, Andy Warhol, Francis Bacon, Arshile Gorky and Jasper Johns. More recent acquisitions include works by Jenny Holzer, Kiki Smith and Matthew Barney.

In 2007 the Albright-Knox sparked an international debate about ethics and public galleries when it sold off a group of pre-twentieth-century works including the Hellenic bronze Artemis and the Stag that sold at auction to a private collector for $25.5 million. None of the cash raised by the controversial sale can be used to repair the neoclassical museum's bricks and mortar, even though parts of the building — notably its interior marble floors and exterior stairs — are quite literally crumbling.

Still, the setting and collection are spectacular. Located in one of the many parks designed for the city of Buffalo by seminal landscape architect Frederick Law Olmstead, the Albright-Knox is surrounded by some truly remarkable private homes built by Buffalo's once-affluent business leaders. Frank Lloyd Wright's 1909 Heath House, for example — a stylistic precursor to Wright's famous Robie House in Chicago — is located within walking distance of the gallery on Bird Avenue.

Henri Matisse, *La Musique*, 1939, Albright-Knox Art Gallery

Wine and Food

Brian Heard

Prince of Wales' grilled venison chop

For lovers of fine food and wine, the Niagara region is a magical corner. Tucked between Lake Ontario, the Niagara Escarpment and "the falls" themselves, the Niagara wine country is an increasingly popular destination. Visitors range from day-trippers from Toronto to tour groups from Europe and the Far East.

Besides wine tasting, wine touring offers pleasant drives along tree-lined roads (the fruit trees are typically in bloom during the first half of May); browsing in gift shops (best of all for local, artisanal preserves); sampling bakery goods and freshly harvested local fruit (cherries, peaches and plums) at roadside farm fruit stalls; and the nearby Shaw Theatre Festival. There are also plenty of wonderful places to stay, luxurious spas and an amazing assemblage of restaurants — from casual to formal, and humble to haute cuisine.

Niagara's Wine Industry

Ontario winemaking — even compared to other "New World" wine regions — has a very short history. In the early nineteenth century, some wine was made by Jesuit missionaries and a few enterprising settlers. However, commercial-scale, premium winemaking did not begin here until the 1970s. Just a few decades later the local industry is thriving, more than making up for any disadvantage of its youth with diversity, dynamism and determination.

As befits its tender age, the Niagara region's industry is still trying to "find itself." Many historic wine regions have established traditions of growing only a few types of grapes. Ontario vignerons, in contrast, are experimenting with scores of grape varieties, making wine in dozens of styles. For visitors, this translates into a richly varied wine-tasting experience, especially suitable for novices.

Icewine: Niagara's Specialty

Although Niagara is known for a very wide range of wine styles, it is certainly fair to single out icewines as a local specialty. These wines are made from grapes left on the vines until the first hard freeze. Local vignerons have found that Niagara's climate is — among grape-growing regions — almost uniquely suitable.

Above and below: Icewine Harvest

Icewines are fantastically sweet. Rather than just sticky, however, a good example is balanced by lively, and even mouth watering, tanginess. The greatest icewines are made from (white) Riesling grapes. Right behind these are those made from (red) Cabernet Franc.

Wine Tasting

Understanding the potential value of wine tourism, most wineries put a great deal of effort into welcoming visitors. Some wineries offer guided tours (most with a small fee). Almost all run a "tasting bar" where visitors may sample wines. The staff — of varying levels of expertise — are happy to answer questions and guide visitors through a variety of wines. As a general rule, the less busy the winery, the more likely you are to be hosted by someone particularly knowledgeable. On particularly lucky occasions, this may even be the grape-grower or winemaker.

Fees for tastings vary. Some wineries are happy to waive a fee ($1 to $3 per sample) if you purchase at least one bottle of wine. A few offer complimentary

Tasting bar,
Inniskillin

samples of their "table" wines, but charge $2 to $3 to sample an icewine. Still others invite visitors to taste through a standardized "flight" (series) of wines. In this case a $10 fee is typical.

There is no need to feel intimidated by the tasting-bar experience. Begin by choosing a wine to try. Next, swirl and sniff. The aroma may offer half of a wine's magic; it is also the most difficult aspect for the winemaker to successfully capture. Then sip and consider: do you like it, and why or why not? Finally, based on what you have just learned, and with the help of your host, return to step number one.

For novices, here are two brief notes on etiquette. Firstly, there is no need to drink everything that is poured. There will always be a "spittoon" (easily confused with an empty vase), which serves two functions: it is perfectly acceptable to dump out part of a sample, and it is also perfectly acceptable to "sip & spit" (admittedly not easy to do so gracefully).

Wine tasting

Secondly, fellow guests will be appreciative if you avoid wearing perfumes.

Winery Events

Wineries with their own restaurants often hold special dinners. These might comprise a seasonal tasting menu, a meal with the winemaker or dinner al fresco in the vineyard.

Guided tasting seminars are offered at some wineries, including Cave Spring Cellars, Hillebrand, Peller, Strewn and Stratus. These seminars feature a knowledgeable host (often the winemaker) and a flight of wines gathered around a theme. Contact the individual wineries for schedules and reservations.

Many wineries ramp up their welcome during Niagara's three annual wine-focused festivals: the New Vintage Festival in June, the Niagara Wine Festival in September and the Niagara Icewine Festival in January.

Once each year, Henry of Pelham Family Estate hosts Shakespeare in the Vineyard. Also at Henry of Pelham, an annual event offers wine lovers some hands-on vineyard experience during Harvest with Henry day. Jackson-Triggs' estate includes an outdoor amphitheatre for Twilight in the Vineyard musical performances. Chateau des Charmes also hosts occasional music performances.

The Wine Council of Ontario publishes an ongoing schedule of wine country events on its website (www.winesofontario.org).

Getting from Winery to Winery

A well-signed "Wine Route" helps guide visitors through the midst of Niagara's wineries. Those wineries located on side roads are individually signed. Most helpful of all, the Wine Council of Ontario publishes an annual guide composed of a pullout map and brief introduction to member wineries. This is available on the website and from local wineries, hotels and restaurants.

Le clos Jordanne Wine

For those not wishing to drive during a day of wine tasting, there are several options. Plenty of tour companies offer the opportunity to join bus and/or van tours. Others offer private tours for groups as small as two. Typically, these tours visit a number of prelisted wineries. You may wish to look for one escorted by a wine-savvy guide.

For the actively inclined, bicycling within a cluster of wineries is a popular option. The Niagara-on-the-Lake area, with several wineries located along a lovely bicycle trail, is particularly well suited. Two local shops, Zoom Leisure and Niagara Rowing School, rent bicycles for this purpose. Cyclists may make their own way or join a guided cycling tour. Two other companies, Steve Bauer Bike Tours and Niagara Wine Tours International, also offer guided cycling tours that include rental of a bicycle.

Niagara's "Wine Route"

Any tour should include a variety of wineries, and at least one small operation in addition to one of the larger ones. The very brief winery descriptions that follow are intended to help plan a tour, and at the end of this section there are four suggested itineraries.

As of 2009, there are roughly sixty wineries in the Niagara region that are open (to varying degrees) to the

Jackson Triggs Winery

public. The twenty described here have been selected as being especially good to visit, and some offer regularly scheduled public tours. All the wineries listed (except Henry of Pelham) are wheelchair accessible to their retail shop and tasting area. Accessibility for tours varies.

It is helpful to divide the Niagara region into four areas: Beamsville, Vineland/Jordan, St. Catharines and Niagara-on-the-Lake.

Beamsville Area

At the far eastern edge of the Niagara region, Puddicombe Estate Farms & Winery offers something quite unusual. Being a fruit farm first and vineyard second, they make a range of not just grape but also fruit wines (raspberry, peach and so on).

Peninsula Ridge Estates is a well-established and respected winery. This is a mid-size operation, with a Burgundian winemaker who chose to take up the challenge of making premium wines in Ontario. The estate also includes a restaurant for lovely lunches and dinners.

Peninsula Ridge

Next is a cluster of three smaller wineries: Angels Gate, Fielding Estate and Thirty Bench. During patio season, lunch is available at Angel's Gate. The atypical tasting format at Thirty Bench is worthy of note: instead of the usual tasting bar, guests sample four wines while enjoying a tutorial with a knowledgeable host. (Booking ahead is optional, but recommended during busy times). One more Beamsville winery especially worth a visit is the Malivoire Wine Company. They are at their best making elegant whites and a very popular rosé.

Vineland/Jordan Area

Heading east, the most picturesque part of Niagara's wine country is gathered around the villages of Vineland and Jordan. Especially worth a visit are Vineland Estates and Cave Spring Cellars. These two mid-size operations both make an excellent range of wines. They also each host their own fine-dining restaurants. Nearby is Kacaba, a small winery that is at its best making powerful reds.

Also worth a visit — especially when the sun is shining — is the smaller Flat Rock Cellars. This winery is perched up on the escarpment, with a view that sweeps over its vineyards and down towards Lake Ontario. Unlike many other wineries, Flat Rock has chosen to specialize in wines made exclusively from just three grape varieties: Riesling, Chardonnay and Pinot Noir.

St. Catharines Area

The St. Catharines area is home to only a few wineries. Most worth a visit is Henry of Pelham Family Estates. This is a mid-size operation with an outstanding variety of wines. Light lunches are available (May to October) at the Coach House Café and Cheese Shoppe. Unfortunately, this winery is not wheelchair accessible.

Niagara-on-the-Lake Area

There are several larger wineries in this area to choose from: Chateau des Charmes, Inniskillin Wines, Rief Estates, Strewn, Hillebrand, Jackson-Triggs and Peller Estates. Of these, Strewn, Hillebrand and Peller each has its own fine-dining restaurant.

Several smaller wineries are also worthy of a visit. Lailey Vineyards (almost next door to Peller Estates) and Stratus both make wines of exceptional quality. Stratus, in particular, aims at the super-premium end of the market.

Four Suggested Itineraries

Here are a few suggestions for three short and one longer "do-it-yourself" wine tours. For a two-winery tour within the Niagara-on-the-Lake area: Inniskillin and Lailey Vineyards; for two wineries within the Vineland/Jordan area: Vineland Estates and Flat Rock Cellars; and for two wineries within the Beamsville area (closest to Toronto): Thirty Bench and Peninsula Ridge Estate. A four-winery tour of the Niagara wine country might take in Thirty Bench, Cave Spring Cellars, Henry of Pelham Family Estate and Stratus.

Below: Henry of Pelham vineyards
Bottom: Stone Road appetizer

Dining

In Niagara, several local factors combine to make the region a particularly exciting destination for those who love fine food.

An unusually large number of potential guests has encouraged a vibrant marketplace of cuisine. Wine and food go naturally together, and people who enjoy wine tasting are almost certain to be people who seek out fine cuisine. In addition, the Shaw Festival brings even more people likely to be looking to enjoy a special dinner out.

Another great boost is provided by local cooking schools (Niagara College and two private schools) that fuel the area's kitchens with talent, creativity and youthful energy.

Fine and Stunning Cuisine: Three Locations

Several wineries have added restaurants to their estates. For wine tourists, this is a popular and convenient option. Generally, the cuisine is artful and places great emphasis on local ingredients and Niagara

wines. Options include a light lunch on (seasonal) patios overlooking the vineyard, as offered at Angel's Gate or Henry of Pelham, right through to a much more formal dinner. Some of the region's finest restaurants are linked to wineries. Peller, Hillebrand, Vineland, Cave Spring Cellars (Inn on the Twenty) and Peninsula Ridge each have beautiful formal dinning rooms, serving the finest cuisine. At the Strewn Winery, Terroir le Cachette is a little less formal.

Grilled Ontario pork tenderloin from Hillebrand Estates

Many of the region's other fine restaurants are associated with inns and hotels in Niagara-on-the-Lake. The dining rooms tend towards posh and the food is not only fantastically delicious but also lavishly chic. A few illustrative examples: lobster tail served with caramelized fennel risotto and preserved lemons; fire-baked pizza with duck, caramelized onion, walnuts and warmed camembert; or Quebec foie gras served with brioche French toast, rhubarb compote and pomegranate molasses.

Finally, there are several excellent independent restaurants around the region. Zee's Patio & Grill, for example, and the especially good Stone Road Grille both combine delicious chic and local wines with dining rooms that might be described as more stylish than formal.

Hillebrand Yard

Excursions for…

The Art Goer

Emily Orford

Art Gallery of Hamilton

Art enthusiasts travelling in southwestern Ontario and the Niagara region are in for a treat. The region boasts more than 300 years of local history and art, not to mention the centuries of First Nations history and culture that predates European settlement. The area is well known for its artists, artisans and craftspeople, who are featured prominently in the many local art galleries, both public and commercial.

Kleinburg

With almost 6,000 Canadian artworks, the McMichael Canadian Art Collection in Kleinburg is a national treasure. The collection began in 1952 when Robert and Signe McMichael purchased a large parcel of land in Kleinburg, just north of Toronto, and constructed a pioneer-style log home, which they called Tapawingo, a "place of joy." Their first art purchases, a Lawren Harris and a Tom Thomson, launched a lifelong commitment to supporting Canadian art and artists. The McMichael family donated their home and collection to the province of Ontario, and the McMichael Conservation Collection of Art officially opened in 1966. Covering 85,000 square feet, it includes thirteen exhibition spaces, a theatre and the Gallery Shop. In spite of its size, the gallery maintains the rustic charm of a log cabin in the woods.

It is truly a Canadian experience to visit the McMichael Collection and marvel at the creative genius of Thomson, the Group of Seven artists, Emily Carr, Edwin Holgate and many more. There is also a large collection of First Nations artists like Norval Morrisseau, and Inuit artists like Kenojuak Ashevak. The McMichael has the unique role of being the only major public gallery devoted exclusively to the exhibition and collection of Canadian art.

Niagara Peninsula

The Niagara Peninsula, best known for its popular wine industry, is also an artist's haven. There are numerous commercial galleries and craft shops and the major communities like Niagara-on-the-Lake and Niagara Falls boast both public and private galleries featuring local as well as international talent.

The Niagara Falls Art Gallery is conveniently located in downtown Niagara Falls. Its dominant feature is the fascinating William Kurelek Art Collection. Internationally renowned for his folk art depictions of rural Canadian life in the early twentieth century, William Kurelek (1927—1977) is an icon of Canadian art and culture.

As well as its excellent Kurelek collection, the Niagara Falls Art Gallery is very supportive of the regional history and the arts of the Niagara peninsula. A key component of the permanent collection is the John Burtniak Niagara Collection, which focuses on historical Niagara Falls artwork from the early 1700s to the 1950s.

There are at least a dozen arts and craft galleries in and around the Old Town area of Niagara-on-the-Lake. The community features the artistic avant-garde of local artists like Angie Strauss, Walter Campbell and Trisha Romance, whose works can be seen in their own personal galleries. The gallery of popular Victorian romantic artist Trisha Romance, the Romance Collection Gallery, is appropriately located in a gorgeous Victorian mansion overlooking Simcoe Park. Although the gallery features predominantly the work of Romance, it also represents internationally renowned super-realist painter Alex Colville, and the expressionist figure-painter Tanya Jean Peterson.

The Preservation Gallery is a restored Victorian mansion in Niagara-on-the-Lake

Hamilton Area

Nestled at the edge of the Niagara region, on the western tip of Lake Ontario, Hamilton has a long history as a steel and manufacturing town. The local economy has always provided a strong cultural basis to support the arts, and over the years Hamilton has developed into a thriving art centre with two major public galleries and numerous smaller galleries and commercial enterprises.

The Art Gallery of Hamilton houses one of the finest permanent collections in Canada. With more than 8,500 works of art, primarily Canadian historical and contemporary works, the collection is highly respected both nationally and internationally. The gallery was founded in 1914 in the old library building to house twenty-nine paintings donated from the estate of Hamiltonian William Blair Bruce (1859–1906). The work of this internationally renowned artist, who trained and worked abroad, reflects the regional, national and international scope of the gallery's collection. Researchers will especially appreciate its library and archival reference materials and rare book special collection.

The permanent collection of the McMaster Museum of Art, across from the University Student Centre at McMaster University, officially opened in 1994. The collection consists of more than 6,000 works, including the Denner Wallace Collection of German Expressionist prints, the Levy Collection of Impressionist and Post-Impressionist paintings, a large collection of European Old Masters, Canadian historical paintings and prints and Inuit art, primarily Cape Dorset prints and sculpture.

The Burlington Art Centre is unique in its role of collecting contemporary Canadian ceramics. The gallery features more than 1,000 ceramic artworks from practising Canadian and international artisans as well as historic pieces.

Art Gallery of Hamilton

The Carnegie Gallery in downtown Dundas was founded in 1910 with funds donated by American industrialist Andrew Carnegie. Striving to promote and preserve the arts and crafts of the region, the Gallery supports the Dundas Art and Craft Association by exhibiting and promoting works by local artists and craftspeople.

Six Nations Reserve

A trip along the Grand River just outside Brantford is a time-travel adventure through Canada's history. The art and history of the First Nations can be discovered and explored at the Six Nations Reserve in Ohsweken. Chiefswood National Historic Site, the birthplace of the internationally renowned poet E. Pauline Johnson, is one of only four remaining pre-Confederation buildings on the Six Nations Reserve. The Mohawk Chapel houses an interesting collection of artifacts of historical, religious and cultural importance.

The Woodland Cultural Centre celebrates the history, traditions and culture of the Eastern Woodland, the Algonquian and the Iroquoian. The collection includes historic artifacts as well as contemporary First Nations work. There are also numerous First Nations arts and crafts shops in the area featuring the work of local artisans. Two Turtle Iroquois Fine Art Gallery in Ohsweken showcases contemporary spirit art of the Six Nations Reserve, including paintings by Arnold Aron Jacobs, sculpture by Tonia Hill and the work of many other fine First Nations artists.

Peel County

Peel County and the city of Brampton are proud of their heritage and are devoted to the cultural diversity and artistic talent of the region.

The Art Gallery of Peel is part of the Peel Heritage Complex in downtown Brampton. The Gallery is dedicated to preserving the region's history and rich artistic heritage. With more than 2,500 works of art, it holds the largest public collection in the region. Its permanent collection features internationally renowned artists such as Andy Warhol, as well as Canadian artists such as Tom Thomson, Michael Snow, Joyce Weiland and Doris McCarthy. The Gallery also gives emphasis to notable local artists, including William Ronald, Ronald Bloore, David Urban and Sadko Hadzihasanovic. The permanent collection includes Peel historical paintings and prints, specifically a collection of more than 500 prints by the early twentieth-century artists Caroline and Frank Armington.

Also in the Peel Heritage Complex are the Peel Archives and the Whitney Community Gallery, which showcases contemporary Peel artists, craftspeople and collectors.

Koningstrasse,
Art Gallery of Peel

Kitchener-Waterloo and Cambridge

Situated about halfway between Toronto and London, the Kitchener-Waterloo and Cambridge region is alive with artists in all media. One of the biggest international names of this region is Homer Watson (1855–1936), whose landscapes depict the sublime, rugged beauty of Canada in the nineteenth century.

The Homer Watson House and Gallery in Kitchener preserves the artist's home and displays the Homer Watson Foundation collection of paintings. The Doon School of Fine Arts used Watson's Victorian house in the 1950s and 1960s: famous Canadian artists such as Fred Varley and Carl Schaefer studied there. The legacy of Watson's creative spirit thrives at the Gallery with frequent exhibitions of local artists and vibrant educational programs.

The Kitchener-Waterloo Art Gallery focuses its

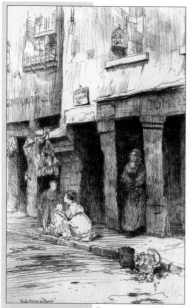

Vielle maison,
Art Gallery of Peel

collection on Canadian artists, including the Group of Seven and Tom Thomson.

The Canadian Clay and Glass Gallery in downtown Waterloo is the only public art gallery in Canada dedicated to exhibiting, interpreting and preserving contemporary clay, glass, stained glass and enamel objects of art. Amidst the fast-paced, high-tech environment of twenty-first century mass-production, this Gallery appreciates the ancient creative traditions of the handmade object. The Gallery displays its permanent collection as well as work by local, national and international artisans.

Textile arts are also prominent in this region. The Cambridge Galleries is a part of the Cambridge Public Library system, with three galleries and exhibition spaces at the Queen's Park, Preston and Riverside libraries. The exhibitions feature local, national and international art, both historical and contemporary. Since 1986, the Cambridge Galleries has focused its collection on Canadian fibre art to reflect the community's historic connection with the textile industry.

Stratford and Middlesex County

Stratford has long been famous for its theatre, but it is also a thriving haven for artists. Further west, London boasts a large art community and educational degree programs in art at the University of Western Ontario and Fanshawe College. Local galleries in both communities support and regularly feature local and international artists and craftspeople.

The old 1883 pump house on the Avon River in Stratford provides an ideal space for Gallery Stratford to combine both history and the arts. Over the past forty years the Gallery has established itself as one of the leading art venues in the region, with a collection of more than 1,000 works of art, primarily by Canadian artists including Jack Shadbolt, Harold Town, Ken Danby and Christopher Pratt. The Gallery also features a regular schedule of exhibits by major Canadian artists, as well as international travelling exhibits, including summer exhibits that highlight the theatre art of the Stratford Festival.

Museum London (prior to 2001, the London Regional Art Gallery and Historical Museum), in downtown London, has a scenic view overlooking the forks of the Thames River. The building itself is a work of art, designed by renowned Toronto architect Raymond Moriyama and officially opened in 1980.

Built as a multi-purpose museum for both art and history, Museum London houses a collection that includes historical artifacts and art from early nineteenth-century London as well as a contemporary collection of more than 2,500 works in various media representing 840 Canadian and international artists. The Canadian collection includes well-known local artists such as Paterson Ewen, Jack Chambers and Greg Curnoe as well as Canadian artists Attila Richard Lukacs, Joanne Todd and Barbara Steinman.

Paterson Ewen (1925–2002) was one of Canada's leading landscape painters. His works, which he often called "weatherscapes," revitalized interest in landscape as valid subject matter in art. His paintings were large, sculpted works on plywood, with added elements of sheet metal and linoleum to highlight the dramatic effects of weather. Greg Curnoe (1936–1992) challenged the way Canadians look at and think about art. He was an eccentric colourist and an avid bicyclist: many of his works depict parts or the complete image of his bicycle in bright, vivid colours. He was very critical of the society in which he lived, a view he shared in a number of his critical lettered text paintings.

The McIntosh Gallery at the University of Western Ontario has the distinction of being the oldest university art gallery in Canada. Its permanent collection of more than 3,000 works in various media dates from the early nineteenth century. The collection includes the work of major Canadian artists such as Arthur Lismer and Anthony Urquhart.

There is a thriving hub of artistic activity in southwestern Ontario and the Niagara region. With a wealth of resources to study and appreciate Canadian and international arts and crafts of all media, the opportunities are endless. Local communities often feature studio tours, providing art enthusiasts with the privilege of meeting the artists in their own milieu and seeing them at work. The region is alive with creative possibilities.

Museum of London

The Theatre Lover

Jeniva Berger

Stratford Shakespeare Festival

The Stratford Shakespeare Festival

"The play's the thing…"

It started out with a dream by Stratford journalist Tom Patterson. It became a reality in a giant tent on a warm July night in 1953, when celebrated British actor Alex Guinness stepped onstage at the newly launched Stratford Festival as the star of Shakespeare's dark tragedy, *Richard III*. It was a "momentous occasion," said Canadian author Robertson Davies, not only for Canada, but "wherever theatre is taken seriously in the world."

The Stratford Festival's first season was inaugurated with only two productions, running in repertory for six weeks. Today's audiences can choose from fourteen productions spread over an eight-month

Avon Theatre

season from April to November and presented in four theatres: the 1,825-seat Festival Theatre, built in 1958, which is called "The Cathedral" by the actors and has been credited with reinventing the Elizabethan thrust stage; the Avon Theatre, a former vaudeville house and

movie theatre that was bought in 1963 and extensively renovated in 2002 for the Festival's 50th anniversary celebrations; the 480-seat Tom Patterson Theatre, which undergoes a metamorphosis every winter when it becomes the home of the Stratford Badminton Club; and the baby of the quartet, the 260-seat Studio Theatre built in 2002. Called "The Chapel" by the actors, the Studio is an intimate place for exploring new and experimental works and rarely produced classics.

Not only does the Stratford Festival have its own conservatory for training actors in classical performance — the only one of its kind in the English-speaking theatre world — it has welcomed on its stages some of the finest actors in the world. William Hutt, Brian Bedford, Lorne Greene, Uta Hagen, Julie Harris, Paul Scofield, Maggie Smith, Alan Bates and Peter Ustinov are only a handful of great actors who have appeared at Stratford. Stratford's new artistic director, Des McAnuff, who holds both US and Canadian citizenship, was raised in Toronto and worked in theatre in that city before he left for the US. A two-time Tony Award-winning director and former artistic director of the famed La Jolla Playhouse in California, McAnuff won acclaim for his Stratford productions of Shaw's *Caesar and Cleopatra* in 2008 starring Christopher Plummer — which was subsequently seen on movie screens across the country — and *A Funny Thing Happened on the Way to the Forum* in 2009.

Tom Patterson Theatre

With its full complement of stage productions, which include the plays of William Shakespeare, modern classics, new works and Broadway musicals, the Festival and its annual $54-million-plus budget welcomes more than 600,000 visitors a year, offering such fringe benefits as workshops and courses, backstage and costume-department tours, lectures and music-workshop concerts, the Celebrated Writers Series and family adventures and activities. This gracious southwestern Ontario town of 30,000 has something for just about anyone spending a day or more here. Visitors can take their pick from some of the finest restaurants in the area (Stratford has its own Chef School) as well as explore the lush farming areas of the surrounding countryside and its Mennonite villages.

As the jewel in the crown of summer theatre dotting southwestern Ontario, Stratford, like Broadway, is an anomaly. But among the roster of Canadian actors appearing on the Festival's stages throughout its fifty years there are many who honed their craft in summer

177

theatre. Summer theatre has changed much over the years. Its "cottage country" motif has become much more than cottages on a pristine lake and now includes condos, apartments and custom-designed summer homes scattered throughout the towns and villages of southwestern Ontario. But summer remains the season with the liveliest theatrical entertainment.

Drayton Theatre Festival

A true summer theatre success story is Drayton Entertainment, which incorporates six thriving summer theatres under the guiding hand of artistic director Alex Mustakas. Mustakas, who immigrated to Canada from his native Greece as a child, was so intrigued with the idea of providing live theatre to the people in Drayton, his adopted town, that the Drayton Theatre Festival became the nucleus of his enterprise. Drayton Entertainment today entertains more than 220,000 theatre-goers at six venues in southwestern Ontario.

The theatres that comprise Drayton Entertainment and its program of musicals, comedies and concerts, and which have proven so popular with audiences include the following: the Drayton Festival Theatre, housed in a renovated 1902 Opera House; the atmospheric King's Wharf Theatre in Penetanguishene,

nestled in Discovery Harbour and surrounded by British history; Huron Country Playhouse and the intimate Playhouse II, working out of a century-old barn located in the very lively summer resort town of Grand Bend; and the St. Jacobs Country Playhouse and Schoolhouse Theatre, originally a winery and cidery, in the village of St. Jacobs.

Visitors staying in Stratford can easily drive to the community of St. Jacobs in less than forty-five minutes. St. Jacobs, which grew from a quiet Mennonite village in the 1970s, now offers a huge, renowned Ontario open-air and indoor market selling Mennonite crafts as well as baked

Red Barn Theatre

goods, fresh fruit and vegetables from local farmers. A popular discount mall located conveniently in the market area also attracts tourists.

The Blyth Festival

While most of the Ontario summer theatres include plays and musicals written by Canadians in their season's lineup, one festival in southwestern Ontario stands out as the premier summer theatre for new and developing Canadian works. The Blyth Festival in Blyth, Ontario was founded in 1975 by James Roy to produce theatre that reflected the culture of southwestern Ontario and beyond. Located in a small village with a population of 1,000 in rural Huron County, it was a bold move but reflected the country's growing interest in new Canadian works. In addition, the Festival recognized that people who lived in the surrounding area wanted to see themselves reflected in their local culture.

Since its founding, the Festival has produced 100 world premieres — plays that have gone on to win national awards, have been produced across Canada (including productions at the Stratford Festival) and have enjoyed international exposure. Housed in the town's Memorial Hall, which dominates its main street, the Blyth Centre for the Arts (including the Blyth Festival), also includes an Art Gallery that showcases three professional shows a year and hosts the Ontario Open Country Singing Contest.

Drayton Festival Theatre

The Festival's six-show summer season, under the artistic directorship of Eric Coates, attracts more than 24,000 people throughout the summer, proof that visitors as well as local residents have an ongoing interest in new and quality plays by Canadian writers.

Summer Theatre

Summer theatre in Ontario takes place in many different kinds of venues: proud established theatre spaces and new ones such as St. Jacobs Country Playhouse; converted barns like those of the Huron Country Playhouse and the thriving 4th Line Theatre in Millbrook, which presents regionally based, environmentally staged, historical dramas in the open air of the Winslow Farm. Other venues are once-upon-a-time vaudeville and movie houses (like the charming Gayety Theatre, now located in one of the fastest expanding resort areas in Ontario, the town of Collingwood, whose major drawing card in the summertime is its famous — and boisterous — outdoor Elvis Festival the third week of July), and borrowed locales such as Barrie's Gryphon Theatre, which operates out of facilities located in Georgian College.

Port towns, which appeal to vacationers because of their many water activities, offer numerous other cultural and historical attractions to draw visitors to their shores. Called one of "Ontario's best kept secrets," picturesque Port Dover two miles north of Lake Erie has long been known for its tourism and hospitality. Visitors can spend an afternoon on its wonderful sandy beach, dine at restaurants filled with tourists and locals alike enjoying Lake Erie perch, pickerel and other favourites, and in the evening take in a theatre production at the renowned Lighthouse Summer Festival, which presents high quality

Blyth Memorial Hall

productions of Canadian scripts.

The 32-year-old Port Stanley Theatre Festival — with the beautiful beaches of north Lake Erie at its doorstep — is in another town with many noteworthy attractions in addition to its full summer theatre season of comedies and musicals. Port Stanley is committed to becoming a destination theatre town; while there, visitors can also enjoy the natural beauty of the meandering Kettle Creek, ride an authentic old rail car from 1940 and take in the historic King George VI lift bridge, the oldest in Ontario, located in the centre of town.

Summer residents and tourists shore up the summer theatre scene, but it's the regional theatres that command the theatre scene from fall to springtime. One of the newest and most spectacular is the Brampton Performing Arts Centre with its 880-seat Rose Theatre, a $55-million edifice that has been called the "eighth wonder of the world" by Brampton's jubilant mayor, Susan Fennell. The acoustically perfect Rose, home to the Brampton Symphony Orchestra, crowns the atmospheric historic centre of Brampton, Canada's tenth largest city. Its full-programming slate ranges from live theatre to concerts, comedy and choral groups, and dance and ballet, and features headliners such as Diana Krahl. Few events run for

The Rose Theatre

more than two or three nights except for the indoor and outdoor summer Flower City Theatre Festival, which stages Shakespeare plays and contemporary works.

Unlike the Rose Theatre, which looks to professional touring shows and guest artists for the bulk of its programming, but also rents to local community arts groups, the Grand Theatre in London, Ontario, one hour away from the Stratford Festival, presents its own in-house seven-show season, with runs lasting anywhere from two to four weeks. The program includes original adaptations and new works, musicals and dramas in an impressive mix of productions that play its main stage as well as the smaller McManus Studio. Under the artistic directorship of Susan Ferley, its renowned High School Project is unique in North America, giving students from London and the surrounding area the chance to work with professional directors, choreographers and stage managers. Scaled down for the high school set are ambitious musicals such as *Les Miserables, School Edition*.

Considered a cultural icon in London, the Grand was once home to the amateur London Little Theatre before it became a professional company in 1971. It underwent complete reconstruction a few years later and today is known for its exceptionally beautiful 889-seat theatre. It also has the dubious distinction of having its own ghost. The theatre opened on September 9, 1901, under the ownership of theatre magnate Ambrose Small, who disappeared in 1919. It's rumored that he haunts the building to this day.

As well as professional-producing theatre companies like the Grand, regional theatres in southwestern Ontario include larger, mainly non-producing performing-arts centres such as the Rose Theatre Brampton, the Oakville Centre for the Performing Arts and the Kitchener-Waterloo Centre in the Square — a 2,047-seat design that boasts one of the largest stages in North America and is home to the Kitchener-Waterloo Symphony as well as the city's Art Gallery.

Hamilton, Ontario, is a mid-size city that has both a significant centre for the performing arts and a well-known professional regional theatre. The huge Hamilton Place Concert Hall is a 2,200-seat theatre that was designed to accommodate a full range of music, opera and musical events. The popular Theatre Aquarius, under the artistic directorship of Ron Ulrich, is comfortably at home in the beautiful three-year-old Dofasco Centre for the Arts, a $12-million-dollar state-of-the-art facility. The company offers not only an eleven-show season that includes dramas, comedies, musicals, children's productions and special performances, but also a year-round theatre school, student matinees and workshops, and the Brave New Works Festival and Community on Stage. Justifiably called a tourist attraction, Theatre Aquarius is the third-largest regional professional theatre in the province, boasting two performing spaces, and welcoming 100,000 patrons to 177 performances each season.

If one could count all the patrons that every year walk through the doors of all the theatres and the performing-arts centres in the province, the numbers would be staggering. To say that theatre is one of Ontario's richest assets is an understatement.

Hamilton Place Concert Hall

The Historian

Julia Browne

Grist Mill built by George and John Ball, located in the Balls Falls Conservation area

History lovers will find no shortage of excursions and side trips through southwestern Ontario, to relive the most important historical events that marked the birth and evolution of Canada and its people: from forts and battlefields in the Niagara Peninsula where the French, Americans and British fought over Upper Canada to lovingly preserved homesteads of early Loyalist settlers; from memorials and exhibits of runaway American slaves to longhouses and chapels of native peoples around Brantford.

Victorian homes of inventors, activists and a future prime minister still share the intimacies of their residents, and poignant First World War exhibits and the in-depth archives of Guelph's poorhouses stir social and political consciences. These stories are retold and re-enacted in both traditional museums and living-history displays, through entrancing performances, audiovisual presentations and many enjoyable interactive opportunities.

Niagara

The Niagara Peninsula was both a fierce battleground dotted with forts and a doorway to safety for fleeing Americans slaves and British Loyalists.

At its hub, Niagara-on-the-Lake, originally called Newark, flourished as the capital of Upper Canada and British headquarters from 1791 through the War of 1812. The Niagara Historical Society and Museum offers an unparalleled 20,000 artifacts of this early Canadian period. On display are many possessions of the United Empire Loyalists who first settled here after the American Revolution. Many of the local documents and relics result from the devoted research of a local retired schoolteacher when the Museum was founded in 1895.

The everyday ailments of nineteenth-century soldiers and farmers were treated at the beautifully restored Niagara Apothecary. Located since 1869 on Niagara-on-the-Lake's main commercial street, the pharmacy could pass for a movie set. The walls are lined with original imported bottles, jars and containers that still bear their gilt labels in Latin, and the lustrous black walnut fixtures and crystal chandeliers still exude the original sense of well-being and financial stability intended to calm a war-torn population.

The Mackenzie Heritage Printery Museum

Political ire, on the other hand, was stoked at the Mackenzie Heritage Printery and Newspaper Museum, located at the foot of Queenston Heights. A champion of local underdogs and reform, the fiery William Lyon Mackenzie, ancestor of Canada's tenth prime minister, published *The Colonial Advocate* here in 1824. During guided tours through Canada's oldest printing museum visitors hear mighty tales that were printed on the Linotype press of 5,000 moving parts, try their hand at setting type or working one of the eight operating presses and glance at rare newspapers.

The courageous effort of Laura Ingersoll Secord saved the Niagara Peninsula from falling into American hands during the War of 1812. Costumed guides at the Laura Secord Homestead in Queenston recount how this young wife of a British officer, upon overhearing Americans planning a surprise attack, promptly set off through enemy lines, climbed the Niagara Escarpment, then was guided by native supporters to warn British officers. The Laura Secord Candy Company restored her home in 1971 with period furniture and artifacts.

Laura Secord Homestead

Chatham-Essex

In 1793 the first parliament of Upper Canada (Ontario) signed a bill outlawing slave ownership and thus Canada, or Canaan, became known as the North Star to fugitive American slaves. Following the "Underground Railroad," a highly secretive network of escape routes, some 40,000 freedom-seekers entered Canada through Niagara and Detroit. In the early 1800s five black families settled along McGregor's Creek, one of the last stops on the Railroad, which is now the town of Chatham.

Chatham First Baptist Church, built by the fledgling

black community in 1841, provided a clandestine meeting place for American abolitionist John Brown and his local supporters. The original clapboard structure, though humble, can be viewed from outside, but visitors are welcome inside for rousing Sunday-morning services. Farther down the same street, at the WISH Centre, stands the Mary Ann Shadd Cary plaque, a tribute to the life of North America's first black female attorney and the first black woman to own and edit a newspaper.

A few miles north in Dresden, the Uncle Tom's Cabin Historical Site and Josiah Henson House give a real sense of the elements and experiences that made up the groundbreaking 1841 Dawn Settlement of early black settlers. On this 2-hectare site stands a restored period church, a sawmill, two cemeteries, a smokehouse made from the trunk of a sycamore tree and the original Henson residence with its square nails and wavy glass windows. Interpretive videos, exhibitions and tours bring to life the drama of early black pioneer life as effectively as did Harriet Beecher Stowe's bestseller *Uncle Tom's Cabin*, which was based on Josiah Henson's autobiography.

Just south of Chatham, North Buxton became the model for prosperous, self-sufficient black communities. At the Buxton National Historic Site & Museum visitors can pay tribute to the original founders of the 2,000-strong Elgin Settlement at the old cemetery and to the world-renowned classical education system they created in the original 1861 schoolhouse. Every Labour Day their Annual Homecoming draws thousands of descendants to celebrate with historical re-enactments, a genealogical conference and family fun.

Eldon House

Brantford Area

A trip along this stretch of the Grand River brings visitors to the homesteads of several inventive Canadians and aboriginal heroes.

On Blue Lake Road, between the towns of Paris and St. George, stands the childhood home of Adelaide Hunter Hoodless, "The Domestic Crusader." The tragedy of her fourth child's death inspired this activist and organizer to help women learn better domestic science and childcare. She is credited with helping to establish the Victorian Order of Nurses, the YWCA, the National Council of Women and McGill University's School of Household Science. The 1857 house is open year round.

The nearby City of Brantford was nicknamed "The Telephone City" by its famous resident, Alexander Graham Bell. Visitors can explore telephone technology at the Bell Homestead, where the inventor first conceived the idea for a telephone in 1874 and made the world's first long-distance call. Thanks to the Bell Telephone Memorial Association and the City visitors can marvel at the original Bell family furnishings and household items as well as enjoy lively tours, audiovisual presentations and demonstrations given by costumed staff.

Brantford boasts a long-standing connection with aboriginal people. "Brant's ford" marks the shallow spot where native Captain Joseph Brant first forded the Grand River and in 1785 began a Mohawk settlement, which has since grown into Six Nations, Canada's largest aboriginal community. The magnificent Joseph Brant Memorial in Victoria Park exalts his larger-than-life persona as an outstanding warrior and ally for the British during the American Revolution, and principal war chief for the Six Nations Iroquois.

Grand River in Brantford

Visitors can pay a final tribute to Brant at his tomb and the tomb of his son John Brant in nearby Six Nations at Her Majesty's Royal Chapel of the Mohawk. In the tradition of storytelling for those who cannot read, eight stained-glass windows, installed between 1959 and 1962, recreate major events in the history of the Six Nations people. Next to Brant's tomb lies a boulder-memorial honouring native poet E. Pauline Johnson, who wielded not a musket but a powerful pen. Johnson's rise to fame at the turn of the century as one of the best-known performers and writers of her time is carefully documented at Chiefswood National Historic Site on the Six Nations Reserve, her birthplace and childhood home.

Guelph

The grandiose vision and wealth of Guelph's founding father, John Galt, included the use of local amber-grey limestone to build magnificent public buildings, churches and private homes that make this city a walk-through museum.

Guelph City Hall is classified as a National Historic Site for its elaborate stone carvings, arched openings and decorative details. The masterpiece of the Royal City, however, is the stunning Church of Our Lady of the Immaculate Conception, built between 1876 and 1888 in the style of a thirteenth-century European cathedral. Down the side streets, more modest Ontario cottage-style houses, once the homes of craftsmen and skilled workers, are a common sight. One in particular, McCrae House, is open to visitors, as the birthplace in 1872 of soldier-physician-poet John McCrae, author of *In Flanders Fields*. This 1858-built homestead was saved from demolition in extremis by an action group in 1966. The site museum displays McRae's life and wartime activities, a copy of the poem as originally published in a British newspaper, recreated family spaces and a family photo album. The grounds offer a restful stroll through an award-winning garden, and out back there is a replica of the original outhouse.

The horrors of the First World War have been impressively recreated in the Far From Home permanent exhibit at the Wellington County Museum & Archives, located north of Guelph between Fergus and Elora. One amazing feature of the installation is

Guelph City Hall

the real earthen trenches manned by life-size soldiers, modelled after the grandsons of Wellington County soldiers. Guelph is known for its social conscience, as is evident from the building's inception in 1877 as the House of Industry and Refuge, providing shelter for the poor, aged and homeless. The exhibit If These Walls Could Talk is a superb scale model of a typical fall day in 1892, with photos and riveting stories displaying attitudes towards poverty, charity and a community's social responsibility.

Kitchener-Waterloo

This area offers some of the finest recollections and live history of the eighteenth-and nineteenth-century immigrant experience.

Unlike the fleeing United Empire Loyalists, Mennonites arrived from Pennsylvania with their Conestoga wagons packed with possessions and their German-Swiss-Dutch language and traditions intact. One farm, the Brubacher House, built in 1850 and restored in 1975, has opened as a museum on its original location, which is now part of the University of Waterloo north campus. Tours give a glimpse into the life of Pennsylvania-German Mennonites, and a video shows a barn raising and historical depiction of settling in the Waterloo Region.

Going one step closer, the Joseph Schneider Haus offers adventurous visitors the chance to try their hand at the Mennonite tasks of sheep-shearing, apple schnitzing, a quilting bee and the creation of period crafts. Year-round activities are animated by costumed staff.

Doon Heritage Crossroads has painstakingly recreated a 1914 village, where visitors can wander from the blacksmith's stall and through the general store, decipher names on the gravestones or try the lost art of walking on stilts. Seasonal events are frequent and popular, with Christmas sleigh rides, old-style Halloween and Canada Day/Dominion Day celebrations and the summer-long A Day in the Life... 1914.

Mennonite buggy, Kitchener-Waterloo

For a taste of how the upper class lived, Castle Kilbride in Baden puts on a fine show of lavish furnishings and the lifestyle of the Victorian era. The owner, Scottish immigrant James Livingston, built this Italianate mansion of his dreams, complete with surprising three-dimensional trompe l'oeil paintings and geometric paintings adorning the ceilings of every room.

Canada's political roots are firmly planted in Kitchener at the boyhood home of William Lyon Mackenzie King. A stroll from the beautiful 4.5 hectares of lawns and gardens of Woodside National Historic Site leads visitors into the elegant interior of the Woodside residence. Costumed interpreters re-enact the times of Canada's longest-serving prime minister and offer details on clothing and other domestic facts.

The Naturalist

Adam Paul Bourret

Niagara Escarpment

Horseback riding

All year round southwestern Ontario offers a wide range of outdoor activities, such as canoeing, cycling, horseback riding, touring around town or even sitting in an easy chair enjoying the sun and the breeze. But one of Ontario's most enduring and rewarding outdoor traditions will always be hiking. Every town and city — even major urban centres like Hamilton and Toronto — has its own particular green spaces set aside for rugged natural adventures or just simple walks in the woods.

The hiking in this region reflects an essentially Canadian love of nature and respect for the land. Most of the trails found here are designed to accommodate a variety of ages and skill levels, making them suitable for young families and large groups, as well as seasoned naturalists. While some natural attractions charge admissions (generally $5 to $10), most of the trails and parks in southwestern Ontario are absolutely free. The volunteer organizations that maintain them ask only that you tread lightly and be respectful of the space.

The Bruce Trail

One factor that makes the parks and trails of this region unique is that they are all connected by one lengthy, winding path known as the Bruce Trail. Stretching from the Niagara region all the way to Tobermory, the trail is the longest uninterrupted footpath in Canada. No matter how far you may wander in this region, you can always find your way along the Bruce by looking for white paint marks on the trees.

The trail is maintained by the Bruce Trail Association, a coalition of nine clubs who each care for a particular section. The association is the ultimate source of information on finding hikes, planning trips or attending events along the trail.

Southern Ontario

Point Pelee is the southernmost tip of Canada, and the site of one of its most moving natural phenomena. Each September, thousands of monarch butterflies descend on the National Park to feast on the native milkweed plant and prepare for their long flight to Mexico. Flocks of visitors come as well, to settle in the nearby town of Leamington and participate in outings, butterfly counts, festivals and special exhibitions.

Butterfly travel is difficult to track, as it relies on weather conditions and availability of plants, so arriving in time to see the butterflies en masse can be tricky. The park has set up an information line that provides updates throughout the fall.

Monarch Butterfly

Niagara Falls

The first thing visitors to Niagara Falls want to see are the falls themselves, a succession of three of the most enormous waterfalls in the world. But while the falls remains a large draw, there is more natural beauty to be found nearby, for free or at a small expense.

Located on the Niagara Parkway, roughly 8 km north of the falls, is the Niagara Glen, a designated nature reserve since 1992. The Glen overlooks the Great Gorge, an enormous rock depression created by the Niagara River. The Glen has a lovely picnic pavilion and a shop where visitors can buy gifts and tickets for Whirlpool Jetboat tours, which travel down the Niagara River to a natural whirlpool. But the real attraction is the beautiful trails that lead into the gorge to the base of the river.

There are two major trail systems in the Niagara Glen. The first is accessed by a set of metal stairs. From there visitors travel through a landscape of mighty rocks to the river's side. The second begins with a long descent down wooden steps, leading to a

Niagara Falls

succession of picturesque spots: a fishing point, a natural waterfall and a view of the whirlpool. For the ambitious there is even a "trail" composed of ropes and pulleys, so that visitors can pull themselves up the side of the gorge.

Despite its beauty, the Glen can be a difficult hike for the uninitiated. It involves an elevation change of more than 60 m and the terrain is rough and uneven. The stairs in particular can be difficult and extremely tiring for seniors and children. Visitors for whom a hike is too strenuous can see the region from above, in an aero car that travels from one side of the gorge to the other.

Visitors can find more natural beauty by travelling farther down the Parkway, or hiking on the Niagara Trail, which follows the Parkway from Fort Erie to the town of Niagara-on-the-Lake. Along the way there is the Floral Clock, the Niagara Parks Botanical Gardens, the Niagara Parks Butterfly Conservatory, Bird Kingdom (the world's largest free-flying aviary) and a plethora of orchards, lookout points and natural gardens.

Interior of the Niagara Parks Butterfly Conservatory

Historical church in the Ball's Falls Conservation Area

The Niagara Region

One of the prettiest spots in southern Ontario, Ball's Falls is an excellent place to take the family for an enjoyable lesson in history and natural appreciation. Located on Niagara Road 75 in the town of Vineland, it was once the site of a small town. Two of the town's earliest settlers were John and George Ball, former soldiers who were granted the land for remaining in Canada.

Now considered a ghost town, the site has many beautiful hiking trails that lead down to a breathtaking natural waterfall, two-thirds the height of Niagara Falls. At the Ball family's original sawmill visitors can learn about the lives of Ontario's settlers. Every October, Ball's Falls is the site of one of Ontario's largest outdoor craft shows, which also has live entertainment, an abundance of foods and a variety of exhibits and demonstrations.

Located just outside St. Catharines, Short Hills Provincial Park runs along the Niagara Escarpment, and can be accessed by three rural roads: Cataract, Roland or Pelham. The park is composed of deposits of sedimentary rock and glacial till, eroded by Twelve Mile Creek. It is popular not only for its natural beauty, but also for the range of activities it offers. There are a series of easy, well-kept trails ideal for families, with fun destinations such as a frog pond and a waterfall lookout. Serious hikers can find trails that lead down into the heart of the Niagara Gorge, or up to the top of the escarpment. The wide paths and open grassland are also good for cyclists, dirt bikers and people on horseback. Botany and herbology enthusiasts favour the area for its variety of plants, flowers and natural edibles, and even the noisiest of visitors will stumble on a few of the park's indigenous animals, such as the beautiful white-tailed deer.

For shorter excursions there is the Woodend Conservation Area on Taylor Road just east of St. Catharines. This area is a particular favourite with tree enthusiasts. It boasts a spectacular collection of indigenous hardwood trees, including black cherry, black oak, pawpaw and tulip trees. In the thick of the forest visitors find themselves in the remains of an abandoned estate belonging to the United Empire Loyalist family of Peter Lampman. St. John's Conservation Area on Barron Road is another favourite spot, with its magnificent deep-water pool.

More Trails

In addition to the Bruce, there are several other long paths through southwestern Ontario that offer a variety of hikes, either for day trips or multi-day excursions. The ever-expanding Thames Valley Trail is becoming a popular alternative to the Bruce. Following the Thames River, it is a 109-km hike beginning at the Elgin Trail at the Elgin-Middlesex county line, travelling around London and meeting the Avon Trail at St. Mary's. The trail is a mix of natural areas and farm country. But be warned, much of the trail passes through private land, and use depends on the landowners' discretion. This trail also changes a great deal to suit the needs of local farmers. It's a good idea to check with the Thames Valley

Below: Spectacular view from heights of Rattlesnake Point
Bottom: Hiking the trails in winter

Trail Association for the most updated version of the trail. The Guelph Radial Trail is popular for hiking the Guelph area and is run on similar terms.

Hamilton and Halton

Simply by following the Bruce Trail hikers can discover many beautiful parks and conservation areas from Niagara to Tobermory. Just outside Hamilton they can find two majestic waterfalls in the Spencer Gorge/Webster's Falls Conservation Area. Webster's Falls is a stunning, tiered waterfall, and Tews Falls is a straight drop, only a few metres shorter than Niagara. The park is considered an important stop along the Bruce Trail and many hikers diverge to visit nearby Crook's Hollow. By car, the park has two entrances, from Fallsview Road and Harvest Road.

There's also a particularly diverse collection of beautiful spots in and around the town of Milton. Hilton Falls Conservation Area, for example, offers an easy stroll through an extensive marsh, one of the best places in Ontario to spot beavers at work. Rattlesnake Point has hiking trails and five observation points for beautiful views from the top of the escarpment, as well as designated points for natural rock climbing, though more-experienced rock climbers will want to check out nearby Mount Eden. An ambling boardwalk surrounds pristine, meromictic Crawford Lake at the Crawford Lake Conservation Area, which also features a reconstructed Iroquois village. All these sites (and others) are protected and operated by the Conservation Halton foundation. They are all within a ten- to twenty-minute drive from each other and many are close enough to hike or bike. It's no surprise that people from Niagara and Toronto choose this region for a quick day trip or weekend getaway.

Webster's Falls

Listings: Contents

Getting There

Set on the northwestern shore of Lake Ontario, and located farther south than Minnesota and much of Michigan, Metropolitan Toronto is one of the most accessible cities in North America by highway, air, rail and water.

By Air

Lester B. Pearson International Airport: Located in the northwestern corner of Metro Toronto, the airport is accessible from highways 401, 427 and 409. Terminal 1 serves Air Canada, Air Canada Jazz, Air New Zealand, Air Transat, Alitalia, All Nippon Airways, Austrian Airlines, Emirates, Lufthansa, Singapore Airlines, and others. Some twenty-four major airlines offer regularly scheduled flights. Terminal 3 serves over fifty-two airlines such as Air France, Air India, American Airlines, British Airways, Cathay Pacific Airways, Cubana, Delta, EL AL, KLM, Korean Airlines, Northwest, Olympic, QANTAS, US Airways, Westjet and others. For information on Terminal 1 call 416-247-7678; for Terminal 3 call 416-776-5100. www.gtaa.com.

Toronto City Centre Airport: Located on the western tip of a series of islands in Toronto Harbour, this island airport handles scheduled, private and corporate flights. The airport serves Porter Airlines. For information call 416-203-6942.

By Road

Whether approaching Toronto by car or by bus, the traveller will reach Toronto by one of several major routes paralleling the shore of Lake Ontario. Highways 401 and 2 and the Queen Elizabeth Way enter Toronto from the west. Highways 401 and 2 also enter Toronto from the east. Hwy. 400 runs from the north and connects with Hwy. 401. Major bus routes converge in Toronto. Out-of-town buses arrive and depart from the Toronto Coach Terminal, located at 610 Bay St.

Service to points all over Ontario and Canada is frequent and fast. National and regional bus lines serve Metro Toronto. Call 416-393-7911 for bus company fares and schedules.

By Rail

Toronto is served by the VIA Rail Canada System, the network that provides all rail service throughout Canada (with connections to the Amtrak system through Niagara Falls, New York). Union Station is located on Front Street, between Bay and University (across the street from the Royal York Hotel). The station is right on Toronto's subway line, and is within walking distance of the Rogers Centre, the CN Tower, the financial district and many downtown hotels, shops and restaurants. Call 1-888-842-7245 or 416-366-8411.

Travel Essentials

Money

Currency can be exchanged at any Toronto bank at the prevailing rate. If you use a small local branch, it's best to call ahead to confirm their capacity to exchange, on the spot, any currency other than American funds. There are currency exchange booths at the airport and at many of Ontario's Travel Information Centres near the U.S./Canada border. Ontario Travel Information Centres can exchange Canadian dollars for most major international currencies, and vice versa. If you wish to exchange a large amount, or to exchange a less common currency, telephone ahead to ensure the centre can serve you. Units of currency are similar to those of the United States, excepting the Canadian one-dollar (loonie) and two-dollar (toonie) coins.

Most major North American credit cards and traveller's cheques are welcome in Toronto, including American Express, Carte Blanche, Diners Club, EnRoute, MasterCard and Visa. Many stores and services will accept U.S. currency, but the exchange rate they offer may vary greatly. Since there are no laws enforcing foreign currency rates of exchange, we strongly recommend that you convert to Canadian funds before you make your purchases.

American visitors may also use bank or credit cards to make cash withdrawals from automated teller machines that are tied into international networks such as Cirrus and Plus. Before you leave home, check with your bank to find out what range of banking services its cards will allow you to use.

Passports

American visitors may be asked to verify their citizenship with a document such as a passport, or a birth or baptismal certificate. Naturalized U.S. citizens should carry a naturalization certificate. Permanent U.S. residents who are not citizens are advised to bring their Alien Registration Receipt Card. Please note, as of January 31, 2008, all American citizens and residents are required to show a valid passport or other secure documents in order to return to the United States following your visit to Canada. Please consult U.S. Customs and Border Protection, or a Canadian embassy or consulate in the U.S. for details. Citizens of all other countries, except Greenland and residents of St.-Pierre et Miquelon, must bring a valid passport. Some may be required to obtain a visitor's visa. For details, please consult the Canadian embassy or consulate serving your home country.

Customs

Arriving

As a nonresident of Canada, you may bring in any reasonable amount of personal effects and food, and a full tank of gas. Special restrictions or quotas apply to certain specialty goods, and especially to plant-, agricultural- and animal-related materials. All items must be declared to Customs upon arrival and may include up to 200 cigarettes, 50 cigars,

200 grams of manufactured tobacco, and 200 tobacco sticks. Visitors are also permitted 1.14 litres (40 oz) of liquor, 1.5 litres (53 oz) of wine, or 8.5 litres (24 x 12-oz cans or bottles) of beer.

You may bring in gifts for Canadian residents duty-free, up to a value of $60.00 (Canadian) each, provided they do not consist of alcohol, tobacco, or advertising material. For more detailed information, please see the website www.cbsa-asfc.gc.ca or the Customs information booklet "I DECLARE," or call the Canada Border Services Agency at 1-800-461-9999 from within Canada, or 204 983-3500 from outside of Canada.

Departing

For detailed customs rules for entering or re-entering the United States, please contact a U.S. Customs office before you visit Toronto. Copies of the U.S. Customs information brochure "Know Before You Go" are available from U.S. Customs offices or by mail. You can also call the U.S. Customs office in Toronto at 905-676-2606. Travellers from other countries should also check on customs regulations before leaving home.

Taxes

Ontario Harmonized Sales Tax (HST)

The Ontario Harmonized Sales Tax is proposed to combine the 8% Ontario sales tax and the 5% GST into a single 13% value-added sales tax that would be federally administered, starting July 1, 2010.

Goods and Services Tax (GST)

The federal Goods and Services Tax is 5%. This is a value-added consumption tax that applies to most goods, purchased gifts, food/beverages and services, including most hotel and motel accommodation.

Provincial Sales Tax (PST)

The Ontario provincial sales tax is 8% on any goods you buy, but not on services or accommodation.

Room Tax

A 5% provincial tax (in place of PST) is added to most tourist accommodation charges, as well as the 5% GST.

Food Service

In restaurants, 5% GST and 8% PST will be added to the food portion of your final bill, as well as a 10% provincial tax on alcoholic beverages (in addition to the 5% GST).

Guides and Information Services

Toronto offers docking facilities and complete services for boaters. For information on harbour facilities, call the Toronto Port Authority at 416-863-2000.

The City of Toronto: Toronto City Hall, 100 Queen Street W., Toronto ON M5H 2N2; call Access Toronto at 416-338-0338. Or dial 311 to access Toronto's system for non-emergency city services, programs and information.

Tourism Toronto: Queen's Quay Terminal at Harbourfront, Box 126, 207 Queen's Quay W., Toronto ON M5J 1A7; 416-203-2600, 1-800-499-2514; torontotourism.com.

Visitor Information Ontario: for comprehensive travel information about the Province of Ontario (including Toronto), visit the Ontario Ministry of Tourism's Travel Centre in the Eaton Centre; or call 1-800-ONTARIO (English), 1-800-268-3736 (French). In Toronto, call: 416-314-0944 (English), 416-314-0956 (French).

Getting Acquainted

Time Zone

Toronto falls within the Eastern Standard Time Zone.

Climate

Here are average Toronto temperatures, highs and lows; fluctuations from the norm are common:

Jan.	-30.1°F to 18.1°F
	-4.1°C to -7.7°C
Feb.	31.5°F to 18.9°F
	-4.3°C to -7.3°C
March	39.5°F to 26.7°F
	2.2°C to 2.9°C
April	53.4°F to 37.8°F
	11.9°C to 3.2°C
May	64.3°F to 47.2°F
	17.9°C to 8.4°C
June	75.6°F to 57.4°F
	24.2°C to 14.1°C
July	80.3°F to 62.3°F
	26.8°C to 16.1°C
Aug.	78.7°F to 61.2°F
	25.9°C to 16.2°C
Sept.	70.8°F to 54.2°F
	21.6°C to 12.3°C
Oct.	59.6°F to 44.8°F
	15.3°C to 7.1°C
Nov.	46.1°F to 35.3°F
	7.8°C to 1.8°C
Dec.	34.2°F to 23.4°F
	1.2°C to -4.8°C

Average annual rainfall: 27.25"/68.9 cm.
Average annual snowfall: 53.2"/135 cm.
Average temperatures: +7.4°C (45.3°F) in spring, +20.7°C (69.3°F) in summer, +10.8°C (51.4°F) in autumn, and -3.3°C (26.1°F) in winter.

Getting Around

Travelling in Toronto

Metro Toronto is laid out in a grid pattern of major north-south and east-west arteries. Streets not on the grid follow natural features such as ravines and escarpments. The following expressways provide access to the city from the major highways: the Don Valley Parkway, the Gardiner Expressway, and the Allen Expressway. If you're a member of any recognized auto club affiliates (AAA, CAA, etc.), CAA Travel at 100 Yonge St., 416-593-7375, will provide all club services. Head Office: 905-771-3242 or toll free at 1-866-988-8878.

Public Transportation

Toronto's clean, safe and efficient public transit is operated by the TTC (Toronto Transit Commission), and consists of over 4,000 kilometres of subway, bus, RT and streetcar routes. Many of the principal downtown bus and streetcar routes, including those which run along Queen, College, St. Clair and Eglinton, operate 24 hours a day. Night bus service is also available along Yonge and Bloor streets and Danforth Avenue. Exact fares are required and day, weekly and monthly passes are available. For information on subway, streetcar and bus routes, schedules and fares, call Customer Information at 416-393-4636 (7a.m.-10p.m.).

GO Transit

Regular GO Bus and Train service to Oshawa, Hamilton, Georgetown, Brampton, Milton, Newmarket, Richmond Hill, as well as limited service to Barrie, Guelph, Sutton and Uxbridge. Call 416-869-3200 for more information.

Ferry boats to the Toronto Islands are operated by the City of Toronto Parks and Recreation Dept., Island and Ferry division. They leave from the foot of Bay Street on a regular basis. Call 416-392-8193 for schedules and rates.

By Car

A valid driver's license from any country is good in Ontario for three months. Evidence of a car's registration is required (a car-rental contract will also serve). If you are driving into Ontario or importing a vehicle, bring with you its registration documents, and either a Canadian Non-Resident Motor Vehicle Liability Insurance Card (obtained from your insurance agent), or else the insurance policy itself. If you're driving a rented car, bring a copy of the rental contract. Speed limits are measured in kilometres per hour and vary depending on the type of road, with 400-level controlled-access highways having the highest limit. Speed limits on most highways are 80 to 90 kph, and 100 kph on freeways. On city streets the normal speed is 50 kph unless otherwise posted. Seat belt use by passengers and drivers is mandatory in Ontario. One kilometre equals about 5/8 of a mile. To convert from kilometres to miles, multiply kilometres by 0.6. To convert from miles to kilometres, multiply miles by 1.6. Metric measurements are used for motor fuel: 1 litre equals about one-quarter of an American gallon, or about one-fifth of an Imperial gallon. A litre of gasoline costs approximately one dollar a litre at time of publishing.

Car Rentals

- Avis, 1-800-TRY-AVIS, downtown: 416-777-AVIS, www.avis.com
- Discount Car Rentals, Yonge and Bloor, Charles Promenade, 730 Yonge Street: 416-921-1212
- Dollar Rent-a-Car, downtown: 416-921-1346, airport: 416-213-8811
- National Car Rental: 1-800-227-7368, www.nationcar.ca
- Thrifty Car Rental, Royal York Hotel: 416-231-2217
  Consult the Yellow Pages for more agencies.

Tours

- A Taste of the World — Neighbourhood. Unearth off-beat nooks and crannies of Toronto's ethnic neighbourhoods: Chinatown, Kensington Market, etc. 416-923-6813
- All About Toronto. Step-on guide service, very professional, yet fun and exciting. 27 Clovercrest Rd., 416-495-8687
- Haunted Toronto. Ghost walks throughout Toronto. 416-487-9017
- Helicopter Company. Offers a bird's-eye view of Toronto. 416-203-3280
- National Helicopters Inc. Spectacular sightseeing rides featuring the Toronto Islands, CN Tower, Rogers Centre and Casa Loma. Operates May to September; 11339 Albion-Vaughan Rd., Kleinburg ON; 1-866-361-1100

- Summer Walking Tours. The Heritage Toronto summer walking tour series offers a wide variety of walks exploring many areas and topics of Toronto. For more details call 416-338-0684 or visit www.heritagetoronto.org
- Toronto Footsteps. Become a Torontonian for a day; smaller groups and families welcome. 416-483-5483
- Tripmate Travel and Tour Guide Company. Experienced multilingual guides highlight the beauty, history and culture of Toronto and Niagara. 7077 Kennedy Rd., Markham ON; 905-305-8892
- Unique Views. Dynamic, interactive and interesting tours of Toronto. 171 Parkside Drive, Unit 1; 416-531-7770

Boat And Yacht Tours

- Empress of Canada. Toronto's luxury yacht cruises around the Toronto Islands. 260 Queen's Quay W., #1408; 416-260-8901, Fax: 416-260-5547, www.empressofcanada.com
- Great Lakes Schooner Company. See Toronto's skyline from the open deck of a tall ship. April to Oct. 249 Queen's Quay W., #111; 416-260-6355, Fax: 416-260-6377, www.greatlakesschooner.com
- Jubilee Queen Cruises. Tour Toronto's harbour aboard a luxury 120-foot river showboat. April to Oct. 207 Queen's Quay W.; 416-203-7245, Fax: 416-203-7177, www.jubileequeencruises.ca
- Klancy's Yacht Charters Incorporated. Cruise Lake Ontario aboard the Klancy II, 100-passenger custom-designed yacht. 1001-480 Queen's Quay W.; 416-866-8489, www.klancyscharters.com
- Mariposa Cruise Line Limited. One-hour narrated harbour tours, private charters, lunch cruises and dinner cruises. 207 Queen's Quay W., #415; 416-203-0178, www.mariposacruises.com
- Miss Toronto Yacht Charters and Tours. Unique 70-foot Florida-style yacht suitable for all occasions. 549 Queen's Quay W.; 416-525-8881, www.chartermisstoronto.com
- Nautical Adventures. Two unique ships for corporate functions, receptions, parties, special events and public cruises. 416-364-3244, Fax: 416-593-0478, www.nauticaladventure.com

Accommodation

Tourism Toronto operates a central reservation service representing 123 member properties throughout the Greater Metropolitan Toronto Area. Contact them at Queen's Quay Terminal at Harbourfront Centre, P.O. Box 126, 207 Queen's Quay West, Toronto ON M5J 1A7; 416-203-2600, 1-800-363-1990 (North America), Fax: 416-203-6753. The services of the Travellers Aid Society include providing tourist information, maps and suggestions on what to see and do in Toronto, and acting as a link between stranded travellers and social services agencies. Contact them at Room B23, Union Station, Toronto ON M5J 1E6; 416-366-7788, Fax: 416-366-0829. Approximate prices are indicated, based on the average cost, at time of publishing, for two persons staying in a double room (excluding taxes): $ = $50-$90; $$ = $90-$180; $$$ = $180-$300; $$$$ = above $300.

For the locations of downtown and midtown hotels, see the map on page 8.

Hotels: Airport

- Delta Toronto Airport West, 5444 Dixie Rd., Toronto ON L4W 2L2; 905-624-1144, 1-800-737-3211, deltanet@deltahotels.com, www.deltahotels.com. Continuous airport shuttle. Swimming pool and spa/fitness centre. $$
- Holiday Inn Express Toronto-North York, 30 Norfinch Drive, North York ON M3N 1X1; 416-665-3500, 1-800-465-4329, Fax: 416-665-0807, www.ichotelsgroup.com. Complimentary continental breakfast. $
- Holiday Inn Select Toronto Airport, 970 Dixon Rd., Etobicoke ON

M9W 1J9; 416-675-7611, 1-800-465-4329, Fax: 416-675-9162, www.ichotelsgroup.com. Complimentary airport shuttle service. Indoor/outdoor pools, sauna and whirlpool. $$

- International Plaza Hotel and Conference Centre, 655 Dixon Rd., Toronto ON M9W 1J4; 416-244-1711, 1-800-668-3656 (Canada and USA), Fax: 416-244-9584. Indoor waterslide park, nightclub, swimming pool/fitness centre. $$

- Sheraton Gateway Hotel, Terminal 3, Departure Level, PO Box 3000, Mississauga ON L5P 1C4; 905-672-7000, Fax: 905-672-7100. Attached to Terminal 3 of Pearson International Airport; saunas and a restaurant. $$-$$$

- Toronto Airport Marriott Hotel, 901 Dixon Rd., Rexdale ON M9W 1J5; 416-674-9400, 1-800-905-2811, Fax: 416-674-8292, www.marriott.com. Volleyball and basketball court on property, golf and tennis nearby. Swimming pool and spa/fitness centre. Secretarial services and business centre. $$

- Travelodge Toronto Airport, 925 Dixon Rd., Etobicoke ON M9W 1J8; 416-674-2222, 1-888-483-6887, Fax: 416-674-5757, www.travelodge.com. Swimming pool, health club and sauna. $$

- Westin Bristol Place Hotel, 950 Dixon Rd., Toronto ON M9W 5N4; 416-675-9444, 1-800-996-3426, Fax: 416-675-4426, www.westin.com. Five-star property with business centre and women travellers' business select rooms. Swimming pool and spa/fitness centre. $$$

Hotels: Downtown

See the Toronto Accommodation Map on page 8 where each of the following can be located by number.

- Best Western Primrose Hotel Downtown Toronto, 111 Carlton St., Toronto ON M5B 2G3; 416-977-8000, 1-800-268-8082, Fax: 416-977-4874, www.torontoprimro sehotel.com. Saunas/exercise room

and an outdoor swimming pool. $$ (map: 12)

- Bond Place Hotel, 65 Dundas St. E., Toronto ON M5B 2G8; 416-362-6061, 1-800-268-9390, Fax: 416-360-6406, www.bondplace.ca. Walking distance to all top tourist attractions. $$ (map: 16)

- Cambridge Suites Hotel, 15 Richmond St. E., Toronto ON M5C 1N2; 416-368-1990, 1-800-463-1990, Fax: 416-601-3751, www.cambridgesuitestoronto.com. Complimentary continental breakfast, spa/fitness centre. $$$ (map: 21)

- Days Inn Toronto Downtown, 30 Carlton St., Toronto ON M5B 2E9; 416-977-6655, 1-800-367-9601, Fax: 416-977-0502. Heated indoor pool, sauna and fitness centre. $-$$ (map: 11)

- Delta Chelsea Inn, 33 Gerrard St. W., Toronto ON M5G 1Z4; 416-595-1975, 1-800-243-5732, Fax: 416-585-4375, reservations@deltachelsea.com, www.deltahotels.com. Swimming pool and spa/fitness centre; business centre. $$ (map: 14)

- InterContinental Toronto Centre, 225 Front St. W., Toronto ON M5V 2X3; 416-597-1400, 1-800-227-6963 (Canada), Fax: 416-597-8128, www.crowneplazatoronto.com. Swimming pool and spa/fitness centre. $$ (map: 25)

- Grand Hotel and Suites Toronto, 225 Jarvis St., Toronto ON M5B 2C1; 416-863-9000, 1-800-324-7263, Fax: 416-863-1100, reservations@ grandhoteltoronto.com, www.grandhoteltoronto.com. Spa/fitness centre. $$ (map: 15)

- Hilton Toronto, 145 Richmond St. W., Toronto ON M5H 2L2; 416-869-3456, 1-800-267-2281, Fax: 416-869-3187, info_toronto@hilton.com, www.hilton.com. Heated indoor/outdoor pool with health club. $$$ (map: 20)

- Holiday Inn on King, 370 King St. W., Toronto ON M5V 1J9; 416-599-4000, 1-800-263-6364, Reservation

Fax: 416-599-4785, info@hiok.com, www.hiok.com. Swimming pool and spa/fitness centre. $$ (map: 28)

- Hotel Le Germain Toronto, 30 Mercer St., Toronto ON M5V 1H3; 416-345-9500, 1-866-345-9501, Fax: 416-345-9501, reservations@germaintoronto.com, www.germaintoronto.com. New boutique hotel is a small, luxurious cross between a bed and breakfast and a large luxury hotel. In the entertainment district. $$$-$$$$ (map: 27)

- Hotel Victoria, 56 Yonge St., Toronto ON M5E 1G5; 416-363-1666, Toll Free: 1-800-363-8228, Fax: 416-363-7327, reception@hotelvictoria.on.ca, www.hotelvictoria-toronto.com. A small historic property located in the heart of Toronto's theatre and financial district. $$ (map: 23)

- Le Royal Meridien King Edward Hotel, 37 King St. E., Toronto ON M5C 1E9; 416-863-9700, 1-800-543-4300, Fax: 416-863-4102, www.lemeridien-hotels.com. An elegant hotel, renowned for its Edwardian splendour. Spa/fitness centre; business centre. $$$ (map: 22)

- Madison Manor Boutique Hotel, 20 Madison Avenue, Toronto ON M5R 2S1; 416-922-5579, 1-877-561-7048, Fax: 416-963-4325, info@madisonavenuepub.com, www.madisonavenuepub.com/madisonmanor/rooms.html. Four floors in a Victorian manor; no elevator. Non-smoking. Complimentary continental breakfast. $$-$$$ (map: 1)

- Marriott Eaton Centre, 525 Bay St., Toronto ON M5G 2L2; 416-597-9200, 1-800-905-0667, Fax: 416-597-9211, www.marriott.com. Swimming pool, spa/fitness centre and business centre. $$ (map: 17)

- Metropolitan Hotel, 108 Chestnut St., Toronto ON M5G 1R3; 416-977-5000, 1-800-668-6600, Fax: 416-977-9513. Swimming pool and spa/fitness centre. $$ (map: 18)

- Novotel Toronto Centre, 45 The Esplanade, Toronto ON M5E 1W2; 416-367-8900, 1-800-668-6835, Fax: 416-360-8285, www.novotel.com. Swimming pool and spa/fitness centre. $$ (map: 33)

- Radisson Plaza Hotel Admiral, 249 Queen's Quay W., Toronto ON M5J 2N5; 416-203-3333, 1-888-201-1718, Fax: 416-203-3100. Business centre; swimming pool. $$ (map: 31)

- Ramada Hotel and Suites Downtown, 300 Jarvis St., Toronto ON M5B 2C5; 416-977-4823, 1-800-567-2233 (Canada and US), Fax: 416-977-4830, www.ramadaplazatoronto.com. Indoor swimming pool and spa/fitness centre. $$-$$$ (map: 13)

- Renaissance Toronto Hotel at Rogers Centre, 1 Blue Jays Way, Toronto ON M5V 1J4; 416-341-7100, 1-800-237-1512, Fax: 416-341-5091. One quarter of the rooms have floor-to-ceiling windows that offer an exclusive view of the stadium. Business centre; swimming pool and spa/fitness centre. $$ (map: 30)

- Royal York Hotel, 100 Front St. W., Toronto ON M5J 1E3; 416-368-2511, 1-800-441-1414, Fax: 416-368-9040, www.fairmont.com/royalyork. Business centre; swimming pool and spa/fitness centre. $$-$$$ (map: 24)

- Sheraton Centre Toronto Hotel and Towers, 123 Queen St. W., Toronto ON M5H 2M9; 416-361-1000, 1-800-325-3535, Fax: 416-947-4874. Olympic-sized pool, sauna, hot tub, sundeck, spa/fitness centre and children's playroom. $$$ (map: 19)

- The SoHo Metropolitan Boutique Hotel, 318 Wellington St. W., Toronto ON M5V 3T3; 416-599-8800, 1-866-764-6638, Fax: 416-599-8801. New luxury boutique hotel in the entertainment district with all the amenities. $$$-$$$$ (map: 29)

- Strathcona Hotel, 60 York St., Toronto ON M5J 1S8; 416-363-3321, 1-800-268-8304, Fax: 416-363-4679, www.thestrathconahotel.com. $-$$ (map: 26)

- The Town Inn Suites, 620 Church Street, Toronto ON M4Y 2G2; 416-

964-3311, 1-800-311-5045, Fax: 416-924-9466, www.towninn.com. Apartment suites with kitchen facilities. $$ (map: 7)

- Westin Harbour Castle, 1 Harbour Sq., Toronto ON M5J 1A6; 416-869-1600, 1-800-228-3000, Fax: 416-869-0573, www.westin.com. Swimming pool and spa/fitness centre. $$-$$$ (map: 32)
- The Windsor Arms, 18 St. Thomas St., Toronto ON M5S 3E7; 416-971-9666, 1-877-999-2767, Fax: 416-921-9121, www.windsorarmshotel.com. Small, centrally located luxury hotel with spa and 24-hour butler service. Small pets allowed. $$$$ (map: 6)

Hotels: Midtown

See the Toronto Accommodation Map on page 8 where each of the following can be located by number.

- Comfort Hotel Downtown, 15 Charles St. E., Toronto ON M4Y 1S1; 416-924-1222, 1-800-228-5150, Fax: 416-927-1369, www.choicehotels.ca. $-$$ (map: 8)
- Four Seasons Hotel, 21 Avenue Rd., Toronto ON M5R 2G1; 416-964-0411, 1-800-268-6282, Fax: 416-964-2301, www.fourseasons.com/toronto/. Toronto's only CAA/AAA Five Diamond hotel. Swimming pool and spa/fitness centre. $$$ (map: 3)
- Hotel InterContinental Toronto, 220 Bloor St. W., Toronto ON M5S 1T8; 416-960-5200, 1-800-267-0010, Fax: 416-960-8269, www.toronto.intercontinental.com. Swimming pool and spa/fitness centre. $$$ (map: 5)
- Howard Johnson Hotel – Downtown Toronto-Yorkville, 89 Avenue Rd., Toronto ON M2R 2G3; 416-964-1220, 1-800-446-4656, Fax: 416-964-8692, www.hojo.com. $-$$ (map: 2)
- Park Hyatt Toronto, 4 Avenue Rd., Toronto ON M5R 2E8; 416-925-1234, 1-800-233-1234, Fax: 416-924-4933, parktoronto.hyatt.com/. Spa/fitness centre. $$$ (map: 4)
- Sutton Place Hotel, 955 Bay St.,

Toronto ON M5S 2A2; 416-924-9221, 1-866-378-8866, Fax: 416-924-1778, www.toronto.suttonplace.com. Indoor swimming pool and spa/fitness centre. $$$ (map: 10)
- Toronto Marriott Bloor-Yorkville Hotel, 90 Bloor St. E., Toronto ON M4W 1A7; 416-961-8000, 1-800-859-7180, Fax: 416-961-4635, www.marriott.com. Spa/fitness centre. $$-$$$ (map: 7)

Beds and Breakfast

Toronto has over 200 bed and breakfast establishments, operating either independently or grouped together in association, several of which are listed below in our introductory selection. You may also want to visit www.bbcanada.com, under Toronto, to view a select list of B & Bs online.

- Abodes of Choice Bed and Breakfast Association of Toronto, 102 Burnside Dr., Toronto ON; 416-537-7629. Co-op group of homes in desirable neighbourhoods with affiliates across Canada. Various locations. $
- Allenby Bed and Breakfast, 351 Wolverleigh Blvd., Toronto ON M4C 1S7; 416-461-7095, www.theallenby.com. AAA approved renovated house, centrally located. Shared baths. $$
- B & B in the Annex, 31 Dalton Rd., Toronto ON M5R 2Y8; 416-962-2786, Fax: 416-964-8837, English, German, Italian spoken. Reservations required. $
- Beaches Bed and Breakfast, 174 Waverly Rd., Toronto ON M4L 3T3; 416-699-0818, Fax: 416-699-2246. Close to the lake, streetcars, parks, shops and cafes. $
- Beaconsfield Bed and Breakfast, 38 Beaconsfield Ave., Toronto ON M6J 3H9; Tel/Fax: 416-535-3338. Brochure available. $$
- Bed and Breakfast Homes of Toronto, P.O. Box 46093, College Park P.O., 777 Bay St., Toronto ON M5G 2P6; 416-363-6362. Thirty welcoming homes, all near transit.

Call or write for a free brochure and then contact chosen host directly. $

- Beverley Place, 226 Beverley St., Toronto ON M5T 1Z3; 416-977-0077, Fax: 416-599-2242. $-$$
- Downtown Toronto Association of Bed and Breakfast Guest Houses, P.O. Box 190; Station B, Toronto ON M5T 2W1; 416-410-3938, Fax: 416-483-8822, info@torontobedandbreakfast.com, www.bnbinfo.com. "Toronto's largest selection B & B homes since 1980." Non-smoking. $-$$
- Feathers Bed and Breakfast, 132 Wells St., Toronto ON M5R 1P4; 416-534-2388. An artistic Victorian home in a great downtown location; five-minute walk to subway, a choice of European-style cafes, live theatre and antique shops. Close to ROM, Casa Loma, Yorkville and U of T. $$
- French Connection Bed and Breakfast, 102 Burnside Drive, Toronto ON M6G 2M8; 416-537-7741, 1-800-313-3993, Fax: 416-537-0747, www.thefrenchconnection.com. Freshly baked European-style breakfast. $-$$
- Homewood Inn, 65 Homewood Ave., Toronto ON M4Y 2K1; 416-920-7944, Fax: 416-920-4091, www.homewoodinn.com. All rooms with colour TV and fridge, some with kitchens. $-$$
- Jarvis House (A Bed and Breakfast in Downtown Toronto), 344 Jarvis Street, Toronto ON M4Y 2G6; 416-975-3838, Fax: 416-496-1357, www.jarvishouse.com. Central downtown Toronto. Private bathrooms. $-$$
- Palmerston Inn Bed and Breakfast, 322 Palmerston Blvd., Toronto ON M6G 2N6; 416-920-7842, 1-877-920-7842, Fax: 416-960-9529. Non-smoking only. $-$$
- Toronto Bed and Breakfast Inc., Box 269, 253 College St., Toronto ON M5T 1R5; 1-877-922-6522, beds@torontobandb.com, www.torontobandb.com. Eighteen homes in the registry. $-$$
- Vanderkooy Bed and Breakfast, 53 Walker Ave., Toronto ON M4V 1G3; 416-925-8765, Fax: 416-925-8557. Relax and enjoy the pond in the garden with resident cats, Blue and Quila. $

Hostels and College Residences

Almost all of the residences listed below are available in summer only, but they provide a safe, economical alternative to hotels. Make sure you book in advance.

- Hospitality York, York University, 4700 Keele St., North York ON M3J 1P3; 416-736-5020, Fax: 416-736-5648. Swimming pool and spa/fitness centre. May to September. $
- Hostelling International Toronto, 76 Church St., Toronto ON M5C 2G1; 416-971-4440, 1-877-848-8737, Fax: 416-971-4088. Central location. Rooms have vanity ensuite and air conditioning. Kitchen and laundry. $
- Neill-Wycik College-Hotel, 96 Gerrard St. E., Toronto ON M5B 1G7; 416-977-2320, 1-800-268-4358, Fax: 416-977-2809. Shared kitchens and washrooms. Sauna. May to August. $
- The Residence, 90 Gerrard St. W., 22nd floor, Toronto ON M5G 1J6; 416-351-1010, Fax: 416-340-3923. Central downtown location. Shared kitchen, bathroom and laundry facilities. $
- University of Toronto at Scarborough, 1265 Military Trail, Scarborough ON M1C 1A4; 416-287-7369, Fax: 416-287-7323, www.scar.utoronto.ca. East Metro location. Mid-May to August. $
- University of Toronto, 89 Chestnut Residence, 89 Chestnut St., Toronto ON M5G 1R1; 416-977-0707, Fax: 416-977-1136, www.89chestnut.com. Central location. Rooms with ensuite bathrooms, fitness centre, laundry room. Mid-May to August. $
- Victoria University, 140 Charles St. W., Toronto ON M5S 1K9; 416-585-4524, Fax: 416-585-4530,

www.vicu.utoronto.ca. May to August. $-$$

- YWCA Woodlawn Residence, 80 Woodlawn Ave. E., Toronto ON M4T 1C1; 416-923-8454, Fax: 416-923-1950. Women's residence, centrally located. Rates include breakfast. $

Top Attractions

Toronto is replete with attractions. Here we have chosen to provide a selective listing of many of the points of interest. Check local newspapers, *Toronto Life* magazine, *eye weekly*, *NOW* magazine, www.torontotourism.com and www.toronto.com for more information.

- Allan Gardens. Huge greenhouses. Carlton and Sherbourne streets.; 416-392-7288.
- Black Creek Pioneer Village. A recreated nineteenth-century village. Open year-round. 1000 Murray Ross Pkwy., North York ON M3J 2P3; 416-736-1733, www.blackcreek.ca
- Campbell House. Toronto's only Georgian historic house. Restored 1822 residence of Sir William Campbell. Open year-round. 160 Queen St. W.; Toronto, ON M5H 3H3; 416-597-0227, www.campbellhousemuseum.ca
- Canada's Walk of Fame. Pays tribute to renowned Canadians through a series of inlaid "sidewalk stars" over fifteen blocks centered around Toronto's Theatre District. 416-367-9255, www.canadaswalkoffame.com
- Canada's Wonderland. Canada's 300-acre premier theme and water park. Open weekends in May and fall, daily late-May through Labour Day. 9580 Jane St. (400 North to Rutherford Rd. Exit), Vaughan ON L6A 1S6; 905-832-8131, www.canadaswonderland.com
- Canadian Broadcasting Centre (CBC). See behind the scenes at a world-class radio and television production facility. Open year-round weekdays. 250 Front St. W., Room 3C409, P.O. Box 500, Station A, Toronto ON M5W 1E6; 416-205-3311, www.cbc.ca
- Canadian National Exhibition, Exhibition Place, Lakeshore Blvd., between Strachan and Dufferin; For over 100 years, Canada's largest annual fair (fifth largest in North America), with the world's largest over-the-water air show on Labour Day weekend. Runs eighteen days from mid-August through Labour Day. 416-393-6300, www.theex.com
- Casa Loma. Toronto's majestic castle estate. Open year-round. 1 Austin Terrace, Toronto ON M5R 1X8; 416-923-1171, Fax: 416-923-5734, www.casaloma.org
- Centreville Amusement Park. A turn-of-the-century theme amusement park located on the Toronto Islands, a short ferry ride away. Open Victoria Day to Labour Day and weekends only in September. Toronto Islands, 84 Advance Rd., Toronto ON M8Z 2T7; 416-203-0405, www.centreisland.ca
- City Hall, 100 Queen St. W.; An architectural ambassador of Toronto situated in Nathan Phillips Square. Book a tour of City Hall. 416-338-0338 (Access Toronto), www.toronto.ca
- CN Tower. The world's tallest free-standing structure at 553 metres (1815 ft.). Stand and look down on Toronto through a glass floor 113 stories above the ground. Open year-round. 301 Front St. W., Toronto ON M5V 2T6; 416-86TOWER (86937), www.cntower.ca
- David Dunlap Observatory. Site of the largest optical telescope in Canada. 123 Hillsview Dr., Richmond Hill; 416-978-2016, www.astro.utoronto.ca/DDO/
- Distillery District. Established in the preserved remains of an enormous distillery, home to cafés, galleries, restaurants, shops and live entertainment. 55 Mill St., Toronto ON M5A 3C4; 416-364-1177, Fax: 416-364-4793, www.thedistillerydistrict.com

Top Attractions: Toronto

- Enoch Turner Schoolhouse. Toronto's first school; call ahead to book a visit. 106 Trinity St.; 416-863-0010

- Fantasy Fair. This indoor amusement park features a Victorian town with eight rides, games, restaurants and a children's play area. Woodbine Shopping Centre, 500 Rexdale Blvd.; 416-674-5437

- Gibson House. Restored 1851 farmhouse of rebel, politician and surveyor, David Gibson, his wife Eliza and their family. Open year-round, closed Mondays. Special weekend events. 5172 Yonge St.; 416-395-7432

- Grange Historic House. The oldest brick house in Toronto built in the 1830s. Open year-round. 317 Dundas St. W. at the Art Gallery of Ontario, Toronto ON M5T 1G4; 416-979-6648, www.ago.net

- Harbourfront Centre. Year-round centre features cultural and recreational activities. 235 Queen's Quay W., Toronto, ON M5J 2G8; 416-973-4600, www.harbourfrontcentre.com

- Kortright Centre for Conservation. There are 16 km of trails for hiking, snowshoeing and skiing at Canada's largest environmental education centre. Open year-round. 9550 Pine Valley Dr., Vaughan ON L4L 1A6; 905-832-2289

- Lillian H. Smith Children's Library. Houses the Osborne Collection of Early Children's Books – over 80,000 rare and notable children's books. 239 College St.; 416-393-7753, www.tpl.toronto.on.ca/uni_spe_osb_collection.jsp

- Medieval Times Dinner anD Tournament. Re-enactment of an eleventh-century medieval banquet. CNE near Dufferin Gate, Exhibition Place, Toronto, ON M6K 3C3; 1-888-935-6878, Fax: 416-260-1179, www.medievaltimes.com/findcastles/toronto/

- Old City Hall. A showplace of history and exquisite craftsmanship, celebrated its centennial birthday in September 1999. 60 Queen St. W., Toronto ON, www.toronto.ca/old_cityhall/

- Ontario Place. Unique entertainment complex on Toronto's waterfront. Open mid-May to Labour Day. 955 Lakeshore Blvd. W., Toronto, ON M6K 3B9; 416-314-9900 or 416-314-9811, 1-866-ONE-4-FUN (663-4386), www.ontarioplace.com

- Ontario Science Centre. Over 800 interactive exhibits emphasizing fun with science. Open year-round. 770 Don Mills Rd., Don Mills ON M3C 1T3; 416-696-1000, www.osc.on.ca

- Osgoode Hall. A heritage building located in downtown Toronto. This historic site is the focus for legal activity in Ontario and has garnered attention for over 170 years. 100-130 Queen St. W., Toronto ON M5H 2N6; 416-947-3300, www.osgoodehall.com

- Queen's Quay Terminal: A specialty retail centre with unique shopping and dining on Toronto's waterfront. 207 Queen's Quay W., www.queens-quay-terminal.com

- Rogers Centre (formerly known as SkyDome). Downtown multipurpose stadium with a retractable roof. Home to the MLB Toronto Blue Jays and the CFL Toronto Argonauts. Tours. 1 Blue Jays Way, 416-341-1707, www.rogerscentre.com

- Royal Ontario Museum. The Dawn of the Crystal Age – the stunning five-story Michael Lee-Chin Crystal has opened at Canada's largest museum; the design was fully completed in 2008. Exhibit areas are now open throughout the year – most notably the permanent return of the dinosaur collection in late 2007. 100 Queen's Park; Sat.–Thurs. 10–5:30, Fri. 10–9:30; 416-586-8000, www.rom.on.ca

- Toronto Police Museum and Discovery Centre. Exciting new museum with interactive displays featuring police and crime memorabilia. Exhibits include vehicles, weapons and infamous criminal cases. Open Mon.–Fri. 40 College St.; 416-808-7020, www.torontopolice.on.ca/museum/

- Toronto Zoo. World-class zoological park featuring over four thousand animals. Open year-round. 361A Old Finch Ave., Hwy. 401 and Meadowvale Rd., Scarborough, ON M1B 5K7; 416-392-5929, www.torontozoo.com
- Waterfront Regeneration Trust. The Trust coordinates the 325-km Waterfront Trail that stretches along the shore of Lake Ontario. 372 Richmond St. W., Suite 308, Toronto ON M5V 1X6; 416-943-8080, Fax: 416-943-8068, www.waterfronttrail.org/
- Wild Water Kingdom. Canada's largest outdoor water park. Open June through Labour Day (water park), April to October (mini-golf). 7855 Finch Ave. W., Brampton ON L6T 0B2; 905-369-WILD (9453), www.wildwaterkingdom.com

Museums

- Bata Shoe Museum, 327 Bloor St. W.; Mon.–Wed. 10–5, Thurs. 10–8 (free after 5), Fri.–Sat. 10–5, Sun. 12–5; 416-979-7799, www.batashoemuseum.ca
- CBC Museum, 250 Front St. W.; weekdays 9–5; 416-205-5574, www.cbc.ca/museum
- City of Toronto Archives and Research Hall, 255 Spadina Rd.; Mon.–Fri. 9–4:30, Saturdays during October to April (closed on long weekends), 10–4:30, 416-397-5000, archives@city.toronto.on.ca, www.city.toronto.on.ca/archives
- The Design Exchange. Museum and research centre of design in arts and everyday life, housed in the old Toronto Stock Exchange, 234 Bay St.; Mon.–Fri. 9–5, Sat.–Sun. 12–5; 416-363-6121, www.designexchange.org
- First Post Office. Free admission. 260 Adelaide St. E.; 416-865-1833, www.townofyork.com
- Gardiner Museum of Ceramic Art, 111 Queen's Park; Mon.–Thurs. 10–6, Fri. 10–9, Sat.–Sun. 10–5; 416-586-8080, Fax: 416-586-8085, www.gardinermuseum.on.ca

- Heritage Toronto. Visit one of four historic sites: Colborne Lodge, home of John George Howard, at High Park, 416-392-6916, www.toronto.ca/culture/museums/colborne-lodge.htm; Fort York, the nineteenth-century fort that recreates the drama of the war of 1812, off Fleet St., east of Strachan, 416-392-6907, www.fortyork.ca; Mackenzie House, home of William Lyon MacKenzie, Toronto's first mayor, 82 Bond St., 416-392-6915, www.toronto.ca/culture/mackenzie_house.htm; and Spadina House, a magnificent 1866 estate with fine art and elegant furnishings, 285 Spadina Rd., 416-392-6910, www.toronto.ca/culture/spadina.htm. Contact Toronto Convention & Visitors Association, PO Box 126, 207 Queen's Quay West Toronto ON M5J 1A7; 416-203-2600, 1-800-499-2514, Fax: 416-203-6753, Toronto@torcvb.com, www.torontotourism.com.
- Hockey Hall of Fame, Brookfield Place (formerly BCE Place), 30 Yonge St. Open seven days a week, hours vary by season. 416-360-7765, www.hhof.com
- Holocaust Education and Memorial Centre, 4600 Bathurst St. Open to the public by appointment only. 416-635-2883, bookavisit@ujafed,org, www.holocaustcentre.com
- Riverdale Farm, 201 Winchester St. See the animals and tour the farm's scenic 7.5 acres along pathways through wooded areas, around ponds, and into butterfly-herb-flower-vegetable gardens. Daily 9–5; 416-392-6794, www.toronto.ca/parks/riverdalefarm.htm
- Scarborough Historical Museum, 1007 Brimley Rd. Hours of operation vary by season. 416-338-8807
- Textile Museum of Canada, 55 Centre Ave.; daily 11–5, Wed. 11–8, open statutory holidays in summer only; 416-599-5321, www.textilemuseum.ca

- Todmorden Mills Heritage Museum and Arts Centre, Pottery Rd. between Broadview Ave. and Bayview Ave. Operating hours vary by season; 416-396-2819, www.toronto .ca/culture/todmorden_mills.htm
- Redpath Sugar Museum, 95 Queen's Quay E. Group tours are by appointment; other visitors are also required to call in advance. Mon.–Fri. 10–12 and 1–3:30; 416-933-8341, www.redpathsugars. com/museum_index.htm
- Zion Church Cultural Centre, 1650 Finch Ave. E. The Centre has no drop-in hours; please call for viewing and tour information. 416-392-3671, www.toronto.ca /culture/zion_church.htm
- Zion Schoolhouse, 1901 Finch Ave. E. The Schoolhouse has no drop-in hours; please call for viewing and tour information. 416-395-7435, www.toronto.ca/culture/zion_school house.htm

Galleries

This list of public galleries is a select one. Consult the latest edition of *Slate*, available at most galleries, for listings of current shows.

- A Space, 401 Richmond St. W., Suite 110; Tues.–Fri. 11–6, Sat. 12–5; 416-979-9633, Fax: 416-979-9683
- The Angell Gallery, 890 Queen St. W.; Wed.–Sat. 12–5; 416-530-0444, www.angellgallery.com
- Art Gallery of Ontario, 317 Dundas St. W.; Tues.–Fri. 11–6, Wed. 11–8:30, Sat.–Sun. 10–5:30, closed all Mondays (including holidays); 416-979-6648, Fax: 416-979-6646, everyone@ago.net, www.ago.net
- Art Metropole, 788 King St. W.; Tues.–Fri. 11–6, Sat. 12–5; 416-703-4400, artmet@interlog.com, www.artmetropole.org
- Bau-Xi Gallery, 340 Dundas St. W.; Mon.–Sat. 10–5:30, Sun. 11–5:30; 416-977-0600, Fax: 416-977-0625, toronto@bau-xi.com, www.bau-xi.com
- Christopher Cutts Gallery, 21 Morrow Ave.; Tues.–Sat. 11–6; 416-532-5566, Fax: 416-532-7272, www.cuttsgallery.com
- Deleon White Gallery, 1139 College St.; Wed.–Sat. 12–5, or by appt.; 416-597 9466, Fax: 416-597 9455, White@emmersive.org, www.eco-art.com
- The Drabinsky Gallery, 114 Yorkville Ave.; Tues.–Sat. 10–5; 416-324-5766, Fax: 416-324 5770, www.drabinskygallery.com
- Gallery One, 121 Scollard St.; Tues.–Sat. 10:30–5; 416-929-3103, www.artgalleryone.com
- Gallery 44, Centre for Contemporary Photography, 401 Richmond St. W., Suite 120; Tues.–Sat. 11–5; 416-979-3941, Fax: 416-979 1695, info@gallery44.org, www.gallery44.org
- Gallery Moos Ltd., 622 Richmond St. W.; Tues.–Sat. 11–6; 416-504-5445, Fax: 416-504-5446, info@gallerymoos.com, www.gallerymoos.com
- Gallery TPW (Toronto Photographers' Workshop), 56 Ossington; Tues.–Sat. 12–5; 416-645-1066, Fax: 416-645-1681, info@gallerytpw.ca, www.gallerytpw.ca
- Jane Corkin Gallery, 55 Mill St., Building 61; Tues.–Sat. 10–6, Sun. 12–5; 416-979-1980, Fax: 416-979-7018, exhibitions@corkin gallery.com, www.corkingallery.com
- Kaspar Gallery, 86 Scollard St.; Tues.–Sat. 10–6; 416-968-2536, www.tomaskaspar.com
- Katharine Mulherin, 1086 Queen Street W.; Wed.–Sat. 12–5; 416-537-8827, info@katherinemulherin.com, www.katherinemulherin.com
- Leo Kamen Gallery, 80 Spadina Ave., #406; Tues.–Sat. 11–5; 416-504-9515, Fax 416-504-9514, info@leokamengallery.com, leokamengallery.com
- Lonsdale Gallery, 410 Spadina Rd.; Wed.–Sun. 12–5; 416-487-8733, Fax 416-487-9604, info@lonsdalegallery.com, www.lonsdalegallery.com
- The McMichael Canadian Collection, 10365 Islington Ave.,

Kleinburg; daily 10–4; 905-893-1121, www.mcmichael.on.ca
- Mira Godard Gallery, 22 Hazelton Ave.; Tues.–Sat. 10–5; 416-964-8197, Fax: 416-964-5912, godard@godardgallery.com, www.godardgallery.com
- Museum of Contemporary Canadian Art (MOCCA), 952 Queen St. W.; Tues.–Sun. 11–6; 416-395-0067, Fax: 416-395-7598, www.mocca.ca
- Olga Korper Gallery, 17 Morrow Ave.; Tues.–Sat. 10–6; 416-538-8220, info@olgakorpergallery.com, www.olgakorpergallery.com
- Paul Petro Contemporary Art, 980 Queen Street W.; Wed.–Sat. 11–5; 416-979-7874, info@paulpetro.com, www.paulpetro.com
- Peak Gallery, 23 Morrow Ave.; Tues.–Sat. 11–6; 416-537-8108, Fax: 416-537-9618, zack@peakgallery.com, www.peakgallery.com
- The Power Plant, Harbourfront Centre, 231 Queen's Quay W.; Tues.–Sun. 12–6, Wed. 12–8, holiday Mondays 12–6; 416-973-4949, www.thepowerplant.org
- Propeller Centre for the Visual Arts, 984 Queen St. W.; Wed.–Sat. 12–6, Sun. 12–5; 416-504-7142, gallery@propellerctr.com, www.propellerctr.com
- Stephen Bulger Gallery, 1026 Queen St. W.; Tues.–Sat. 11–6; 416-504-0575, Fax: 416-504-8929, info@bulgergallery.com, www.bulgergallery.com
- Susan Hobbs Gallery, 137 Tecumseth St.; Thurs.–Sat. 1–5, or by appt.; 416-504-3699, Fax: 416-504-8064, info@susanhobbs.com, www.susanhobbs.com
- The Red Head Gallery, 401 Richmond St. W., Suite 115; Wed.–Sat. 12–5; 416-504-5654, art@redheadgallery.org, www.redheadgallery.org
- Toronto Imageworks, 80 Spadina Ave., Suite 207; Mon. & Wed. 8:30–10, Tues., Thurs. & Fri. 8:307, Sat. 10–4; 416-703-1999, www.torontoimageworks.com
- Toronto Sculpture Garden, 115 King St. E.; daily 8:00 a.m.–dusk; 416-515-9658, www.torontosculpturegarden.com
- Wynick/Tuck Gallery, 401 Richmond Street W., Suite 128; Tues.–Sat. 11–5; 416-504-8716, Fax: 416-504-8699, wtg@wynicktuckgallery.ca, www.wynicktuckgallery.ca
- Ydessa Hendeles Art Foundation, 778 King St. W.; Sat. 12-5 and by appt. (please fax or mail requests); 416-413-9400, Fax: 416-969-9889.

Entertainment

Theatre and Dance/Performance Venues

For tickets to most theatres, contact Ticketmaster, 1 Blue Jays Way, 416-870-8000 or online at www.ticketmaster.ca. For same-day tickets, contact T.O. Tix, Toronto's Half-price Ticket Centre, for a wide variety of theatre, dance and musical events. Half-price tickets are available Tuesdays through Saturdays, from noon to 6:30 p.m., on the day of the performance, and tickets for Sunday or Monday shows can be purchased the Saturday before. Tickets must be purchased in person at the booth on the southeast corner of Yonge-Dundas Square, or online at www.totix.ca. Call 416-536-6468 for recorded information.

- Alumnae Theatre. 70 Berkeley St., 416-364-4170, www.alumnaetheatre.com
- Artword Theatre, 128 Portland St., 416-204 3437, www.artword.net
- Ballet Jorgen. 160 Kendal Ave., 416-961-4725, www.balletjorgen.ca
- Buddies in Bad Times. Theatre by and about the gay and lesbian community and experience. 12 Alexander St., 416-975-8555, www.artsexy.ca
- Canadian Stage Company (CanStage). Bluma Appel Theatre in the St. Lawrence Centre, 27 Front St. E., and at the Berkeley Street Theatre, 26 Berkeley St., 416-368-3110, www.canstage.com

- Canon Theatre, 244 Victoria St., 416-364-4100, www.canon-theatre.com
- Convocation Hall. 31 King's College Circle, 416-978-8849, www.arts.utoronto.ca
- Danceworks. 55 Mill St., 416-204 1082, www.danceworks.ca
- Danny Grossman Dance Company. 157 Carlton St., Suite 202, 416-408-4543, www.dannygrossman.com
- Elgin and Winter Garden Theatres, 189 Yonge St., 416-314-2871
- Enwave Theatre. (Harbourfront Centre). 231 Queen's Quay W., 416-973 4000, www.harbour frontcentre.com
- The Factory Theatre, 125 Bathurst St., 416-504-9971, www.factorytheatre.ca
- Famous People Players, 343 Evans Ave., 416-532-1137, www.fpp.org
- Four Seasons Centre for the Performing Arts. Home to the National Ballet of Canada and Canadian Opera Company. 145 Queen St. W., 416-363 6671, www.fourseasonscentre.ca
- George Weston Recital Hall. Home to Amadeus Choir and Toronto Philharmonia. Toronto Centre for the Arts, 5040 Yonge St., 416-733-9388
- Harbourfront Centre. Various performance spaces and venues. 235 Queen's Quay W., 416-973-3000, www.harbourfrontcentre.com
- Lorraine Kimsa Theatre for Young People (formerly Young People's Theatre), 165 Front St. E., 416-353-5131, www.lktyp.ca
- Massey Hall. Venerated historical concert hall. 178 Victoria St., 416-872-4255, www.masseyhall.com
- Molson Amphitheatre. (Ontario Place) 909 Lakeshore Blvd. W. Outdoor concert stage. www.ontarioplace.com/en/02_events/amphitheatre.html
- Music Hall. Former vaudeville hall and movie house reinvented as concert theatre.147 Danforth Ave., 416-778 8163, www.themusichall.ca
- National Ballet of Canada, Walter Carsen Centre, 470 Queen's Quay W., 416-345-9686, www.national.ballet.ca

- Panasonic Theatre, 651 Yonge St., 416-928-5963, www.mirvish.com
- Premiere Dance Theatre, Queen's Quay Terminal, 235 Queen's Quay W., 3rd floor, 416-973-4000, www.harbourfrontcentre.com
- Princess of Wales Theatre, 300 King St. W., 416-872-1212 or 1-800-461-3333, www.mirvish.com
- Roy Thomson Hall. Home of the Toronto Symphony Orchestra. 60 Simcoe St., 416-872-4255, www.roythomson.com
- Royal Alexandra Theatre, 260 King St. W., 416-872-1212, www.mirvish.com
- Shaw Festival, Niagara-on-the-Lake, 1-800-511-7429, www.shawfest.com
- Solar Stage Children's Theatre, Madison Centre, 4950 Yonge St., 416-368-8031, www.solarstage.on.ca
- Sony Centre for the Performing Arts, 1 Front St. E., 416-393-7469, www.sonycentre.ca
- St. Lawrence Centre for the Arts. Houses the Bluma Appel Theatre and the Jane Mallet Theatre. 27 Front St. E., 416-366-7723, www.stlc.com
- Stratford Festival, Stratford, 416-363-4471 or 1-800-567-1600, Fax: 519-273-6173, orders@stratford-festival.on.ca, www.stratford-festival.on.ca
- Tarragon Theatre, 30 Bridgman Ave., 416-531-1827, www.tarragontheatre.com
- Theatre Passe Muraille, 16 Ryerson Ave., 416-504-7529, www.passemuraille.on.ca
- Toronto Centre for the Performing Arts, 5040 Yonge St., 416-733-9388, www.tocentre.com
- Toronto Dance Theatre, 80 Winchester St., 416-967-1365, www.tdt.org
- Young Centre for the Performing Arts. Home of Soulpepper classical repertory theatre company. 55 Mill St., Building 49, 416-866-8666, www.soulpepper.ca

Cinemas

For current movies, showtimes and venues check the entertainment pages of the *Toronto Star*, *NOW* magazine or *eye weekly*.

Comedy and Dinner Theatre

- Bad Dog Theatre. Home of Theatresports Toronto. Improv comedy with shows and drop-in classes. 138 Danforth Ave., 416-491-3115, www.baddogtheatre.com
- BigTime Murder Mystery. Weekly interactive comic murder mystery and dinner show. Vineyards Restaurant, 55 John St., 416-855-3306, www.bigtimemurder.com
- Diesel Playhouse. Theatrical comedy and musical cabaret on two stages. 56 Blue Jays Way, 416-971-5656, www.dieselplayhouse.com
- The Laugh Resort. Stand up comedy. 370 King St. W., 416-364-5233
- Medieval Times Dinner and Tournament. Re-enactment of an eleventh-century medieval banquet with knights on horses competing in medieval games, sword fights and jousting. 10 Dufferin St. (Exhibition Place), 416-260-1234 or 1-800-563-1190, www.medievaltimes.com
- Mysteriously Yours. A hilarious "whodunit." Join the fun at this interactive murder mystery! Dinner and show. 2026 Yonge St., 416-486-7469 or 1-800-668-3323, www.mysteriouslyyours.com
- Stage West Mississauga. Vegas style musical show and buffet. 5400 Dixie Rd., 905-238-0159, www.stagewest.com
- Second City. The well-known comedy troupe guarantees laughs. 51 Mercer St., 416-343-0011, www.secondcity.com
- Yuk Yuk's Comedy Club. Canada's original home of stand-up comedy. 224 Richmond St. W., 416-967-6425, www.yukyuks.com

Symphony, Chamber Music, Opera, Choirs

- Amadeus Choir, 75 The Donway W., Suite 410, 416-446-0188, www.amadeuschoir.com
- Aradia Ensemble. Baroque orchestra. 78 Twenty Fifth St., 416-461-3471, www.aradia.ca
- Arraymusic. New music ensemble performs works by contemporary composers. 60 Atlantic Ave., 416-532-3019, www.arraymusic.com
- Art of Time Ensemble, Enwave Theatre, 416-973-4000, www.artoftimeensemble.com
- Canadian Opera Company, Four Seasons Centre for the Performing Arts, 416-363-6671, www.coc.ca
- Elmer Isler Singers. Illustrious chamber choir. 2180 Bayview Ave., 416-217-0537, www.elmeriselersingers.com
- Esprit Orchestra, 174 Spadina Ave., Suite 511, 416-815-7887, www.espritorchestra.com
- Glenn Gould Studio, Canadian Broadcasting Centre, 250 Front St. W., 416-205-5555, www.glenngouldstudio.cbc.ca
- Jubilate Singers. Chamber choir. 416-421-4419, www.jubilatesingers.ca
- MacMillan Theatre, Faculty of Music, Edward Johnson Building, 80 Queen's Park, 416-978-3744
- The Music Gallery. Contemporary and experimental music and dance. 197 John St., 416-204-1080, www.musicgallery.org
- Music Toronto, 8 King St. E., Suite 910, 416-214-1660, www.music-toronto.org
- Nathaniel Dett Chorale. Afrocentric choral ensemble performing in a variety of styles and genres. 40 Baycrest Ave., 416-340-7000, www.nathanieldettchorale.org
- New Music Concerts, 157 Carlton St., Suite 203, 416-961-9594, www.newmusicconcerts.com
- Off Centre Music Series, 968 Logan Ave., 416-466-1870, www.offcentremusic.com
- Opera Atelier (Opera In Concert), St. Lawrence Hall, 157 King St. E., 4th floor, 416-703-3767, www.operaatelier.com
- Orpheus Choir, 416-530-4428, www.orpheuschoirtoronto.com
- Soundstreams Canada. International centre for new directions in music.

57 Spadina Ave., Suite 200, 416-504-1282, www.soundstreams.ca

- Tafelmusik. Baroque orchestra. Trinity-St. Paul's Church, 427 Bloor St. W., 416-964-9562, www.tafelmusik.org
- Tallis Choir of Toronto. Renaissance choral music. St. Patrick's Church, 141 McCaul St., 416-286-9798, www.tallischoir.com
- Tapestry New Opera (Opera Briefs/Opera To Go). Building 58, The Cannery, Studio 316, 416-537-6066, www.tapestrynewopera.com
- Toronto Children's Chorus, 26 Delisle Ave., 416-932-8666, www.torontochildrenschorus.com
- Toronto Consort. Chamber ensemble specializing in music of the Middle Ages, Renaissance, and early Baroque. Trinity-St. Paul's Church, 427 Bloor St. W., 416-966-1045, www.torontoconsort.org
- Toronto Masque Theatre, 416-410-4561, www.torontomasquetheatre.ca
- Toronto Mendelssohn Choir, 60 Simcoe St., 416-598-0422, www.tmchoir.org
- Toronto Symphony Orchestra, 212 King St W. Performances at Roy Thomson Hall, 60 Simcoe St., 416-593-7769, or RTH at 416-872-4255, www.tso.on.ca

Nightlife

This list will help guide you through Toronto after dark. Refer to the Nightlife section for more details and to the map at the beginning of the book. Be sure to check local newspapers; there is something for everyone in Toronto. For up-to-date listings, try the most recent edition of *NOW* magazine or *eye weekly*, both available free of charge in bars and restaurants throughout Toronto.

The Annex

- Dance Cave, 529 Bloor St. W., 2nd floor (above Lee's Palace), 416-532-1598. Alternative, indie and retro music. www.leespalace.com
- Lee's Palace, 529 Bloor St. W., 416-532-1598. Intimate venue for up and

coming live bands. www.leespalace.com

- Madison Avenue Pub, 14 Madison Ave., 416-927-1722. "The Maddy" has something for everyone – six levels in three attached Victorian houses. www.madison avenuepub.com
- Paupers Pub, 539 Bloor St. W., 416-530-1331. Three-level pub with a great street-level patio and an even better one on the roof. www.pauperspub.com/aboutus.html
- Ye Olde Brunswick House, 481 Bloor St. W., 416-964-2242

Bloor-Yorkville

- Bar Italia, 582 College St., 416-535-3621. Attracts all types of people, including families. Billiards, football and live jazz upstairs. www.bar-italia.ca
- Ciao Edie, 489 College St., 416-927-7774. A retro-kitsch home for scenesters.
- College Street Bar, 574 College St., 416-533-2417. Attracts a large student crowd. Filling Italian food and microbrewery beers on tap. www.collegestreetbar.com
- El Convento Rico, 750 College St., 416-588-7800. Late-night dancing and Latin drag performers. www.elconventorico.com
- El Rancho Night Club, 430 College St., 416-921-2752. Dress code in effect. www.elrancho.ca
- Hemingway's, 142 Cumberland St., 416-968-2828. Young or old, indoors or on the rooftop patio – popular with all.
- Lobby, 192 Bloor St. W., 416-929-7169. Sleek and sophisticated. www.lobbyrestaurant.com
- The Midtown, 552 College St., 416-920-4533. A modern café with the classic feel of a neighbourhood pub. Play pool at the back, or sit with creative types up front. www.themidtown.com
- The Mod Club, 722 College St., 416-588-4MOD. Brit indie, pop, rock and electronic pumping on a Saturday night and also an intimate concert venue. www.themodclub.com

- Orbit Room, 580A College St., 416-535-0613. Consistently filled to capacity, this venue is owned by Alex Lifeson of the Canadian power-rock trio Rush. The resident band, the Dexters, plays classic R and B tunes loudly. www.orbitroom.ca
- Plaza Flamingo Restaurant Night Club, 423 College St., 416-603-8884. Dress code in effect.
- The Roof, Park Hyatt Hotel, 4 Avenue Rd., 18th floor, 416-924-5471. Beautiful outdoor patio in summer.
- Sassafraz, 100 Cumberland St., 416-964-2222. Upscale resto-lounge. www.sassafraz.ca
- Sottovoce, 595 College St., 416-536-4564. A wine bar with a wrought-iron fenced patio. The most picturesque place to sit in Little Italy.
- Souz Dal, 636 College St., 416-537-1883. Cozy and dark. Listen to the eclectic mix of music over a few martinis or margaritas (the best in town). www.souzdal.com

Downtown

- Acqua, 10 Front St. W., 416-368-7171. An uptown crowd gathers for an outstanding happy hour, weekdays from 5–7. www.acqua.ca
- Betty's, 240 King St. E., 416-368-1300. An informal, charming, comfortable bar. www.bettysonking.com
- Esplanade Bier Markt, 58 The Esplanade, 416-862-7575. A huge selection of beers from across the world. www.thebiermarkt.com
- Fionn McCool's, 70 The Esplanade, 416-362-2495. Irish is the theme in this comfortable pub. www.fionnmaccools.com
- Phoenix Concert Theatre, 410 Sherbourne St., 416-323-1251. Live music and themed DJ venue. www.libertygroup.com/phoenix/phoenix.html
- Rockit Night Club, 120 Church St., 416-947-9555
- Rosewater Supper Club, 19 Toronto St., 416-214-5888. A forties-style supper club with lavish details.
- Scotland Yard, 56 The Esplanade, 416-364-6572, www.scotlandyard.ca

Entertainment District

- Cha Cha Cha, 11 Duncan St., 416-598-3538. Come to mambo! A supper club with a tiny dance floor and a Latin menu.
- Crocodile Rock, 240 Adelaide St. W., 416-599-9751. Bayou-themed restaurant/club with a rooftop patio featuring classic rock and retro '80s music for the 25-plus crowd on the dance floor. www.crocrock.ca
- Fluid Lounge, 217 Richmond St. W., 416-593-6116. Thursdays are the best night, with progressive house over the sound system. www.fluidlounge.ca
- Horizons, 301 Front St. W., 416-362-5411. Atop the CN Tower, with a spectacular view.
- Jeff Healey's Roadhouse, 56 Blue Jays Way, 416-703-5882. Named after the late Juno award-winning guitarist Jeff Healey, who often played there.
- Joe, 250 Richmond St. W., 416-971-6JOE. A landmark for the student crowd. Three floors take you from the plains to the forest to a Muskoka lake and from lounge to pop to club music.
- Limelight, 250 Adelaide St., 416-593-6126. Crowded and energetic.

Jazz

- Alleycatz Live Jazz Bar, 2409 Yonge St., 416-481-6865. Great live jazz every night. www.alleycatz.sites.toronto.com
- Reservoir Lounge, 52 Wellington St. E., 416-955-0887. A must for the jazz lover. www.reservoirlounge.com
- The Rex Jazz and Blues Bar, 194 Queen St. W., 416-598-2475. Don't be fooled by the run-down appearance. Over eighty performances a month. www.jazzintoronto.com
- Top o' the Senator, 249 Victoria St., 416-364-7517. A cozy club that attracts any top names passing through town.

Queen St. West

- The Beaconsfield, 1154 Queen St. W., 416-516-2550. Friendly, upscale yet casual one-room lounge. www.thebeaconsfield.com
- The Big Bop, 651 Queen St. W., 416-504-0744. Style code in effect. www.thebigbop.com
- Cameron House, 408 Queen St. W., 416-703-0811. Soul, R and B, alternative or acid-jazz. www.thecameron.com
- Gypsy Co-op, 817 Queen St. W., 416-703-5069. An eclectic mix of vintage furniture and herbal teas attracts arty patrons.
- Horseshoe Tavern, 370 Queen St. W., 416-598-4753. Features great local bands. A jeans-and-draught pub. www.horseshoetavern.com
- The Rivoli, 334 Queen St. W., 416-596-1908. Dinner or drinks. The best place for live bands. www.rivoli.ca
- Savage Garden, 550 Queen St. W., 416-504-2178. A gritty, dark, industrial, Goth dance bar. www.savagegarden.ca
- Velvet Underground, 510 Queen St. W., 416-504-6688. Dark and unusual.

Other Neighbourhoods

- 2 Cats, 569 King St. W., 416-204-6261. Chic and relaxed. www.2cats.ca
- Academy of Spherical Arts, 38 Hanna Ave., 416-532-2782. The ne plus ultra of pool halls. www.sphericalarts.com
- Atlantis Pavilions, Ontario Place, West Entrance, 955 Lakeshore Blvd. W., 416-260-8000, www.atlantispavilions.com
- Brant House, 522 King St. W. (at Brant), 416-703-2800, www.branthouse.com
- C Lounge, 456 Wellington St. W., 416-260-9393. A spa-inspired lounge with a faux-pool deck that resembles a scene set at a five-star hotel.
- The Comfort Zone, 480 Spadina Ave., 416-763-9139. Still raving late when other doors are shut. www.comfortzonetoronto.com

- The Docks, 11 Polson St., 416-469-5655. Patrons from all walks of life from bikers to yachters and college kids. www.thedocks.com
- The Guvernment/Kool Haus, 132 Queen's Quay E., 416-869-0045. A huge central dance space gives way to other unique rooms. www.theguvernment.com
- Matador, 466 Dovercourt Rd., 416-533-9311. Open from 1–5 a.m., Friday and Saturday. Live bands.
- Myth, 417 Danforth Ave., 416-461-8383. Primarily a supper club, a mix of crowds and a mythic decor.
- Rebel House, 1068 Yonge St., 416-927-0704. Try the cheese pennies, choose from a plethora of micro-brews and play Abalone, a terrific board game in this pub. www.rebelhouse.ca
- Silver Dollar Room, 486 Spadina Ave., 416-763-9139. A Chicago-style house of blues. An easy-going, good-time place. www.silverdollarroom.com
- Sneaky Dee's, 431 College St.; 416-603-3090. A sticky-floored beer hall. Ignore the feeling of being at a high school party and get caught up in the dancing. www.sneaky-dees.com

Dining

Toronto boasts some of the finest restaurants in North America. With a huge cultural diversity, there is something for everyone. The following is a select list of the restaurants available. Restaurants are listed alphabetically by category (e.g. Asian) and subcategory (e.g. Chinese). The sequence of the categories follows the sequence used in the dining chapter.

The Toronto Dining Map on page 9 shows the restaurants included in this selective listing, which are located in central Toronto. The listings and brief descriptions which follow give you the numbers you can use to find central-city restaurants on the map.

Approximate prices are indicated, based on the average cost, at time of publication, of dinner for two including wine (where available), taxes and gratuity: $ = under $45; $$ = $45–$80; $$$ = $80–$120; $$$$ = $120–$180; $$$$$ = over $180. Meals served are indicated as: B = breakfast; L = lunch; D = dinner; Late = open past midnight; G = "grazing"; T-O = take-out. Credit cards accepted are also indicated: AX = American Express; V = Visa; MC = MasterCard.

Canadian

- 360, CN Tower, 301 Front St. W., 416-362-5411. Seasonal, eclectic menu of fine hearty fare. Prix fixe options. $$, AX/V/MC (map: 37)
- Aunties & Uncles, 74 Lippincott St., 416-324-1375. Closed Mondays and long weekends. Popular local upscale diner fare with patio. B/L $
- Fran's, 20 College St., 416-923-9867; also at 200 Victoria St., 416-304 0085. A 24-hour Toronto institution. Late, B/L/D, $, AX/V/MC
- Frank, 317 Dundas St., 416-979-6688. In Frank Gehry AGO, featuring Ontario ingredients and wines. L/D, $$$, AX/V/MC
- George, 111 Queen St. E., 416-863-6006. Lunch Mon.–Fri., dinner Tues.–Sat. Seasonal "Toronto Cuisine" with recommended wine pairings. L/D, $$$, AX/V/MC (map: 23)
- Jump Café and Bar, Commerce Court East, 18 Wellington St. W., 416-363-3400. Weekday lunches, closed Sunday. L/D, $$, AX/V/MC (map: 32)
- Rebel House, 1068 Yonge St., 416-927-0704. Cheese pennies make a perfect appetizer in this unpretentious restaurant/tavern. Numerous Ontario microbrewery offerings and a great weekend brunch. L/D, $–$$
- Wayne Gretzky's, 99 Blue Jays Way, 416-979-PUCK (7825). Hockey memorabilia featuring The Great One and other players alongside a menu that shoots and scores above a typical sports bar/restaurant. L/D, $$$, AX/V/MC

Asian

Chinese

- Asian Legend, 418 Dundas St. W.,

416-977-3909. Modern Northern Chinese cuisine and dim sum. L/D/T-O, $ V/MC
- Dynasty Chinese Cuisine, 131 Bloor St. W., 416-923-3323. Floor to ceiling windows overlook the swanky Bloor Street shops. Seafood can be chosen from tanks. Daily dim sum. L/D. $–$$$, AX/V/MC (map: 4)
- Lai Wah Heen, 108 Chestnut St., 416-977-9899. Haute Cantonese and superlative dim sum. L/D, $$$, AX/V/MC (map: 21)
- Monsoon, 100 Simcoe St., 416-979-7172. Innovative upscale Asian. Closed Sundays. Late, L/D, $$$, AX/V/MC/DC
- Pearl Harbourfront Chinese Cuisine, 207 Queen's Quay W., 416-203-1233. Elegant Cantonese on the waterfront. B/L/D, $$, AX/V/MC/DC

Japanese

- Hiro Sushi, 171 King St. E., 416-304-0550. Masterful à la carte and omakase sushi. L/D, $$, AX/V/MC
- Kaiseki Sakura, 556 Church St., 416-923-1010. Closed Tuesday. Specializes in kaiseki, the high-end Japanese tasting menu that features intricate, artistically crafted food. D, $$–$$$$$, AX/V/MC (map: 18)
- New Generation Sushi, 493 Bloor St. W., 416-963-8861. Friendly, fresh sushi. Late, L/D/T-O, $, AX/V/MC
- Supermarket, 268 Augusta Ave., 416-840-0501. Oriental-inspired tapas. Closed Sundays. D, $, AX/V/MC
- Sushi Island, 571 College St., 416-535-1515. Simple Japanese fare providing a welcome contrast to surrounding Little Italy. L/D/T-O, $–$$

Thai

- Green Mango, 730 Yonge St., 416-928-0021 and other locations. Favourite local Thai chain — try the jackfruit fritters. L/D/T-O, $, AX/V/MC/DC
- Hungary Thai. 196 Augusta, 416-595-6405. Unusual but tasty combination of Hungarian and Thai menu items. Prix fixe available. L/D, $

- King's Café. 192 Augusta Ave., 416-591-1340. Healthy Asian fare with vegetarian ingredients. L/D, $

Latin

- Churrasco of St. Lawrence, 91 Front St. E. in the St. Lawrence Market, 416-862-2867. BBQ chicken lunch on the go in the heart of the Market. L, $
- Jumbo Empanadas, 245 Augusta Ave., 416-977-0056. Delicious Chilean turnovers. L/D, $
- Perola's Supermarket, 247 Augusta Ave., 416-593-9728. Groceries and homemade pupusas. $
- Plaza Flamingo, 423 College St., 416-603-8884. Closed Monday, Saturday lunch. Wide-ranging Latin menu including tapas and paella. Live Flamenco show Fri. & Sat. L/D, $$ (map: 48)

Continental

Greek

- Christina's, 492 Danforth Ave., 416-463-4418. Classic Greek cuisine. Late Fri. & Sat. with live music. L/D, $$, AX/V/MC
- Kokkino, 414 Danforth Ave., 416-461-3562. Mediterranean dips and grilled meat and seafood tidbits. Late cocktail menu. D, $$
- Myth, 417 Danforth Ave., 416-461-8383. Mediterranean fare in the heart of Greektown. Weekend lunch. D, $$

Italian

- Bellini's Ristorante, 101 Yorkville Ave., 416-929-9111. D, $$$$ (map: 12)
- Biagio, 155 King St. E., 416-366-4040. Closed Sunday, closed for weekend lunch. Traditional northern Italian fare paired with great Italian wines. L/D, $$$$, AX/V/MC (map: 27)
- Café Diplomatico, 594 College St., 416-534-4637. A Little Italy landmark with one of Toronto's best patios. Casual Italian fare. B/L/D, Late $–$$
- Grappa Ristorante, 797 College St., 416-535-3337. Closed Monday.

Cozy dining room in the heart of Little Italy with an extensive wine list. D, $$–$$$, AX/V/MC
- Il Fornello, 491 Church St., 416-944-9052. Popular chain offering Italian fare. L/D, $$ AX/V/MC
- Mistura, 265 Davenport Rd.,416-515-0009. Closed Sunday. Contemporary pan-Italian fare. D, $$$$ (map: 9)
- The Old Spaghetti Factory, 54 The Esplanade, 416-864-9761. Closed for weekend lunches. L/D, $$, AX/V/MC
- Prego Della Piazza, 150 Bloor St. W., 416-920-9900. Closed Sunday lunch. Spot celebrities over veal chops and a bottle of Barolo. L/D/G, $$$$, AX/V/MC (map: 5)
- Sicilian Sidewalk Café, 712 College St., 416-531-7755. A favourite spot in Little Italy offering light meals and an extensive dessert menu. L/D, $–$$
- Sotto Sotto, 116A Avenue Rd., 416-962-0011. Romantic, subterranean setting. Irresistible grilled dishes, especially the radicchio. D, $$$$, AX/V/MC
- Terroni, 1 Balmoral, 416-925-4020; 720 Queen St. W., 416-504-0320; 106 Victoria St., 416-955-0258. Upmarket pastas and thin crispy pizzas in a relaxed setting. B/L/D, $$, V
- Vittorio's, 1973 Yonge St., 416-482-7441. Lunch Fri. & Sat. Authentic Italian cuisine in an intimate setting. Superb homemade gnocchi. L/D, $$$–$$$$

À La Mode

- Amuse-Bouche, 96 Tecumseth St., 416-913-5830. Closed Sun. & Mon. Seasonal menus in an elegant atmosphere at this small French boîte. D, $$$, AX/V/MC (map: 43)
- Biff's, 4 Front St. E., 416-860-0086. Parisian-style bistro. Outstanding cheeses. Closed Sundays, dinner only on Saturdays. L/D, $$$$, AX/V/MC (map: 33)
- Bonjour Brioche, 812 Queen St. E., 416-406-1250. Hot-from-the-oven sweet baked goods and savories in

this tiny boîte. Closed Mon. Patio. B/L/T-O, $

- Cava, 1560 Yonge St., 416-979 9918. Wine and tapas bar featuring entrees by revered chef Chris McDonald. Weekday lunches, dinner nightly. L/D, $$, AX/V/MC
- Célestin, 623 Mount Pleasant Rd., 416-544-9035. Closed Sun. & Mon. Superb contemporary French cuisine. All breads are baked next door and are available for purchase. D, $$$, AX/V/MC
- Conviction, 609 King St. W., 416-603-2777. As seen on TV's *Conviction Kitchen*. B/L/D, $$$, AX/V/MC
- Cowbell, 1564 Queen St. W., 416-849-1095. Ontario locavore dining at its best. D, $$$, AX/V/MC
- Crêpes à GoGo, 18 Yorkville Ave., 416-922-6765. More than twenty varieties of savory and sweet crepes. L, $ (map: 13)
- Grace, 503 College St., 416-944-8884. Smart, casual bistro dining. D, $$$, AX/V/MC
- La Maquette, 111 King St. E., 416-366-8191. Closed for Saturday lunch, closed Sunday. Imaginative French cuisine overlooking the Toronto Sculpture Garden. L/D, $$$, AX/V/MC (map: 26)
- La Palette, 256 Augusta Ave., 416-929-4900. Charming bistro with classic meaty fare. Weekend brunch. D, $$, AX/V/MC
- Le Select Bistro, 422 Wellington St. W., 416-596-6406. L/D, $$$, AX/V/MC
- Madeline's, 601 King St. E., 416-603-2205 . Opulent and fashionable continental fare. D, $$$, AX/V/MC
- Richtree Market Restaurant, 42 Yonge St., 416-366-8986. Eclectic bistro food, cafeteria style, in fun, bustling atmosphere. Late, B/L/D, $$, AX/V/MC

Four-Star Dining

- AME, 19 Mercer St., 416-599-7246. Fashionable hot spot with refined Japanese cuisine. D, $$$, AX/V/MC
- Bymark, 66 Wellington St. W., 416-777-1144. Closed Sun.

Contemporary twist to classic cuisine. An extensive wine list. L/D, $$$$–$$$$$, AX/V/MC (map: 36)

- Canoe, Toronto Dominion Tower, 66 Wellington St. W., 54th floor, 416-364-0054. Closed weekends. Award-winning Canadian-themed menu. L/D, $$$$, AX/V/MC (map: 35)
- Centro, 2472 Yonge St., 416-483-2211. Closed Sun. Contemporary European cuisine showcasing Canadian ingredients. Awe-inspiring wine cellar. D, Late, $$$$, AX/V/MC
- Chiado, 864 College St., 416-538-1910. Light, elegant Portuguese cooking in graceful surroundings. D, G, T-O, $$$, AX/V/MC
- Didier, 1496 Yonge St., 416-925-8588. Lunch Tues.–Fri., dinner Tues.–Sat., Sunday brunch. True French cuisine in a room that feels transplanted out of Paris. L/D, $$$, AX/V/MC
- Epic, 100 Front St. W., Toronto, 416-860-6949. Modern, French-inspired, in the Royal York Hotel. Afternoon tea daily, Sunday prix fixe brunch B/L/D, $$$$, AX/V/MC
- Harbour Sixty Steakhouse, 60 Harbour St., 416-777-2111. Closed for weekend lunch. Superb steak and seafood set in a historic building. Long dessert list entices. L/D, $$$$–$$$$$, AX/V/MC (map: 35)
- Hemispheres, 110 Chestnut St., 416-599-8000. International menu in the Metropolitan Hotel. Dinner Tues.–Sat. Late, B/L/D, $$$$, AX/V/MC (map: 20)
- Jacobs & Co. Steakhouse, 12 Brandt St., 416-366-0200. Glamorous steakhouse for serious carnivores. D, $$$$, AX/V/MC
- North 44, 2537 Yonge St., 416-487-4897. Canadian-continental fine dining in a sleek atmosphere. D, $$$$, AX/V/MC
- Nota Bene, 180 Queen St. W., 416-977-6400. Voted best new restaurant by *Toronto Life* magazine. L/D, $$$, AX/V/MC

- Opus, 37 Prince Arthur Ave., 416-921-3105. Fine dining in a warm, laid-back atmosphere. *Wine Spectator* Grand Award recipient, with a vast inventory of wines. L/D, $$$–$$$$ (map: 7)
- Oro, 45 Elm St., 416-597-0155. Closed Sunday, and Saturday lunch. Thorough pampering in a lovely dining room. L/D, $$$$, AX/V/MC (map: 19)
- Pangaea, 1221 Bay St., 416-920-2323. Closed Sun. Frequently changing menu featuring internationally inspired selections. L/D, $$$$, AX/V/MC (map: 15)
- Rosewater Supper Club, 19 Toronto St., 416-214-5888. Refined contemporary global dining in a genteel setting. L/D, $$$
- Scaramouche Pasta Bar/Restaurant, 1 Benvenuto Place, 416-961-8011. Closed Sun. A gifted chef, top-drawer service and lavish dining room. D/G, $$$$$, AX/V/MC
- Splendido, 88 Harbord St., 416-929-7788. Closed Sun. Stately, elegant dining room and a wine cellar of over 1,000 bottles. D, $$$$$, AX/V/MC (map: 1)

Neighbourhood Spots

- Avenue, 21 Avenue Rd., 416-964-0411. Upscale luxury bar and lounge with casual snack fare. L/D/Late, $$$
- Barberian's Steakhouse, 7 Elm St., 416-597-0335. Closed for weekend lunches. L/D, $$$$$, AX/V/MC
- Beaver Café, 1192 Queen St. W., 416-537-2768
- Byzantium, 499 Church Street, 416-922-3859. Upscale restaurant and martini bar. D, $$, AX/V/MC
- C5, Royal Ontario Museum, 100 Queen's Park, 416-586-7928. Lunch daily, dinner Thurs.–Sat. At the pinnacle of the striking new Michael Lee-Chin Crystal at the Royal Ontario Museum, diners have a stunning view of the cityscape while noshing on a variety of dishes made with local and artisanal ingredients. L/D, $$–$$$, AX/V/MC (map: 2)
- Cadillac Lounge, 1296 Queen St. W., 416-536-7717. Classic pub fare and extensive beer menu in retro, alt-country club. Weekend brunch. L/D/ Late, $
- Captain John's, 1 Queen's Quay, 416-363-6062. Seafood aboard a permanently docked 1957 cruise ship at the foot of Yonge St. L/D, $$$
- Carman's, 26 Alexander St., 416-924-8697. Glorious beef and seafood. Olives and dill pickles pass as vegetables. Hundreds of celebrity photos. New steak house section. D, $$$$$, AX/V/MC
- Churchmouse and Firkin, 475 Church St., 416-927-1735. Traditional pub fare in popular chain. L/D, $
- Esplanade Bier Markt, 58 The Esplanade, 416-862-7575. A huge selection of beers from across the world complements brasserie food. L/D, $$, AX/V/MC
- Flow, 133 Yorkville Ave., 416-925-2143. Trendy international resto-lounge. D, $$$$, AX/V/MC
- Fuzion, 580 Church St., 416-944-9888. Closed Sun. & Mon., Tues. lunch. Fusion in a contemporary resto-lounge atmosphere. L/D, $$, AX/V/MC
- Hard Rock Café, (279 Yonge St., 416-362-3636. Family dining, rock memorabilia and gift shop. L/D/ G/Late, $–$$$, AX/V/MC (map: 22)
- Hot House Café, 35 Church St., 416-366-7800. Thin crust pizza, steaks, pastas, burgers and sandwiches served in brightly coloured rooms. Award-winning Sunday brunch with live jazz. L/D/Late, $–$$ (map: 28)
- Kalendar, 546 College St., 416-923-4138. Eclectic menu in a cozy neighbourhood setting. Weekend brunch. L/D, $$, V/MC
- The Keg Steakhouse & Bar, 515 Jarvis St., 416-964-6609 (multiple other locations in Toronto). Grilled steaks, seafood and salads in a laid-back setting. The Keg's flagship restaurant is housed in a three-storey historic mansion that some believe is still haunted. L/D, $$$, AX/V/MC

- Lee, 603 King St. W., 416-504-7867. Closed Sun. A variety of sharable dishes drawing from global influences. Substantial wine list. D, $$–$$$, AX/V/MC (map: 41)
- MBCo, 100 Bloor St. W., 416-961-6226. Tucked in a laneway, the freshest fast food known to man, with a quality quotient you'd expect from a five-star restaurant. L/T-O, $
- Mezzrow's, 1546 Queen St. W., 416-535-4906. L/D, $–$$, AX/V/MC
- Mildred's Temple Kitchen, 85 Hanna Ave., 416-588-5695. Bistro fare in a soaring minimalist room in Liberty Village. L/D, $$, AX/V/MC
- Mill Street Brew Pub, Distillery District, 55 Mill St., 416-681-0338. Closed for dinner Sunday; weekend brunch. Housed in an 1870s tankhouse, offering up traditional favourites. L/D, $–$$, AX/V/MC
- Mitzi's Sister, 1554 Queen St. W., 416-532-2570. Homey café with live music nightly. L/D, $
- Moonbean Coffee Company, 30 St. Andrew St., 416-595-0327. Independent gourmet coffee shop in the heart of Kensington with light fare. B/L/D, $
- O'Grady's, 518 Church St., 416-328-2822
- Patrician Grill, 219 King St. E., 416-366-4841. Closed Sun. Classic diner fare along with the standard fast service and vinyl booths. Cash only. B/L, $
- Peter Pan, 373 Queen St. W., 416-593-0917. Sunday brunch. Burgers, warm salads, pastas, steaks and Thai noodles. L/D/Late/G, $$–$$$, AX/V/MC
- Queen Mother Café, 208 Queen St. W., 416-598-4719. Asian-influenced cuisine in an arty atmosphere bistro. L/D/Late, G/T-O, $$, AX/V/MC
- Remy's, 115 Yorkville Ave., 416-968-9429. Smart casual ambience with range of fare from snacks to fine entrees. Rooftop patio. Weekend brunch. L/D, $$ (map: 11)
- Rhino, 1249 Queen St. W., 416-535-8089. Comfy casual pub grub and patio dining complete with wide selection of beers. L/D/Late, $

- The Rivoli, 334 Queen St. W., 416-596-1908. Elegant fare borrows from the Orient. Quirky décor and staff. L/D/Late/G, $$$, AX/V/MC
- The Rosebud, 669 Queen St. W., 416-703-8810. Unpretentious classic fare in a wood-panelled intimate setting. D, $$–$$$, V/MC (map: 45)
- Sightlines, Rogers Centre, 1 Blue Jays Way, 416-341-2364. Open two hours prior to events. Open-air restaurant facing the playing field of the Rogers Centre. L/D, $$$–$$$$, AX/V/MC
- Signatures, Hotel InterContinental, 220 Bloor St. W., 416-324-5885. Closed Sunday evening. B/L/D, $$$$, AX/V/MC
- Sultan's Tent, 49 Front St., 416-961-0601. Closed for weekend lunches. L/D, $$$, AX/V/MC (map: 30)
- Ultra Supper Club, 314 Queen St. W., 416-263-0330. Closed Sun. Upscale dining adjacent to ultra chic nightclub. Rooftop patio. D, $$$$ (map: 44)
- Zelda's, 542 Church St., 416-922-2526. Cheap and cheerful casual fare. Sunday brunch. L/D, $

Shopping

Antiques and Collectibles

- Quasi Modo Modern Furniture, 789 Queen St. W., 416-703-8300. Vintage furniture and collectibles. www.quasimodomodern.com
- Stylegarage, 938 Queen St. W., 416-534-4343. A mix of contemporary and antique furnishings. www.stylegarage.com
- Zig Zag, 985 Queen St. E., 416-778-6495, www.modfurnishings.com

Beauty and Health

- Aveda Environmental Lifestyle Store, 220 Yonge St., 416-979-8892. Other locations in Toronto. Full line of Aveda products, including shampoo, hair care products and cosmetics. www.aveda.com
- The Body Shop, 138 Cumberland St., 416-928-1156; Toronto Eaton

Centre, 220 Yonge St., 416-977-7364; most major malls and assorted other locations. Environmentally-friendly skin care products, cosmetics and toiletries. www.thebodyshop.ca

- Lush, 312 Queen St. W., 416-599-5874; also at Toronto Eaton Centre and Toronto International Airport. A blitz of bath bombs from London, England, along with other bubbly concoctions.
- MAC, 89 Bloor St. W., 416-929-7555, as well as twelve other locations. A makeup store that contributes to AIDS charities through a wide range of cruelty-free products.
- Sephora, Toronto Eaton Centre, 220 Yonge St., 416-595-7227; Yorkdale Mall, 416-785-4400. A seemingly endless array of beauty & body products.

Books

- Indigo, 55 Bloor St. W., 416-925-3536, and other locations of this biggest Canadian bookseller that includes Chapters stores. www.chapters.indigo.ca
- Mabel's Fables Children's Book Store, 662 Mount Pleasant, 416-322-0438, www.mabelsfables.com
- Nicholas Hoare, 45 Front St. E., 416-777-2665. A publisher's dream and cornucopia of colour; almost all the books face out, framed by fine wood display stands and walls. www.nicholashoare.com
- Pages Books and Magazines, 256 Queen St. W., 416-598-1447. Queen West's most popular newsstand and bookroom.
- This Ain't the Rosedale Library, 86 Nassau St. in Kensington Market, 416-929-9912. A great store for fiction in the heart of the Church Street community. www.thisaint.ca

Canadiana

- Bowring Canadiana, 220 Yonge St. in Toronto Eaton Centre, 416-596-1042. Gifts and Canadiana.
- Canadian Naturalist, 207 Queen's Quay W., 416-203-0365, Eaton Centre, 416-581-0044

- First Hand Canadian Crafts, Queen's Quay Terminal, 207 Queen's Quay W., 416-603-7413

China and Crystal

- Bowring Canadiana, 220 Yonge St. in Toronto Eaton Centre, 416-596-1042. Gifts and Canadiana.
- Du Verre, 186 Strachan Ave., 416-593-0182. Hand-blown glassware and handcrafted iron furnishings.
- Muti and Company, 88 Yorkville Ave. 416-969-0253. An ample selection of imported Italian majolica ceramics. www.emuti.com
- William Ashley, 55 Bloor St. W., 416-964-2900. Toronto's largest selection of fine china, crystal, silver and gifts. www.williamashley.com

Clothing: Canadian Designers

- Comrags, 654 Queen St. W., 416-360-7249. Canadian duo Joyce Gunhouse and Judy Cornish offer feminine clothing such as ethereal floral rayon dresses and tight-fitting cotton-Lycra knits. www.comrags.com
- Fashion Crimes, 322 ½ Queen St. W., 416-592-9001. Velvet wear for the Goth crowd, Edwardian morning coats, Empire-waisted bodice gowns and glamourous accessories.
- Lida Baday Studio, 70 Claremont St., 416-603-7661. Simple, elegant, high-end women's fashion, using excellent fabrics and knits.
- Linda Lundstrom, 136 Cumberland St., 416-927-9009; 176 Yonge St. (The Bay), 416-861-9111. Women's outerwear including the four-coats-in-one La-Parka. www.lundstrom.ca
- Lowon Pope Design, 779 Queen St. W., 416-504-8150
- Price Roman, 162 John St.., 416-979-7363. Elegant women's suits and dresses, with simple lines and subtle detailing. www.pricer oman.com
- Psyche, 708 Queen St. W., 416-599-4882

Clothing: Children's
- Baby Gap, 80 Bloor St. W., 416-515-0668; other locations.

Well-made clothing for babies in natural fabrics; a bit on the preppy side. www.gapcanada.ca
- Gap Kids, 2574 Yonge St., 416-440-0187; other locations. Well-made clothing for babies and children in natural fabrics; a bit on the preppy side. www.gapcanada.ca
- Misdemeanours, 322 ½ Queen St. W., 416-351-8758. This wonderful shop makes you step through the looking glass: storybook dresses for girls, accented with Victorian frills.
- Old Navy, Toronto Eaton Centre, 416-593-0065; Yorkdale Mall, 416-787-9384 and other locations. Affordable fashion for men, women and children. www.oldnavy.ca
- Roots, 100 Bloor St. W., 416-323-3289; Toronto Eaton Centre, 416-593-9640; twelve other stores, plus three factory outlets. Look for the Baby Roots line at each of these locations. www.roots.com

Clothing: Men's
- Banana Republic, 80 Bloor St. W., 416-515-0018; Toronto Eaton Centre, 416-595-6336. Trendy chain featuring casual and office wear for young professionals; also carries accessories and shoes. www.bananarepublic.ca
- Boomer, 309 Queen St. W., 416-598-0013. A variety of mid-range to upscale men's clothing.
- Eddie Bauer, Yorkdale Shopping Centre, 1 Yorkdale Rd., 416-783-2692. Outdoor gear, hiking boots, down vests, flannel shirts and other icons of the comfortable male.
- The Gap, 60 Bloor St. W., 416-921-2225; First Canadian Place, 416-777-1332; 375 Queen St. W., 416-591-3517; Toronto Eaton Centre, 416-599-8802. Casualwear for some, workwear for others and dancewear if you watch too much television. www.gapcanada.ca
- Harry Rosen, 82 Bloor St. W., 416-972-0556; Toronto Eaton Centre, 416-598-8885; Yorkdale Shopping Centre, 416-787-4231. Upscale men's business and casual wear, including Giorgio Armani, Hugo

Boss, Canali, Brioni and Versace and the V2 collection; also shoes and accessories. www.harryrosen.com
- H&M, 13-15 Bloor St. W., 416-920-4029; Toronto Eaton Centre, 416-593-0064; other locations. Cheap faddish finds from this popular European retailer. www.hm.com
- Holt Renfrew, 50 Bloor St. W., 416-922-2333; Yorkdale Shopping Centre, 416-789-5377. Fine fashions for men; Giorgio Armani, Calvin Klein and Holt Renfrew's own label. www.holtrenfrew.com
- Hugo Nicholson, Hazelton Lanes, 416-927-7714, www.hugonicholson.com
- Old Navy, Toronto Eaton Centre, 416-593-0065; Yorkdale Mall, 416-787-9384 and other locations. Affordable fashion for men, women and children. www.oldnavy.ca
- TNT, 388 Eglinton W., 416-488-8210 as well as Hazelton Lanes, 416-975-1810

Clothing: Second-Hand
- Cabaret Nostalgia, 672 Queen St. W., 416-504-7126, www.cabaretvintage.com
- Courage My Love, 14 Kensington Ave., 416-979-1992. Standby funky vintage clothing with all the trappings (beads, chains, charms); reasonably priced.
- Dancing Days, 17 Kensington Ave., 416-599-9827, www.dancingdays.com
- Preloved, 881 Queen St. W., 416-504-8704. Features clothes from the 1970s. www.preloved.ca

Clothing: Women's High-end
- Annie Thompson, 1 Wiltshire Ave., Studio 205, 416-703-4445. Canadian designer boutique. www.anniethompson.ca
- Betsey Johnson, 102 Yorkville Ave., 416-922-8164. Dresses and more.
- The Cashmere Shop, 24 Bellair St., 416-925-0831. Sweaters, scarves,

throws and blankets; you can have them customized, too. www.thecashmereshop.com

- Chanel Boutique, 131 Bloor St. W., 416-925-2577. Fragrances, shoes, clothes and leather bags.
- Gucci, 130 Bloor St. W., 416-963-5127. Internationally famous fashion retailer.
- Lileo, 55 Mill St. (Distillery District), 416-413-1410
- Nancy Moore for Motion Clothing Co., 106 Cumberland St., 416-968-0090. The Canadian designer's exclusive boutique.
- Over the Rainbow, 101 Yorkville Avenue, 416-967-7448 Designer Denim
- Petra Karthaus, Hazelton Lanes, 416-922-5922. Exclusive boutique. www.petrakarthaus.com
- Plaza Escada 110 Bloor St. W., 416-964-2265. Escada designer lines, including Couture, Elements, Laurèl and Escada Sport.
- Prada, 131 Bloor St. W. 416-513-0400. Clothing, shoes and accessories.
- TNT, 388 Eglinton W., 416-488-8210 as well as Hazelton Lanes, 416-975-1810

Medium Range and Casual Wear

- Banana Republic, 80 Bloor St. W., 416-515-0018; Toronto Eaton Centre, 416-595-6336. Another trendy chain featuring casual and office wear for young professionals; also carries accessories and shoes. www.bananarepublic.ca
- Casual Way, 2541 Yonge St., 416-481-1074
- Club Monaco, 157 Bloor St. W., 416-591-8837; 403 Queen St. W., 416-979-5633; Toronto Eaton Centre, 416-977-2064. Canadian company with trendy, fashionable clothing including suits, dresses, club and athletic wear.
- Daily Fraiche, 348 Queen St. W., 416-341-8606. Clean, European-styled innovative fashions.
- Eddie Bauer, Yorkdale Shopping Centre, 1 Yorkdale Rd., 416-783-2692. Offers jackets and corduroy

pants, as well as classic career wear.
- Esprit, Toronto Eaton Centre, 416-598-2776. Mid-priced clothing.
- Ewanika, 1083 Bathurst St., 416-927-9699. Modern clothing. www.ewanika.ca
- Fairweather, Yonge Eglinton Centre, 416-489-2631; Yorkdale Shopping Centre, 416-781-9105; other locations. Reasonably-priced workwear for young women who want to preserve a touch of funk; a good source for sweaters and T-shirts.
- Fresh Collective, 692 Queen St. W., 416-594-1313. Handmade clothes and accessories. www.freshcollective.com
- The Gap, 60 Bloor St. W., 416-921-2225; First Canadian Place, 416-777-1332; 375 Queen St. W., 416-591-3517; Toronto Eaton Centre, 416-599-8802. Trendy, well-made clothing in the younger line; T-shirts, khakis and cotton. www.gapcanada.ca
- Georgie Bolesworth, 913 Dundas St. W., 416-703-7625. Curvy women's fashions.
- Girl Friday, 740 Queen St. W., 416-364-2511; 776 College St., 416-531-1036. Unique clothing for women. www.girlfriday clothing.com
- H&M, 13-15 Bloor St. W., 416-920-4029; Toronto Eaton Centre, 416-593-0064; other locations. Cheap faddish finds from this popular European retailer. www.hm.com
- Jacob, 55 Bloor St. W., 416-925-9488; Yorkdale Mall, 416-785-3043 and other locations. www.jacob.ca
- Kaliyana Artwear, 2516 Yonge St., 416-480-2397, www.kaliyana.com
- lululemon, 342 Queen St. W., 416-703-1399; 130 Bloor St. W., 416-964-9544; and other locations. Trendy Canadian workout and yoga wear and accessories. www.lululemon.com
- Mendocino, 2647 Yonge St., 416-646-0812 and other locations
- Mango, Toronto Eaton Centre, 416-595-7130; Yorkdale Mall,

416-787-7957. Spanish clothing chain for young, urban women.
- Mink, 550 College St., 416-929-9214
- Mirabelli, 456 Eglinton Avenue W., 416-322-3130; Bayview Village, 416-781-9090, and other locations. www.mirabelli.com
- Nearly Naked, 920 Queen St. W., 416-588-7090. Attractive lingerie.
- Old Navy, Toronto Eaton Centre, 416-593-0065; Yorkdale Mall, 416-787-9384 and other locations. Affordable fashion for men, women and children. www.oldnavy.ca
- Posh Boutique, 2016 Queen St. E., 416-690-5533
- Set Me Free, 653 College St., 416-516-6493. Clothing and occasionally bicycles. www.setmefree.ca
- Skirt, 903 Dundas St. W., 647-436-3357
- Talbots, 2 Bloor St. W., 416-927-7194. Conservative women's clothing, reasonably priced.

Crafts and Hobbies
- Beadworks, 2154 Queen St. E., 416-693-0780, www.beadworksjo.com
- The Paper Place, 887 Queen St. W., 416-703-0089. Imported origami and handcrafted papers. www.thepaperplace.ca

Electronics
- Best Buy, 65 Dundas St. W., 416-642-8321, and other locations. National electronics superstore. www.bestbuy.ca
- Future Shop, 325 Yonge St., 416-971-5377; 2400 Yonge St., 416-489-4726 and other locations. National electronics superstore. www.futureshop.ca

Gourmet
- Chocolate and Creams, 207 Queen's Quay W., 416-368-6767
- Dufflet Pastries, 2638 Yonge St., 416-484-9080; 787 Queen St. W., 416-504-2870. Cakes and other sweet treats. www.dufflet.com
- Magnolia, 548 College St., 416-920-9927. High quality fresh foods and gourmet items.
- The Mercantile, 297 Roncesvalles Ave., 416-531-7563. Fine foods, mostly dry goods. www.themercantile.ca

Hats and Accessories
- Fresh Collective, 692 Queen St. W., 416-594-1313. Handmade clothes and accessories. www.freshcollective.com
- Lilliput Hats, 462 College St., 416-536-5933. Wonderful assortment of handmade hats; fairly pricey, but worth it. www.lilliputhats.com
- Prada, 131 Bloor St. W. 416-513-0400. Clothing, shoes and accessories.
- Wildhagen, 55 Mill St. (Distillery District), Case Goods Warehouse. Fine and fancy hats. wildhagenwear.com

Home Furnishings
- Art Shoppe, 2131 Yonge St., 416-487-3211. Upscale home furnishings in a wide range of styles. www.theartshoppe.com
- Constantine Interiors, 1110 Yonge St., 416-929-1177. Beautiful furnishings, mostly antique, as well as an eclectic assortment of home accessories; great Venetian overhead lamps, some fabrics; friendly service.
- Eye Spy, 1100 Queen St. E., 416-461-4061, www.eyespygifts.com
- Fluid Living, 35 Bathurst St., 416-850-4266
- High-Tech, 106 Front St. E., 416-861-1069. Modern kitchenware. www.hightechonline.ca
- Homefront, 371 Eglinton Ave. W., 416-488-3189
- Home Furnishings, 11 William Kitchen Rd., 416-293-3591 and other locations
- IKEA, 15 Provost Dr., 416-222-4532 and other locations. Sturdy, inventive, diverse and at the extreme end of the subway line.
- Morba, 667 Queen St. W., 416-364-5144
- Pier 1, 1986 Queen St. E., 416-698-3426 and other locations. Cheery housewares and dinnerware. www.pier1.ca

- Pottery Barn, 100 Bloor St. W., 416-962-2276; Toronto Eaton Centre, 416-597-0880; Yorkdale Shopping Centre, 416-785-1233. Contemporary home furnishings, décor and accents. www.potterybarn.com
- Restoration Hardware, 2434 Yonge St., 416-322-9422 and in Bayview Village, 416-223-2055. Upscale U.S. home furnishings chain. www.restorationhardware.com
- Ridpath's, 906 Yonge St., 416-920-4441. Another long-established Toronto quality furniture shop.
- Stylegarage, 938 Queen St. W., 416-534-4343. A mix of contemporary and antique furnishings. www.stylegarage.com
- Up Country, 310 King St. E., 416-366-7477. Comfortable couches, lamps and wooden furniture in a trendy industrial setting; personal items also. www.upcountry.com
- Urban Mode, 145 Tecumseth St., 416-591-8834. Hip modern furnishings. www.urbanmode.com
- Williams-Sonoma, Toronto Eaton Centre, 416-260-1255; Yorkdale Shopping Centre, 416-789-3261; 100 Bloor St. W., 416-962-9455; www.williams-sonoma.ca

Jewellery and Watches

- Birks, 55 Bloor St. W., 416-922-2266; Toronto Eaton Centre, 416-979-9311 and six other locations. Extensive, conservative collection of jewellery, silverware, crystal, watches and china.
- European Jewellery, Toronto Eaton Centre, 416-599-5440
- Experimetal, 742 Queen St. W., 416-363-4114. Unique jewellery.
- Fabrice, 55 Avenue Rd., 416-967-6590, www.fabricetoronto.com
- Gucci, 130 Bloor St. W., 416-963-5127. Internationally famous fashion retailer.
- Tiffany and Co., 85 Bloor St. W., 416-921-3900. The jewellery here includes collections by Elsa Peretti, Paloma Picasso and Jean Schlumberger; also diamonds, pearls, gold, silver and platinum. Watches, flatware, sterling silver, china, fragrances and even stationery. www.tiffany.ca

Leather

- Danier Leather, Toronto Eaton Centre, 416-598-1159; Yorkdale Shopping Centre, 416-783-9526 and other locations. In-house designs at reasonable prices from this Canadian chain.
- Hide House, 49 Eastern Ave., Acton, 519-853-1031. "Worth the drive to Acton."
- Perfect Leather Goods, 555 King St. W., 416-205-9775. A great place for leather, located in Toronto's old garment district.
- Roger Edwards Sport, 2811 Dufferin St., North York, 416-366-2501
- Roots, 100 Bloor Street W., 416-323-3289; Toronto Eaton Centre, 416-593-9640 and other locations. In addition to the trademark clothing and shoes, this Canadian company also produces jackets, handbags and luggage, plus a new line of leather furniture.

Malls

- Bayview Village Shopping Centre, 2901 Bayview Ave. at Sheppard, 416-226-0404. Almost 100 shops, restaurants and services, including Talbots, Havana Tobacconist, La Vie En Rose, Capezio Shoes and Rodier. www.bayviewvillageshops.com
- Eaton Centre, 220 Yonge St., 416-598-8560. The place visitors to Toronto visit first and most often, with over 320 shops, restaurants and services, under the protective wings of Michael Snow's geese.
- Hazelton Lanes, 55 Avenue Road, 416-968-8600. Over eighty unique boutiques and a few chain stores, with mid- to high-end shops for fashion and the home. Toronto's serious shopping zone. www.hazeltonlanes.com www.torontoeatoncentre.com
- Holt Renfrew Centre, 50 Bloor St. W., 416-922-2333. Over twenty-five shops, including HMV, Eddie Bauer,

Sunglass Hut and Science City, as well as unusual boutiques. www.holtrenfrewcentre.ca
- Manulife Centre, 55 Bloor St. W., 416-923-9525. Fifty upscale shops, including Indigo, William Ashley, Mephisto and an LCBO; a Thomas Cook Foreign Exchange is upstairs. www.manulifecentre.com
- Pacific Mall, 4300 Steeles Ave. E., Markham, 905-470-8785. North America's largest indoor Asian mall with over 400 stores is open year round including holidays. www.pacificmalltoronto.com
- Queen's Quay Terminal, 207 Queen's Quay W., 416-203-0510. A magnificent Deco terminal building on the waterfront, renovated to house specialty shops with a Canadian focus. Also features restaurants and special events.
- Sherway Gardens, 25 The West Mall, Etobicoke, 416-621-1070. Over fifty shops, including Holt Renfrew and Co., Eddie Bauer, Harry Rosen, Japan Camera and the Gap. www.sherwaygardens.ca
- Square One, 100 City Centre Dr., Mississauga, 905-279-7467. More than 360 stores featuring the Bay, MAC, Sears, Black's Camera and Merle Norman. www.shopsquareone.com
- Vaughan Mills, 1 Bass Pro Mills Dr., Vaughan, 905-879-2110. This 250-store mecca combines fashion, outlets, dining and entertainment. Many are the first of their kind in Canada. www.vaughanmills.shopping.ca
- Yorkdale Shopping Centre, Hwy. 401 and Allen Rd., 416-789-3261. Over 200 shops and services, including Benetton, Club Monaco, Harry Rosen, Holt Renfrew, Nine West, Roots, Tall Girl and La Senza Lingerie. www.yorkdale.com

Museum Shops
- Bata Shoe Museum, 327 Bloor St. W., 416-979-7799. Everything in this unique shop, from jewellery, scarves and umbrellas to books, has a shoe focus. www.batashoe museum.ca

- Fort York, 100 Garrison Rd. (off Fleet St.), 416-392-6907. A small shop dedicated to military books and reproductions from fifes to buttons, plus a selection of prints. You can visit the shop separately from the site, if you wish (but you probably won't; Fort York is an urban gem). www.fortyork.ca
- Gallery Shop, Art Gallery of Ontario, 317 Dundas St. W., 416-979-6648. A great shop with an extensive collection of Canadian and international art prints, plus cards, books, toys for children and grownups, and jewellery. www.ago.net/shop
- Gardiner Museum of Ceramic Art, 111 Queen's Park, 416-408-5066. A fine selection of contemporary Canadian ceramic art highlights this museum shop. www.gardinermuseum.on.ca
- Royal Ontario Museum, 100 Queen's Park Cres., 416-586-5549. Three shops, each with its own emphasis. The ROM Shop carries jewellery, objects d'art, distinctive cards and books; the ROM Reproduction Shop offers sculpture and jewellery inspired by the museum's collections; and the Museum Toy Shop, underground, contains a wide variety of inventive and educative toys. www.rom.on.ca
- Swipe Books on Advertising and Design, 401 Richmond St. W., 416-363-1332. Much more than books; cool setting, and the old Deco Exchange building is always worth a visit, not least for the reliefs outside. www.swipe.com

Music
- Capsule, 921 Queen St. W., 416-203-0202. Beautiful guitars and other instruments. www.capsulemusic.com
- HMV, 333 Yonge St., 416-596-0333; 50 Bloor St. W., 416-324-9979, and other locations. The flagship store on Yonge St. has four floors of music, videos and magazines.
- Rotate This, 801 Queen St. W., 416-504-8447. New and used CDs

and vinyl. www.rotate.com
- Song & Script, 2 Bloor St. W., 416-932-3044. Canada's foremost Broadway specialist; all categories of sheet music, songbooks, CDs and karaoke.
- Soundscapes, 572 College St., 416-537-1620. Wonderful and diverse selection of CDs. www.soundscapesmusic.com

Outfitters and Sports
- Europe Bound, 47 Front St. E., 416-601-1990. A worthy challenger to Mountain Equipment Co-op when both were on Front St. www.europebound.com
- lululemon, 342 Queen St. W., 416-703-1399; 130 Bloor St. W., 416-964-9544, and other locations. Trendy Canadian workout and yoga wear and accessories. www.lululemon.com
- Mountain Equipment Co-op, 400 King St. W., 416-340-2667. From tents and sleeping bags to cycling helmets and bike parts, Mountain Equipment Co-op is a leading supplier of outdoor gear and clothing.
- Sporting Life, 2665 Yonge St., 416-485-1611; Sherway Mall, 416-620-7750; and Sporting Life Bikes and Boards, 2454 Yonge St., 416-485-4440. An excellent all-round sports shop, but especially good if you cycle; also a great shoe selection. www.sportinglife.ca

Outlets
- Danier Leather Factory Outlet, 2650 St. Clair W., 416-762-8175. Quality leather and suede clothing for men and women; discounts of up to 70 per cent. www.danier.com
- Roots Canada Clearance Outlet, 120 Orfus Rd., 416-781-8729. Great bargains year round from Canada's retailing wunderstore.
- Tom's Place, 190 Baldwin St. (Kensington Market), 416-596-0297. Racks and racks of high quality business and casual clothing for men and women; don't forget to haggle. www.toms-place.com

Shoes
- Aldo Shoes, Toronto Eaton Centre, 416-597-3809, and various other locations
- B2, 399 Queen St. W., 416-595-9281, www.brownsshoes.com
- Browns, Toronto Eaton Centre, 416-979-9270; Sherway Gardens, 416-620-1910, other locations. Three in-house lines complement a good selection of fine footwear for men and women. www.brownsshoes.com
- Capezio, 70 Bloor St. W., 416-920-1006 and 218 Yonge St., 416-597-6662, other locations. Trendy, cutting-edge women's shoes by Guess, Steve Madden, Nine West, Unisa and others; also stocks belts, handbags and leather goods. www.capezioshoes.ca
- Corbo Boutique, 119 Yorkville Ave, 416-928-0954
- Davids, 66 Bloor St. W., 416-920-1000. Top designer shoes and accessories for men and women, including David's own line. Large selection of fashionable boots. www.davidsfootwear.com
- Get Outside, 437 Queen St. W., 416-593-5598
- Groovy, 323 Queen St. W., 416-595-1059. Hip running shoes.
- Gucci, 130 Bloor St. W., 416-963-5127. Internationally famous fashion retailer.
- Harry Rosen, 82 Bloor St. W., 416-972-0556. The upscale men's clothier also has a shoe salon upstairs.
- John Fluevog, 242 Queen St. W., 416-581-1420. Wild platform shoes, go-go boots and more. Not for the tame or weak of sole.
- Nine West, Toronto Eaton Centre, 220 Yonge St., 416-977-8126; First Canadian Place, King west of Bay, 416-368-0611; 93 Bloor St. W., 416-920-3519
- Prada, 131 Bloor St. W., 416-513-0400. Clothing, shoes and accessories.
- Town Shoes, 95 Bloor St. W., 416-928-5062; Toronto Eaton Centre,

220 Yonge St., 416-979-9914;
Toronto-Dominion Centre, 416-362-1921; St. Clair Centre,
416-967-4131, other locations.

Toys

- Disney Store, Toronto Eaton Centre, 416-591-5132; Yorkdale Mall, 416-782-3061
- Kol Kid, 670 Queen St. W., 416-681-0368
- Mastermind, 3350 Yonge St., 416-487-7177; 2134 Queen St. E., 416-699-3797, and other locations. A treasure-trove of educational toys, books, software, lego, arts and crafts. www.mastermindtoys.com
- The Toy Shop, 62 Cumberland St., 416-961-4870. Wonderful selection of children's toys, dolls, books, arts and crafts supplies, as well as other items. Great place to visit; lots of fun. www.thetoyshop.ca
- Toys R Us, 690 Evans Ave. (at Sherway Gardens), 416-621-8697, and other locations. The classic toy store. www.toysrus.ca

Weird and Wonderful

- Paper Things, 99 Yorkville Avenue, 416-922-3500, www.paperthings.ca

Sports

Pro Sports

- Canadian Squash Classic. John Bassett Theatre, Metro Toronto Convention Centre, 255 Front St. W.; individual tickets 416-585-3585, www.prosquash.ca
- Grand Prix Racing. 171 East Liberty St., Suite 207. Exhibition Place, Lakeshore Blvd.; information: 416-588-7223, tickets: 416-872-5000, www.grandprixtoronto.com
- Toronto Argonauts Football. See the CFL at its best. Rogers Centre, 1 Blue Jays Way; individual tickets: 416-872-5000, or 416-341-2746; www.argonauts.ca
- Toronto Blue Jays Baseball. Another season of exciting American League baseball. Rogers Centre, 1 Blue Jays Way; individual tickets: 416-872-5000; bluejays.mlb.com

- Toronto FC. Toronto's professional Major League Soccer club. BMO Field, Exhibition Place; 416-360-4625, web.mlsnet.com.
- Toronto Maple Leafs Hockey. Toronto's National Hockey League team. Air Canada Ctr., 40 Lower Bay St.; individual tickets: 416-872-5000, www.mapleleafs.nhl.com
- Toronto Marlies. American Hockey League team. Ricoh Coliseum, 100 Princes' Blvd., Exhibition Place; individual tickets: 416-872-5000, www.torontomarlies.com
- Toronto Raptors Basketball. See the Toronto Raptors hit the court. Air Canada Ctr., 40 Lower Bay St.; individual tickets: 416-872-5000, www.nba.com/raptors/
- Toronto Rock Lacrosse Club. Air Canada Ctr., 40 Lower Bay St.; individual tickets: 416-872-5000, www.torontorock.com
- Rogers Cup Tennis. Professional tennis tournament, alternating men's and women's series each year with Montreal. Rexall Centre, Pond Road, York University; tickets and information: 416-665-9777 or 1-877-283-6647, www.rogerscup.com
- Woodbine Racetrack. Home of the Queen's Plate, Breeders' Stakes race in Canada's Triple Crown Series, and several other thoroughbred and standardbred horseracing competitions, as well as harness racing. 555 Rexdale Blvd., 1-888-675-RACE, www.woodbineentertainment.com

Halls of Fame

- Canadian Motorsport Hall of Fame. Canada's leading collection of racing vehicles and motorsport history. 8220 Fifth Line, Halton Hills, 905-876-2454, www.cmhf.ca
- Canada's Sports Hall of Fame, 115 Princes' Blvd., Exhibition Place, 416-260-6789, www.sportshall.ca
- Hockey Hall of Fame. The ultimate tribute to Canada's beloved sport. Open year-round. Brookfield Place, 30 Yonge St. (formerly BCE Place), 416-360-7765, www.hhof.com

Fishing

- Albion Hills Conservation Area, 16500 Hwy. 50, Caledon, 905-880-0227, www.trca.on.ca
- Canadian Trophy Fishing. Fishing and sightseeing charters on 27- or 40-foot craft. Bluffers Park (east of Toronto Harbour), Scarborough, 416-540-0839, www.cdntrophyfishing.com
- Klancy's Fishing Charters. Try Klancy's for fishing or a lazy afternoon cruise. 480 Queen's Quay W., Suite 1001, 416-866-8489.

Golf

- Dentonia Golf Course. Par 3 facility ideal for beginners and advanced players alike. 781 Victoria Park, 416-392-2558, www.toronto.ca/parks/golf
- Don Valley Golf Course, 4200 Yonge St., south of Hwy. 401, 416-392-2465, www.toronto.ca/parks/golf
- Glen Abbey Golf Club. Home of the Royal Canadian Golf Association and public 18 hole championship layout. 1333 Dorval Dr., Oakville, 905-844-1800, www.glenabbey.ca
- Humber Valley Golf Course. Moderately difficult par 70 golf course. 40 Beattie Ave., 416-392-2488, www.toronto.ca/parks/golf
- Scarlett Woods Golf Course, 1000 Jane St., 416-392-2484, www.toronto.ca/parks/golf

Recreation

- Harbourfront Canoe and Kayak Centre. Canoe and kayak lessons and rentals. 283A Queen's Quay W., 416-203-2277, www.paddletoronto.com
- Ice skating. Various locations, including at Harbourfront's Natrel rink (see Harbourfront), city parks and Nathan Phillips Square in front of City Hall, where rentals are available, 416-338-7465, www.toronto.ca
- Playdium. Canada's first physical and interactive entertainment centre. Open daily. Twenty minutes west of downtown, in Mississauga. 99 Rathburn Road West, 905-273-9000, www.playdium.com

- ProKart Indoor Raceway. Paved indoor kart-racing facility. Must have a valid driver's licence. 120 North Queen St., 416-236-5278
- Toronto Island Bicycle Rental. Regular bikes, tandems, two-seaters and four-seaters available for island exploration. Centre Island, 416-203-0009

Festivals and Events

All winter

- Harbourfront Centre's Skating Rink. Outdoor skating, skate rentals, change rooms, rental lockers and skate-sharpening. Open daily, 10–10. The Rink at Harbourfront, York Quay Centre, 235 Queen's Quay W., 416-973-3000

November

- The Hobby Show. The International Centre, 6900 Airport Rd., www.thehobbyshow.com
- Royal Agricultural Winter Fair. Featuring the Agricultural Show, the Royal Horse Show, and the Winter Garden Show among other attractions. Direct Energy Centre, Exhibition Place; 416-263-3400, www.royalfair.org
- Santa Claus Parade. This crowd-pleasing parade takes place the third Sunday in November each year. 416-249-7833

All of December

- Allan Gardens Victorian Christmas Flower Show. A display of seasonal Christmas plants. Allan Gardens Conservatory, 19 Horticultural Ave., 416-392-7288
- The Nutcracker. National Ballet of Canada at the Sony Centre for the Performing Arts, 416-345-9595, www.national.ballet.ca
- Tafelmusik's Sing Along Messiah, 416-964-6337

Mid-December

- Cavalcade of Lights Christmas Carol Concert. Features Toronto's finest choirs, including the Toronto

Mendelssohn Choir. Rotunda, Toronto City Hall, Queen and Bay streets. Events Hotline: 416-395-0490

- The Christmas Story. Mimed story of the nativity with narration, organ music and carols. Christmas Eve. Church of the Holy Trinity, Trinity Square (behind Toronto Eaton Centre), 416-589-4521

New Year's Eve

- Cavalcade of Lights New Year's Eve Celebration. Toronto's alcohol-free New Year's party. Nathan Phillips Square, Toronto City Hall, Queen and Bay Streets. Events Hotline: 416-395-0490
- First Night. An alcohol-free New Year's Eve celebration for all ages with theatre, dance, musical and visual-arts performances, People's Parade and Imagination Market. Multiple locations along Front St., between John St. and Jarvis St.; 416-395-0490

Mid-January

- Toronto International Boat Show. Direct Energy Centre, Exhibition Place, www.torontoboatshow.com

February

- Canadian International Auto Show. Canada's premier automotive showcase. Metro Toronto Convention Centre, 255 Front St. W., 905-940-2800
- Cavalcade of Lights Canadian Flag Day. A salute to our nation's flag. Nathan Phillips Square, Toronto City Hall, Queen and Bay streets.; Events Hotline: 416-395-0490
- Cottage Show. West Annex Bldgs., Exhibition Place, 416-393-6000
- Psychics, Mystics and Seers' Fair. Queen Elizabeth Bldg., Exhibition Place, 416-461-5306
- Toronto Festival of Storytelling. Storytelling, workshops, evening concerts and free afternoon storytelling; over seventy storytellers from Canada and beyond. York Quay Centre, Harbourfront Centre, 416-656-2445

Mid-March

- Canada Blooms. Direct Energy Centre, 416-447-8655, www.canadablooms.com
- International Home and Garden Show. The International Centre, 6900 Airport Rd., 416-512-1305, www.home-show.net
- Toronto International Bicycle Show. Better Living Centre, Exhibition Place, 416-363-1292, www.bicycleshowtoronto.com
- Toronto Sportsmen's Show. Metro Toronto Convention Centre, 905-361-2677, www.torontosportshow.ca

Late March

- National Motorcycle Swap Meet and Bike Show. A retail motorcycle and custom bike show. Better Living Centre, Exhibition Place, 705-778-2275
- One of a Kind Spring Canadian Craft Show and Sale. Direct Energy Centre, Exhibition Place, 416-960-3680

Early April

- National Home Show/National Kitchen and Bath Showcase. Direct Energy Centre, Exhibition Place, 416-263-3000

Mid-April

- Creative Sewing and Needlework Festival. National Trade Centre, Exhibition Place, 905-709-0100
- International Spring Bike Show. International Centre, 6900 Airport Rd., 416-674-4636
- Postage Stamp Show. Queen Elizabeth Exhibit Hall, Exhibition Place, 416-393-6000

Late April

- Old Clothing Show and Sale. Better Living Centre, Exhibition Place, Lakeshore Blvd. W., 416-393-6000
- Travel and Leisure Show. Metro Toronto Convention Centre, 6900 Airport Rd., 416-674-4636

May

- Victoria Day Fireworks. Celebrate Victoria Day while witnessing an exciting fireworks presentation.

Paramount Canada's Wonderland, 9580 Jane St., 905-832-8131
- Victoria Day Musical Fireworks. Celebrate the Queen's birthday and witness an exciting fireworks extravaganza put to music. Ontario Place, 955 Lakeshore Blvd. W., 416-314-9990

Early May
- Cabbagetown's Forsythia Festival in Riverdale Park W.; 416-921-0857
- The Good Food Festival. International Centre, 6900 Airport Rd., 905-677-6131
- Hot Docs Canadian International Documentary Festival. Showcasing the best in documentary film and television. 416-637-5150

Early June
- Toronto Aviation and Aircraft Show. Canadian Airline Hangar, Pearson International Airport, 1-800-776-5976, www.canadianaviationexpo.com

All of June
- Milk International Children's Festival. North America's largest performing arts festival for the whole family. Performers from around the world, as well as right here in Canada. For seven days visitors can see the very best the world has to offer in theatre, dance, music, visual arts, storytelling, physical comedy and puppetry for young audiences. Harbourfront Centre, 416-973-3000

Mid-to-late June
- Bloom in the Beaches. A literary festival. Various venues. 416-365-7877, www.pathcom.com
- Downtown Jazz Festival. Featuring high-profile international and Canadian jazz favourites. Various venues. Information: 416-928-2033; Tickets: 416-870-8000. www.torontojazz.com
- North by Northeast. Enjoy up-and-coming rock bands over a three-day festival. June 16–20, 2010. Various venues. 416-863-6963, www.nxne.com

- Pride Week-Toronto. The largest Lesbian and Gay Pride event in North America. Church and Wellesley neighbourhood. 65 Wellesley St. E, Suite 501, 416-927-7433, www.pridetoronto.com
- Queen's Plate. The running of this internationally renowned race. Woodbine Racetrack, 555 Rexdale Blvd., 416-675-7223 or 416-675-6110
- Toronto International Dragon Boat Race Festival. Dragon boat racing and multicultural performances on the Toronto Islands. 416-595-0313, www.torontodragonboat.com
- Toronto Worldwide Short Film Festival, 416-445-1446, ext. 815, www.worldwideshortfilmfest.com

July
- Grand Prix of Toronto. Features the superstars of Champ Car racing. Exhibition Place, Lakeshore Blvd. Tickets: 416-870-8000, www.grandprixtoronto.com
- Toronto Outdoor Art Exhibition. This free outdoor exhibit showcases the original paintings, ceramics, jewellery, sculpture and mixed-media creations of talented Canadian and international artists. July 9–11, 2010. Nathan Phillips Square, 100 Queen St. W., 416-408-2754, www.torontooutdoorart.org

Late July
- Beaches International Jazz Festival. This popular jazz street fest features over forty bands performing everything from calypso, to Latin, fusion and steel drum nightly on selected street corners, balconies and parks. Queen St. E., between Woodbine Ave. and Victoria Park Ave.; 416-698-2152, www.beachesjazz.com
- CHIN Picnic, Exhibition Place, 416-531-9991, www.chinradio.com
- Fireworks, Ontario Place, 955 Lakeshore Blvd. W. June 27–July 4, 2010. Information: 416-314-9900; tickets: 416-870-8000, www.ontarioplace.com
- Toronto Fringe Theatre Festival.

June 30–July 11, 2010. Ten days of theatre in the Annex area (near Bloor and Spadina). 416-966-1062, www.fringetoronto.com

August

- Caribana. A two-week celebration attracting more than one million people, capped with a parade. Various venues; July 14–Aug. 2, 2010, www.caribanatoronto.com
- Circle Ball Fair. A ten-day fair with busker competitions, 416-929-5566
- Fringe Festival of Independent Dance Artists. Various indoor and outdoor sites. July 1–11, 2010, www.torontodance.com
- Rogers AT&T Cup. New box seating and upper stand seating available. National Tennis Centre, York University, Aug. 9–15, 2010. Ticket info: 1-800-398-8761, www.tenniscanada.com
- SummerWorks. Ten days of theatre. Various venues. 416-504-7529, www.summerworks.ca

Mid-August to Labour Day

- Canadian National Exhibition. The largest annual fair in Canada. Featuring midway rides, display buildings, top-name concert performers, roving entertainers, live music and much more. Exhibition Place, Lakeshore Blvd. W., 416-393-6300, www.theex.com

Fall

- Bell Canadian Open. St. George's Golf & Country Club, 1-800-571-6736
- International Festival of Authors. The world's largest literary festival. Harbourfront Centre, 235 Queen's Quay W., 416-973-4760
- Made in Canada Festival of Canadian Music. 416-593-7769, ext. 335
- Toronto International Film Festival. Sept. 9–18, 2010, 416-968-3456, www.bell.ca/filmfest
- Word on the Street. Open-air book and magazine festival celebrating literacy and the printed word. Queen St. W. between Spadina Ave.

and Simcoe St. 416-504-7241, www.thewordonthestreet.ca/wots/toronto

Day Trips

- Bruce Trail Association, 905-529-6821 or 1-800-665-4453, www.brucetrail.org
- Butterfly Conservatory at the Niagara Parks Botanical Gardens, www.niagaraparks.com
- Crawford Lake Conservation Area. May through October. At Steeles Ave. and Guelph Line, 905-847-7430, www.conservationhalton.on.ca
- Elora Festival. July/August. P.O. Box 370, Elora ON N0B 1S0, 519-846-0331, Fax: 519-846-5947, info@elorafestival.com, www.elorafestival.com
- Fort George, Niagara-on-the-Lake. A recreated British garrison. Open Apr. 1–Oct. 31; 905-468-4257
- Kortright Centre for Conservation, 9550 Pine Valley Dr., Woodbridge; daily 10–4; 905-832-2289, www.kortright.org
- Maid of the Mist, Niagara Falls, 905-358-5781, www.maidofthemist.com
- Marineland Theme Park, open May 22–Oct. 10, 2010, 7657 Portage Rd., Niagara Falls, 905-356-9565, www.marinelandcanada.com
- The McMichael Canadian Collection, 10365 Islington Ave., Kleinburg, 1-888-213-1121, 905-893-1121, www.mcmichael.on.ca
- Niagara Parks Botanical Gardens and School of Horticulture, on the Niagara Parkway, 9 km north of Niagara Falls. 905-356-2241 (Niagara Parks) or 1-877-642-7275
- Niagara Wine Festival. A ten-day celebration of the grape harvest, featuring winery tours, concerts and parades. 905-688-0212, www.niagarawinefestival.com
- Presqu'ile Provincial Park. Off the 401, 155 km east of Toronto, 613 475-4324, www.ontarioparks.com
- Shaw Festival, Niagara-on-the-Lake; Apr. 1–Oct. 31, 2010, 1-800-511-7429,

www.shawfest.com
- South Simcoe Railway, Tottenham, www.steamtrain.com
- St. Jacobs Farmers' Market and Flea Market. In the heart of Mennonite country. markets@stjacobs.com, www.stjacobs.com
- Stratford Festival, Stratford, 416-363-4471 or 1-800-567-1600, Fax: 519-273-6173, orders@stratfordshakespearefestival.com, www.stratfordfestival.ca

Gay Toronto

Festivals and Events
- Fashion Cares. Toronto's high-fashion, star-studded spring fundraiser for the fight against AIDS. Distillery District, 416-340 2437, www.fashioncares.com
- Halloweek. A week-long series of Halloween-themed events highlighting costumes and dressing up. Includes events for children. Church and Wellesley neighbourhood, 416-393-6363, www.halloweek.ca
- Inside Out Lesbian and Gay Film and Video Festival. Canada's largest queer film festival, featuring productions by, or about, gay, lesbian, bisexual and transgendered people. 401 Richmond St. W., Suite 219, 417 977-6847, www.insideout.on.ca
- Pride Week (Pride Committee of Toronto). The largest gay and lesbian pride event in North America, culminating with the Pride Parade at the end of June. Church and Wellesley neighbourhood, 14 Dundonald St., 416-927-7433, www.pridetoronto.com
- Rhubarb Festival, Buddies in Bad Times Theatre. Two weeks of new, queer-themed short plays, performances and installations performed in repertory. 12 Alexander St., 416-975-8555, www.artsexy.ca

Theatres and Community Institutions
- 519 Church Street Community Centre. Meeting place and community centre with events and social programming. 519 Church, 416-392-6874, www.the519.org
- Buddies in Bad Times. North America's largest gay and lesbian theatre company, dedicated to promoting queer expression. 12 Alexander St., 416-977-8555, www.artsexy.ca
- Canadian Lesbian and Gay Archives. Open 7:30–10:00 p.m. Tues.–Thurs. Closed August. 34 Isabella St., 416-777-2755, www.clga.ca
- Metropolitan Community Church. Gay-positive congregation and community hub. 115 Simpson Ave., 416-406-6228, www.mcctoronto.com
- Tallulah's Cabaret Theatre. Cabaret space and late night club. Part of Buddies in Bad Times, 12 Alexander St., 416-977-8555, www.artsexy.ca

Bars, Restaurants and Clubs
- The Barn/Stables, 418 Church St., 416-977-4702
- Beaver Café, 1192 Queen St. W., 416-536-2768
- Black Eagle, 457 Church St., 416-413-1219
- Bulldog Coffee. 89 Granby St., 416-923-3469
- Byzantium, 499 Church St., 416-922-3859
- Cadillac Lounge, 1296 Queen St. W., 416-536-7717
- Churchmouse and Firkin – see dining info
- Crews, 508 Church St., 416-972-6145
- Drake Hotel, 1150 Queen St. W., 416-531-5042, 1–866-372-5386
- El Convento Rico, 756 College, 416-588-7800
- Fly Nightclub, 8 Gloucester St., 416-410-5426
- Fuzion, 580 Church St., 416-944-9888

- Gladstone Hotel, 1214 Queen St. W., 416-531-4635
- Hair of the Dog, 425 Church St., 416-964-2708
- Il Fornello, 491 Church St., 416-944-9052
- Lo'la Martini Lounge, 7 Maitland Ave., 416-920-0946
- Mezzrow's, 1546 Queen St. W., 416-535-4906
- Mitzi's Sister, 1554 Queen St. W., 416-532-2570
- O'Grady's, 518 Church St., 416-323-3822
- The Rhino, 1249 Queen St. W., 416-535-8089
- The Rivoli, 334 Queen St. W., 416-596-1908
- Stone's Place, 1255 Queen St. W., 416-536-4242
- Village Rainbow Restaurant, 477 Church St., 416-961-0616
- Woody's/Sailor, 465-67 Church St., 416-972-0887
- Zelda's, 542 Church St., 416-922-2526

Lesbian
- Tango, 508 Church St., 416-972-6145

Shopping
- Come As You Are, 701 Queen St. W., 416-504-7934. Friendly and helpful erotic boutique. www.comeasyouare.com
- Glad Day Bookshop, 598A Yonge St., 416-961-4161. Gay and lesbian literature, videos and periodicals. www.gladdaybookshop.com
- Good For Her, 175 Harbord St., 416-588-0900. Sex toys, education, art, workshops for women and their admirers. www.goodforher.com
- Priape, 501 Church St., 416-586-9914. Sex shop for the gay audience. www.priape.com
- This Ain't the Rosedale Library, 86 Nassau St., 416-929-9912. A great store for fiction in the heart of the Kensington Market community. www.thisaint.ca

NIAGARA

Getting There

Niagara is usually described as the part of the province south of Toronto across Lake Ontario, bounded by Lake Ontario to the north, the Niagara River (U.S. border) to the east, the eastern city limits of Hamilton to the West, and Lake Erie in the south. See the map on page 144 for an overview of the area.

By Road
If you're coming to Niagara from the Toronto region, the Queen Elizabeth Way (QEW) is your quickest route, accessible by the Gardiner Expressway or Hwy. 401 (via either highways 403 or 427).

For visitors from New York State, the points of entry on the Canadian side are Queenston, Niagara Falls and Fort Erie.

Visitors from Michigan can cross over to Hwy. 402 at Sarnia or the 401 at Windsor.

Greyhound Canada is the most comprehensive bus line serving Niagara. Greyhound can be contacted for fares and information at 1-800-361-1235.

By Rail
Niagara is served by VIA Rail. For general information and reservations call 1-888-842-7245.

By Air
The largest airport close to Niagara is the Lester B. Pearson International Airport in Toronto. Located in the northwestern corner of Metro Toronto, the airport is accessible from Highways 401, 427 and 409. For information on Terminal 1, call 416-247-7678; for Terminal 3, call 416-776-5100, www.gtaa.com. There are also smaller international airports in Hamilton and Buffalo, NY:
- Hamilton International Airport, Airport Rd., Mount Hope, ON, 905-679-1999, www.flyhi.ca

- Buffalo International Airport, 4200 Genesee St., Cheektowaga, NY, 716-630-6000, www.buffaloairport.com

Ontario Travel Information Centres

Ontario Travel Information Centres are operated by the Ministry of Economic Development, Trade and Tourism; they provide tourist information on every aspect of Ontario, and are open daily. Call 1-800-ONTARIO to check for extended hours in summer.

Fort Erie
- 350 Bertie St. (near the Peace Bridge), 905-871-3505, Fax: 905-871-6461

Niagara Falls
- 5355 Stanley Ave. (West on Hwy. 420 from the Rainbow Bridge), 905-358-3221, Fax: 905-358-6441

St. Catharines
- QEW at Garden City Skyway., 905-684-6354, Fax: 905-684-3634

Sarnia
- Bluewater Bridge, 1455 Venetian Blvd., 519-344-7403, Fax: 519-332-4576

Windsor
- 1235 Huron Church Rd. (East of the Ambassador Bridge), 519-973-1310, Fax: 519-973-1313
- 110 Park St. East (Windsor-Detroit tunnel), 519-973-1338, Fax: 519-973-1341

Accommodation

What follows is a good cross-section of the accommodation options in Niagara. We have given preference to fine, independently run inns, where they exist. Failing these, we have found the best in chain hotels and motels for value and service.

Price alone has never been a factor in making our selections. Approximate prices are indicated, based on the average cost, at the time of publishing, for two persons staying in a double room (excluding taxes): $ = $50–$90; $$ = $90–$180; $$$ = above $180.

The accommodation and travel associations listed below also provide guides to their respective regions, either in print format or on the Internet. The Ontario South Central Trip Planner, available from any Ontario Travel Information Centre (1-800-ONTARIO), also has accommodation listings for each town or city of note.

Accommodation and Travel Associations
- Ontario Accommodation Association, #2, 347 Pido Rd., RR#6, Peterborough ON K9J 6X7, 705-745-4982, Toll Free: 1-800-461-1972, Fax: 705-745-4983, info@ontarioaccommodation.com, www.ontarioaccommodation.com
- Ontario Tourism (general information): 1-800-668-2746

Jordan
- The Vintner's Inn, 3845 Main St., Jordan, ON L0R 1S0, 905-562-5336, Toll Free: 1-800-701-8074, Fax: 905-562-0009. Home of the elegant On the Twenty restaurant, and across the street from Cave Spring Cellars. www.innonthetwenty.com, $$–$$$

Niagara Falls
- Crowne Plaza Hotel, 5685 Falls Ave., Niagara Falls, ON L2E 6W7, 905-374-4444, Toll Free: 1-800-263-7135, Fax: 905-358-0443. Grand old 1929 hotel overlooking the falls with fitness facilities and good public areas. www.niagarafallscrowneplazahotel.com, $$–$$$
- Michael's Inn-By-the-Falls, 5599 River Rd., Niagara Falls, ON L2E 3H3, 905-354-2727, Toll Free:1-800-263-9390, Fax: 905-374-7706. 130-room motor inn overlooking the falls, just north of the Rainbow Bridge. www.michaelsinn.com, $–$$

Niagara-on-the-Lake

- The Charles Inn, 209 Queen St., Niagara-on-the-Lake, ON L0S 1J0, 905-468-4588, Toll Free: 1-866-556-8883. 1832 Georgian-style home within walking distance of the Shaw Festival, with twelve guest rooms. www.charlesinn.ca, $$
- Moffat Inn, 60 Picton St., Niagara-on-the-Lake, ON L0S 1J0, 905-468-4116. Historic country inn with dining facilities. www.moffatinn.com, $$
- Oban Inn & Spa, 160 Front St., P.O. Box 94 Niagara-on-the-Lake, ON L0S 1J0, 905-468-2165, Toll Free: 1-866-359-6226, Fax: 905-468-4165. 26 tranquil, luxurious guest rooms, a spa and home to Restaurant Tony de Luca. www.obaninn.ca
- The Pillar & Post Inn, 48 John St., PO Box 1011, Niagara-on-the-Lake, ON L0S 1J0, 905-468-2123, Toll Free: 1-888-669-5566, Fax: 905-468-3551. 123 well-furnished rooms, spa facilities and Vintages Wine Bar and Lounge. www.vintage-hotels.com/niagara-on-the-lake, $$–$$$
- The Prince of Wales Hotel, 6 Picton St., Niagara-on-the-Lake, ON L0S 1J0, 905-468-3246, Toll Free: 1-888-669-5566, Fax: 905-468-5521. Distinguished 1864 hotel with well-appointed rooms, Prince of Wales dining room and saunas. www.vintage-hotels.com/niagara-on-the-lake, $$–$$$
- Queen's Landing Inn, 155 Byron St., PO Box 1180, Niagara-on-the-Lake, ON L0S 1J0, 905-468-2195, Toll Free: 1-888-669-5566, Fax: 905-468-2227. Spacious rooms, saunas, whirlpool and a marina go toward earning this inn a Four Diamond Award from the CAA. www.vintage-hotels.com/niagara-on-the-lake, $$$
- White Oaks Conference Resort and Spa, 253 Taylor Rd., RR #4, Niagara-on-the-Lake, ON L0S 1J0, 905-688-2550, Toll Free: 1-800-263-5766. Niagara's only 4 Diamond, 5 Star conference resort and spa. www.whiteoaksresort.com, $$

Art Galleries and Studios

Though not so thickly clustered as in the major urban center of Toronto, art galleries in Niagara are varied and unique, sometimes centering on a single, celebrated artist. The galleries below are all worth a visit.

General Information

- Ontario Association of Art Galleries (OAAG), #617, 111 Peter St., Toronto ON M5V 2H1, 416-598-0714, Fax: 416-598-4128, www.oaag.org

Galleries

- Art Gallery of Hamilton, 123 King St. W., Hamilton ON L8P 4S8, 905-527-6610, Fax: 905-577-6940, www.artgalleryofhamilton.com
- Gallery/Stratford, 54 Romeo St., Stratford ON N5A 4S9, 519-271-5271, Fax: 519-271-1642, www.gallerystratford.on.ca
- McMaster Museum of Art, 1280 Main St. W., Hamilton ON L8S 4L8, 905-525-9140, www.mcmaster.ca/museum/
- Romance Collection Gallery, 177 King St. Niagara-on-the-Lake ON L0S 1J0, 1-800-667-8525, www.romancecollection.com

Dining

Niagara boasts some of the finest restaurants in Canada. We have tried to give as broad a sampling as possible, concentrating on establishments that reflect the individual flair of the presiding chef.

The listings below are broken into the regions outlined in the "Food and Dining" chapter in the main body of the Colourguide. Within each region, individual restaurants are then listed alphabetically by city. We advise calling ahead to make reservations for most of them.

Approximate prices are indicated, based on the average cost, at time of publication, of dinner for two, including wine (where available), taxes, and gratuity: $ = under $45; $$ = $45–$80; $$$ = $80–$120; $$$$ = over $120. Meals served are indicated as B = breakfast; L = lunch; D = dinner.

Beamsville

- Restaurant at Peninsula Ridge Estates, 5600 King St. W., PO Box 550, Beamsville ON L0R 1B0, 905-563-0900. Summer patio. Open Wed.–Sun. from 11:30 a.m.; Sunday brunch 11–3. L/D
- Angels Gate Winery Terrace, 4260 Mountainview Rd., Beamsville ON L0R 1B2, 905-563-3942, Toll Free: 1-877-ANG-GATE. Lunch in summer. L

Jordan

- On The Twenty, at Cave Spring Cellars, 3845 Main St., Jordan ON L0R 1S0, 905-562-7313. Fine regional cuisine using local produce. The restaurant is housed in an old winery facing Twenty Mile Creek. L/D, $$$$

Niagara Falls

- Whirlpool Clubhouse Restaurant and Lounge, 3351 Niagara Parkway, Niagara Falls ON, 905-356-7221. Panoramic view of the greens and the tree-lined Niagara Parkway. Open during golf season. L/D
- Wolfgang Puck, 6300 Fallsview Blvd., Niagara Falls ON L2G 2J3, 905-354-5000. L/D

Niagara-on-the-Lake

- Carriages & Cannery Dining Rooms, King St. at John St., PO Box 1011, Niagara-on-the-Lake ON L0S 1J0, 905-468-2123, Toll Free: 1-888-669-5566, Fax: 905-468-3551. This is the restaurant for the luxurious Pillar and Post Inn, and it offers exceptional fresh market cuisine, including full country breakfasts and buffets. B/L/D, $$$$
- Charles Inn Dining Room, PO Box 642, 209 Queen St., Niagara-on-the-Lake ON L0S 1J0, 905-468-4588,

Toll Free: 1-866-556-8883. A relaxed elegant setting; afternoon tea; tasting menu. Open daily. B/L/D
- The Epicurean, 84 Queen St., Niagara-on-the-Lake ON L0S 1J0, 905-468-3408. This café features provençal décor and Mediterranean influences. Chef Ruth Aspinall's specialties include wild mushroom lasagne and a variety of focaccia made on the premises. Live jazz can be heard Thursday through Saturday evening. L/D, $$
- Escabeche, at the Prince of Wales Hotel, 6 Picton St., Niagara-on-the-Lake ON L0S 1J0, 905-468-3246, Toll Free: 1-888-669-5566, Fax: 905-468-5521. Dishes steeped in the traditions of France and England. L/D
- Hillebrand Vineyard Café, 1249 Niagara Stone Rd., Niagara-on-the-Lake L0S 1J0, 905-468-7123, Toll Free: 1-800-582-8412, Fax: 905-468-4789. Offers a wide range of wine country cuisine using local ingredients. Open daily for lunch from 12:00 p.m. and dinner from 5:00 p.m. Reservations are recommended. L/D, $$$
- Little Red Rooster Restaurant, 271 Mary, Niagara-on-the-Lake ON L0S 1J0, 905-468-3072. Light and casual fare. L/D
- LIV Restaurant, at White Oaks Conference Resort and Spa, 253 Taylor Rd., RR #4, Niagara-on-the-Lake ON L0S 1J0, 905-688-2550, Toll Free: 1-800-263-5766. Niagara's only concept restaurant and winner of the 2004 Fetzer Award and the VQA Restaurant Award of Excellence.
- Niagara Culinary Institute Dining Room, NOTL Campus, Niagara College, 135 Taylor Rd., Niagara-on-the-Lake ON L0S 1J0, 905-735-2211. "The culinary stars of tomorrow are cooking in our kitchens today." Lunch Tues.–Sun. 11:30–2; dinner Wed.–Fri. 5–9, Sat. 5–9:30. L/D
- Peller Estates Winery Restaurant, 290 John St. E., Niagara-on-the-Lake ON L0S 1J0, 905-468-4678, Toll Free: 1-888-673-5537. Open

daily for lunch from 12:00 p.m. and dinner Sunday through Friday from 5:30 p.m. and Saturday from 5:00 p.m. L/D

- Queenston Heights Restaurant, 14184 Niagara Parkway, Niagara-on-the-Lake, ON L0S 1J0, 905-262-4274. Overlooking a historic battlefield. Afternoon tea; Sunday brunch. L/D
- Restaurant Tony de Luca, at the Oban Inn & Spa, 160 Front St., P.O. Box 94 Niagara-on-the-Lake, ON L0S 1J0, 905-468-7900, Toll Free: 1-866-394-7900. Cuisine that celebrates the integrity of Niagara and Canadian products. B/L/D
- Ristorante Giardino, Gate House Hotel, 142 Queen St., Niagara-on-the-Lake L0S 1J0, 905-468-3263. Especially good for lunch, where fish or veal are favourites. L/D, $$$, www.gatehouse-niagara.com
- Riverbend Inn & Vineyard, 16104 Niagara River Pkwy, PO Box 1560, Niagara-on-the-Lake ON L0S 1J0, 905-468-8866, Toll Free: 1-888-955-5553. An authentic 1890s salon bar, flanked by marble pillars. B/L/D, www.riverbendinn.ca
- Shaw Café & Wine Bar, 92 Queen St., Niagara-on-the-Lake ON L0S 1J0, 905-468-4772. Elegant, light fare and a stunning patio. L/D, www.shawcafe.ca
- Stagecoach Family Restaurant, 45 Queen St., Niagara-on-the-Lake ON L0S 1J0, 905-468-3133. A charming burger and fries joint for over twenty-five years. B/L/D, $
- Stone Road Grille, 238 Mary Street at Mississauga in the Garrison Plaza, Niagara-on-the-Lake ON L0S 1J0, 905-468-3474. Closed Mondays in winter. Lunch: Tues.–Fri., 11:30–2; dinner: 5–10ish. L/D, $$$, www.stoneroadgrille.com
- Tetley's, 60 Picton, Niagara-on-the-Lake ON L0S 1J0, 905-468-4641. Stone grilling, fonduing and conventional plated dinners. Lunch: 11:30–4; dinner from 5:00 p.m. L/D

- Terroir La Cachette, at Strewn Estate Winery, 1339 Lakeshore Road, RR #3, Niagara-on-the-Lake ON L0S 1J0, 905-468-1222. May to November: open daily, lunch from 11:30 a.m., dinner from 5:00 p.m.; November to April: closed Monday and Tuesday. L/D, www.lacachette.com
- Theatre Deli & Gourmet Shoppe, 29 Queen St., Niagara-on-the-Lake ON L0S 1J0, 905-468-0197. A dine-in restaurant or as take-out/supplies for a picnic.
- Tiara Restaurant at the Queen's Landing Inn, 155 Byron St., PO Box 1180, Niagara-on-the-Lake L0S 1J0, 905-468-2195, Toll Free: 1-888-669-5566, Fax: 905-468-2227. A team of award-winning chefs serve up an eclectic and well-presented cuisine. Try the foie gras with Niagara peach preserve. B/L/D, $$$$
- Zee's Patio & Grill at the Shaw Club Hotel & Spa, P.O. Box 642, 92 Picton St., Niagara-on-the-Lake, ON L0S 1J0, 905-468-5715. Lunch: 11:30–2:30; dinner 5–9 daily. L/D, $$$$, www.zees.ca

St. Catharines / Thorold

- Bansaree, 342 St. Paul St., St. Catharines ON L2R 3N2, 905-684-3411. Great Indian food from a clay oven. L/D, $$
- The Blue Mermaid, 10 Market Square, St. Catharines ON L2R 5C6, 905-684-7465. Steak and seafood for over twenty-five years. Closed Sun.; lunch Mon.–Fri. L/D, www.thebluemermaid.com
- Coach House Café and Cheese Shoppe, at Henry of Pelham Family Estate Winery, 1469 Pelham Rd., RR.#1, St. Catharines ON L2R 6P7, 905-684-8423. Open late May to early October, daily, 11:30–5. L, www.henryofpelham.com
- Keefer Mansion Inn, 14 St. Davids St. W., Thorold ON L2V 2K9, 905-680-9581, Toll-Free: 1-866-680-9581. Honouring the early French roots of the Keefer

family, the kitchen offers the very best in local cuisine. L/D, www.keefermansion.com
- Marie's Seafood Dining Room, 1 Lock Street, St Catharines ON L2N 5B4, 905-934-1677
- Treadwell Farm to Table Cuisine, 61 Lakeport Rd., St. Catharines ON L2N 4P6, 905-934-9797. Overlooking the site of the original 1829 Welland Canal, Stephen Treadwell offers seasonal, mostly local fine dining menus with a spectacular Ontario wine list. Closed Mon. L/D, $$–$$$, www.treadwellcuisine.com
- Wellington Court Restaurant, 11 Wellington St., St. Catharines ON L2R 4W9, 905-682-5518. Fine dining, well presented using local ingredients; the restaurant is Edwardian on the outside and jazzy on the inside. Open Tues.–Sat. L/D, $$–$$$, www.wellington-court.com

Vineland

- About Thyme Bistro, 3457 King St., Vineland ON L0R 2C0, 905-562-3457. Open for lunch at 11, Wed.–Sat., and for dinner at 5, Wed.–Sun. Reservations recommended for Fri. and Sat. L/D, www.aboutthymebistro.com
- Vineland Estates Winery Restaurant, 3620 Moyer Rd., Vineland ON L0R 2C0, 905-562-7088, Fax: 905-562-3071, www.vineland.com. The region's first wine restaurant. Mediterranean cuisine changes seasonally to reflect local harvests and the pasta is made fresh on the premises daily. L/D (2 servings), $$$$

Welland

- Rinderlin's Dining Rooms, 24 Burgar St., Welland ON L3B 2S7, 905-735-4411. Generous servings of a wide variety of European fare, located in the Fortner House, an 1806 Queen Anne Revival building. L/D, $$$

Festivals & Events

There's something festive for everyone in Niagara. The categories of music, cultural, fall and winter festivals are highlighted below. For theatre festivals, see the theatre listings.

General Information

- Festivals and Events Ontario (FEO), 5 Graham St., Woodstock ON N4S 6J5, 519-537-2226, Fax: 519-537-7226, www.festivalsandeventsontario.ca

January

- Niagara Icewine Festival, 8 Church St., Suite 100, St. Catharines ON L2R 3B3, 905-688-0212, www.niagaraicewinefestival.com

May

- Niagara Folk Arts Festival, 85 Church St., St. Catharines ON L2R 3C7, 905-685-6589, Fax: 905-685-8376, www.folk-arts.ca

June

- Niagara New Vintage Festival, 8 Church St., Suite 100, St. Catharines ON L2R 3B3, 905-688-0212. Thirty participating wineries will be welcoming visitors with tours, tastings and special events all celebrating the first taste of Ontario's newest wines. www.niagaranewvintagefestival.com

August

- Royal Canadian Henley Regatta, 12-111 Fourth Ave., Suite 262, St. Catharines ON L2S 3P5, www.henleyregatta.ca

September

- Niagara Wine Festival, 8 Church St., Suite 100, St. Catharines ON L2R 3B3, 905-688-0212, www.niagarawinefestival.com

October

- Oktoberfest, Kitchener-Waterloo ON. Canada's great Bavarian festival. Over forty different family and cultural events. Visit one of sixteen Festhallen, or celebrate with family and friends at the annual Oktoberfest Thanksgiving Day Parade. www.oktoberfest.ca

Winter

- Winter Festival of Lights, Niagara Falls ON, 905-374-1616, Toll Free: 1-800-563-2557. Over 125 animated lighting displays and 3 million tree and ground lights right at the falls. November to early January. www.wfol.com

Gardens and Parks

Greenery is everywhere you look in spring and summer in Niagara, but much of it survives over winter, too, in the greenhouses and conservatories listed below. Dedicated garden-goers may want to contact the provincial association for an informed look at the beauty that abounds here.

General Information

- Ontario Horticultural Association, www.gardenontario.org

Hamilton

- Royal Botanical Gardens, 680 Plains Rd. W., Hamilton ON L7T 4H4; 905-527-1158, Fax: 905-577-0375. A living museum developing and promoting public understanding of the relationship between the plant world, humanity and the rest of nature. www.rbg.ca.

Niagara Falls

- The Niagara Parks Commission, PO Box 150, Niagara Falls ON L2E 6T2, 905-356-2241, Fax: 905-354-6041, www.niagaraparks.com The following sites are administered by the Niagara Parks Commission:
- Butterfly Conservatory, 2405 Niagara Pkwy. Located on the grounds of the Niagara Parks Botanical Gardens, open daily from 9:00 a.m. year-round; closing time varies according to season; admission charge.
- The Floral Clock, located 10 km north of the falls on the Niagara Pkwy.
- Niagara Parks Botanical Gardens, 2565 Niagara Pkwy. Open year-round, dawn until dusk; free admission.
- Niagara Parks Commission Greenhouses, located on the Niagara Pkwy., just south of the Horseshoe Falls; open daily from 9:30–5, June to Labour Day. For the rest of the year, open Sun.–Thurs. 9:30–5, Fri. & Sat. 9:30–6. Wheelchair accessible.
- Niagara Glen, Niagara Pkwy. A unique spot of beauty deep in the Great Gorge that has been a designated Nature Reserve since 1992.
- Queen Victoria Park, located on the Niagara Pkwy., at the falls.

Golf

Ontario Tourism (1-800-ONTARIO) produces an annual directory, *Golf Ontario Style*, which covers all the golf courses in Niagara. Below are some of the best courses.

- Legends on the Niagara, 9561 Niagara Pkwy, Niagara Falls ON, 905-295-9595, Toll Free: 1-866-465-3642. Operating two highly ranked 18-hole courses — Battlefield (the North course) and Ussher's Creek (the South course) — and the 9-hole Chippawa. www.niagaraparksgolf.com
- Niagara-on-the-Lake Golf Club, 143 Front St., PO Box 45, Niagara-on-the-Lake ON L0S 1J0, 905-468-3424. North America's oldest course. www.notlgolf.com
- Peninsula Lakes Golf Club, 569 Highway 20 W., Fenwick ON L0S 1C0, 905-892-8844, Toll Free: 1-877-241-GOLF (4653). Boasting 27 championship holes and located in the heart of the Niagara Peninsula atop the escarpment; impeccably groomed fairways and greens and sparkling lakes. www.penlakes.com
- Royal Niagara Golf Club, One Niagara-on-the-Green Blvd., Niagara-on-the-Lake ON L0S 1J0, 905-685-9501, Toll-free: 1-866-ROYAL-18. Three impressive

9-hole courses — a "must play" course of international standing playing over 7,000 yards from the tips. www.royalniagara.com

- Thundering Waters Golf Club, 6000 Marineland Pkwy., Niagara Falls, ON L2E 6X8, 905-357-6000, 1-877-833-DALY. John Daly's first signature golf course in Canada, located within the Niagara Falls Tourist District and a mere 1,500 yards from the Horseshoe Falls. www.thunderingwaters.com
- Whirlpool Public Golf Course, 3351 Niagara Pkwy, Box 150, Niagara Falls ON L2E 6T2, 905-356-1140, Toll Free: 1-866-465-3642, Fax: 905-356-7273, www.niagaraparksgolf.com

Hiking

Either Hike Ontario or the Bruce Trail Association is the best places to start when looking for information about hiking in Niagara. The Bruce Trail Association also produces an excellent, detailed book of maps, which is available at most outfitters and bookstores.

General Information

- Hike Ontario, 165 Dundas St. W., Suite 400, Mississauga ON L5B 2N6, 905-894-7249, Toll Free: 1-800-894-7249, www.hikeontario.com
- The Bruce Trail Association, PO Box 857, Hamilton ON L8N 3N9, 905-529-6821, Toll Free: 1-800-665-4453, Fax: 905-529-6823, info@brucetrail.org, www.brucetrail.org
- Niagara Trail, c/o Hike Ontario, above

Kids' Stuff

Sites listed below will appeal to all ages, but particularly young ones.
- African Lion Safari, 1386 Cooper Road, Flamborough ON, 519-623-2620, Toll Free: 1-800-461-9453, Fax: 905-623-9542. Large drive-through wildlife park; view and photograph 1,000 unique and rare mammals and birds who are roaming freely. www.lionsafari.com
- Journey Behind The Falls, Table Rock Centre, 6650 Niagara Pkwy, Niagara Falls ON. Experience the awesome spectacle of one-fifth of the world's fresh water crashing down thirteen stories to the basin below. Open daily from 9:00 a.m.; www.niagaraparks.com
- Marineland, 7657 Portage Rd., Niagara Falls ON L2E 6X8, 905-356-8250. Enjoy entertaining killer whale, dolphin, walrus and sea lion shows; an informative training and educational marine mammal presentation; bears, a deer-petting park, freshwater fish aquarium and amusement rides. www.marinelandcanada.com

Attractions, Historic Sites and Museums

In addition to the wealth of attractions in Niagara Falls, each community in Niagara has its own story to tell, and usually a museum to tell it through. Historic plaques are also strung along the heritage highways enabling you to make history part of your drive. The Ontario Museum Association maintains a comprehensive listing of all local museums on its website.

General Information

- Ontario Museum Association (OMA), George Brown House, 50 Baldwin St., Toronto ON M5T 1L4, 416-348-8672, Fax: 416-348-0438, www.museumsontario.com

Galleries

- Albright-Knox Art Gallery, 1285 Elmwood Ave., Buffalo NY USA 14222-1096, 716 882-8700, Fax: 716-882-1958. Open Tues.–Thurs., Sat.–Sun. noon–5, Fri. noon–10; closed Mondays, Independence, Thanksgiving, Christmas and New Year's Days. www.albrightknox.org
- Bird Kingdom, 5651 River Rd., Niagara Falls ON L2E 7M7, 905-

356-8888, Toll Free: 1-866-994-0090. Home to over 400 free-flying birds. Open 365 days a year; hours vary by season.
www.birdkingdom.ca

- Butler's Barracks (Fort George National Historic Site), John St. at King St., Niagara-on-the-Lake ON L0S 1J0, www.pc.gc.ca/eng/lhn-nhs/on/fortgeorge/natcul/natcul2d.aspx
- Canadian Warplane Heritage Museum, 9280 Airport Rd., Mount Hope ON L0R 1W0, 905-679-4183, Fax: 905-679-4186, www.warplane.com
- Casino Niagara, 5705 Falls Ave., Niagara Falls ON L2H 6T3, 905-374-3598, Toll Free: 1-888-WINFALL (946-3255). Over 1,700 slot and video poker machines, seventy tables of gaming excitement, three restaurants and three bars. www.casinoniagara.com
- Chippawa Battlefield Park, Niagara Pkwy, Niagara Falls ON, www.niagaraparks.com/heritage-trail/chippawa-battlefield-park.html
- Dundurn Castle, Dundurn National Historic Site, 610 York Blvd., Hamilton ON L8R 3H1, 905-546-2872, Fax: 905-546-2875. Discover mid-nineteenth-century Hamilton on a tour of more than forty rooms on three floors.
- Fallsview Casino Resort, 6380 Fallsview Blvd., Niagara Falls ON L2G 7X5, Toll Free 1-888-FALLSVU. Overlooking the falls with more than 3,000 slot machines and 150 gaming tables, a 368-room five-star hotel, fine-dining restaurants, 50,000 square feet of meeting/conference space, a health spa, a retail facility, a 1,500-seat theatre and more.
www.fallsviewcasinoresort.com
- Fort George, 26 Queen St., c/o Niagara National Historic Sites, Parks Canada, PO Box 787, Niagara-on-the-Lake ON L0S 1J0, 905-468-4257, Fax: 905-468-4638, www.pc.gc.ca/lhn-nhs/on/fortgeorge/index_e.asp
- Konica-Minolta Tower Centre, 6732

Fallsview Blvd., Niagara Falls ON L2G 3W6, 905-356-1501, Toll Free: 1-800-461-2492. Situated 500 feet above the Niagara Gorge, offers spectacular view of the falls and the Niagara Region from the observation deck. Restaurant, nearby shops and attractions.
www.niagaratower.com

- Maid of the Mist, 5920 River Rd., Niagara Falls ON L6E 6V6, 905-358-5781. For over 150 years, views of the falls from the river directly below have awed all. April through October. www.maidofthemist.com
- Navy Hall (Fort George National Historic Site), 305 Ricardo St., Niagara-on-the-Lake ON L0S 1J0, (905) 468-4257, Fax: (905) 468-4638; ont-niagara@pc.gc.ca, www.pc.gc.ca/fortgeorge
- Niagara Apothecary, 5 Queen St., Niagara-on-the-Lake ON, www.niagaraapothecary.ca
- Niagara Glen Nature Reserve, 8 km north of the falls on the Niagara Pkwy., Niagara Falls ON. Free access to Niagara Glen Trails. Open year-round, access weather dependent in winter.
www.niagaraparks.com/nature-trails/niagara-glen-whirlpool.html
- Niagara Historical Society & Museum, 43 Castlereagh St., PO Box 208, Niagara-on-the-Lake, ON L0S 1J0, 905-468-3912, www.niagarahistorical.museum/
- Niagara Totem Pole & Wood-Carving Park, located at the Niagara Glen Nature Reserve (see above listing). North America's largest collection (over 500) of hand-carved, one-of-a-kind totem poles. Open daily throughout the summer.
www.niagaraparks.com/nature-trails/totem-pole-park.html
- Queenston Heights Park, 14184 Niagara Pkwy, Queenston ON. Battlefield site and home to Brock's Monument.
www.niagaraparks.com/garden-trail/queenston-heights.html
- Skylon Tower, 5200 Robinson St., Niagara Falls ON L2G 2A3; 905-356-2651. An observation deck 775

feet above the falls, along with a revolving dining room, plaza and concourse levels. Indoor entertainment centre for dynamic family fun; 3D/4D motion theatre. www.skylon.com

- St. Catharines Museum at Lock 3 and Welland Canal Centre, RR #6, 1932 Welland Canals Parkway (formerly Government Road), St. Catharines ON L2R 7K6, 905-984-8880, Toll Free: 1-800-305-5134, Fax: 905-984-6910. Also home to the Ontario Lacrosse Hall of Fame & Museum. www.stcatharineslock3museum.ca
- Whirlpool Aero Car, 3850 Niagara Pkwy., Niagara Falls ON. View the racing Niagara River and Whirlpool from above in an antique cable car. Open March through November, operation is weather dependent. www.niagaraparks.com/attractions/whirlpool-aero-car.html

Theatre

Opportunities to enjoy live theatre abound in Niagara and the surrounding area. Contact each theatre individually for production information and reservations. Most theatres also post brochures at Ontario Travel Information Centres.

General Information

- Theatre Ontario, 215 Spadina Ave., Suite 210, Toronto ON M5T 2C7, 416-408-4556, Fax: 416-408-3402, www.theatreontario.org

Theatres

- Lighthouse Festival Theatre, PO Box 1208, 247 Main St., Port Dover ON N0A 1N0, 519-583-2221, www.lighthousetheatre.com
- Shaw Festival, PO Box 774, 10 Queen's Parade, Niagara-on-the-Lake ON L0S 1J0, 1-800-511-7429, Fax: 905-468-3804. The only theatre festival in the world that specializes in plays by Bernard Shaw and his contemporaries, and plays about his era (1856–1950). Runs April through November.

bxoffice@shawfest.com, www.shawfest.com

- Stratford Shakespeare Festival, PO Box 520, Stratford ON N5A 6V2, 1-800-567-1600, Fax: 705-271-2734. One of the world's premier repertory theatre companies, presenting a challenging roster of the best plays ever written. Runs April through November. www.stratfordfestival.ca
- Theatre Aquarius, 190 King William St., Hamilton ON L8R 1A8, 905-522-7529, Toll Free: 1-800-465-7529, www.theatreaquarius.org

Wine Tasting

The wineries listed below are located on the Niagara Peninsula and Pelee Island.

General Information

- The Wine Council of Ontario, #B205, 110 Hannover Dr., St. Catharines ON L2W 1A4, 905-684-8070, Fax: 905-684-2993, www.wineroute.com
- Wineries of Niagara-on-the-Lake, www.wineriesofniagaraonthelake.com

Wineries

- Angels Gate Winery, 4260 Mountainview Rd., Beamsville ON L0R 1B2, 905-563-3942, Toll Free: 1-877-ANG-GATE, Fax: 905-563-4127. Hours vary by day and by season. www.angelsgatewinery.com
- Cave Spring Cellars, 3836 Main St., Jordan ON L0R 1S0, 905-562-3581. Hours vary by day and season; Tours: June 1–Sept. 30, daily at 3:00 p.m.; Oct. 2 –May 31, Fri., Sat., and Sun. at 3:00 p.m. www.cavespringcellars.com
- Chateau des Charmes Wines, 1025 York Rd., Niagara-on-the-Lake ON L0S 1J0, 905-262-4219. English language public tours are conducted year-round daily at 11:00 a.m. and 3:00 p.m. French tours are conducted daily at noon. www.chateaudescharmes.com
- Colio Estate Wines, 1 Colio Dr., PO Box 372, Harrow ON N0R 1G0,

519-738-2241. Open year round; tours at 1, 2, and 3. www.coliowines.com

- Fielding Estate Winery, 4020 Locust Lane, Beamsville, ON L0R 1B2, 905-563-0668, Toll Free: 1-888-778-7758, Fax: 905-563-0664. Daily tours 10:30–6, May–Oct., and 10:30–5:30 Nov.–Apr. Reservations recommended. For tours from Nov.–Apr., call to book an appointment. www.fieldingwines.com

- Flat Rock Cellars, 2727 Seventh Ave., Jordan ON L0R 1S0, 905-562-8994, Fax: 562-9162. Open year round 10–6 Mon.–Sat.; 11–6 Sunday. www.flatrockcellars.com

- Henry of Pelham Family Estate Winery, 1469 Pelham Rd., RR.#1, St. Catharines ON L2R 6P7, 905-684-8423, Fax: 905-684-8444. From November to Victoria Day (in May), hours are 10–5 daily; from Victoria Day through October, hours are 10–6 daily. www.henryofpelham.com

- Hillebrand Estate Winery, 1249 Niagara Stone Rd., Niagara-on-the-Lake ON L0S 1J0, 905-468-7123, Toll Free: 1-800-582-8412. Daily tours on the hour throughout the day from 10:00 a.m. to 7:00 p.m. www.hillebrand.com

- Inniskillin Wines, 1499 Line 3, at Niagara Pkwy., Niagara-on-the-Lake ON L0S 1J0, 905-468-2187, Toll Free: 1-888-466-4754. Tours daily. www.inniskillin.com

- Jackson-Triggs Niagara Estate Winery, 2145 Regional Road 55, Niagara-on-the-Lake ON L0S 1J0, 905-468-4637, Toll-free: 1-866-589-4637. June to September, open daily 10:30–6:30 with tours every half hour; October to May, open daily with varying tour and operating hours. www.jacksontriggswinery.com

- Lailey Vineyard, 15940 Niagara Pkwy., Niagara-on-the-Lake ON L0S 1J0, 905-468-0503, Fax: 905-468-8012. Tours daily. www.laileyvineyard.com

- Malivoire Wine Company Ltd.,

4260 King St. E., PO Box 475, Beamsville, ON L0R 1B0, 905-563-9253, Toll Free: 1-866-644-2244, Fax: 905-563-9512, www.malivoirewineco.com

- No. 99 Wayne Gretzky Estates Winery, 3751 King St., PO Box 551, Vineland ON L0R 2C0, 905-562-4945. Open year round; call for tour times. www.gretzky.com/wine/

- Pelee Island Winery, 455 Seacliff Drive (County Road #20), Kingsville ON N9Y 2K5, 519-733-6551, Toll Free: 1-800-597-3533. Daily tours Mon.–Sat., 9–6, Sun. 11–5. www.peleeisland.com

- Peller Estates, 290 John St. E., Niagara-on-the-Lake ON L0S 1J0, 905-468-4678, Toll Free: 1-888-673-5537, Fax: 905-468-1920. Tours Sun.–Thurs., 10–7, Fri. & Sat., 1–9. www.peller.com

- Peninsula Ridge Estates, 5600 King St. W., PO Box 550, Beamsville ON L0R 1B0, 905-563-0900, Fax: 905-563-0995. One tour daily for individual visitors from June to October at 11:30 a.m.; November to May, tours are by appointment. www.peninsularidge.com

- Puddicombe Estate Farms & Winery, 1468 #8 Hwy, Winona ON L8E 5K9, 905-643-1015 (farm), 905-643-6882 (winery), www.puddicombefarms.com

- Reif Estate Winery, 15608 Niagara Pkwy., RR #1, Niagara-on-the-Lake ON L0S 1J0, 905-468-7738. Open daily, Apr.–., 10–6, Nov.–Mar., 10–5; tours at 11:30 a.m. and 1:30 p.m., May–Oct. www.reifwinery.com

- Stoney Ridge Winery, 3201 King St., PO Box 566, Vineland ON L0R 2C0, 905-562-1324. Open Sun.–Wed., 10–6, and Thurs.–Sat., 10–8. Tours Sat., Sun. and holidays at 11 and 2. www.stoneyridge.com

- Stratus Wines, 2059 Niagara Stone Rd., Niagara-on-the-Lake, ON L0S 1J0, 905-468-1806, Fax: 905-468-0847. Open May–Oct. daily, 11–5; Nov.–Apr., Wed.–Sun., 12–5. www.stratuswines.com

- Strewn Estate Winery, 1339

Lakeshore Road, RR #3, Niagara-on-the-Lake ON L0S 1J0, 905-468-1229, Fax: 905-468-8305, www.strewnwinery.com

- Thirty Bench Wines, 4281 Mountainview Rd., Beamsville ON L0R 1B2, 905-563-1698. Store hours, Sun.–Fri., 10–5:30; Sat., 10–6; www.thirtybench.com
- Vineland Estates Winery, 3620 Moyer Rd., Vineland, ON L0R 2C0; 905-562-7088, Toll Free: 1-888-846-3526, Fax: 905-562-3071. Daily tours throughout summer until October at 11:00 a.m. and 3:00 p.m. www.vineland.com

Excursions – Art Lovers

- Art Gallery of Hamilton. Ontario's third-largest gallery with a collection including historical European, Canadian and contemporary art. Open Tues.—Sun. and holiday Mondays.123 King St. W., Hamilton, 905-527-6610, www.artgalleryofhamilton.com
- Art Gallery of Peel. Dedicated to preserving and promoting the region's artistic heritage. 9 Wellington St. E., Brampton, 905-791-4055, www.peelregion.ca/heritage/art-gallery
- Burlington Art Centre. Specializing in collecting contemporary Canadian ceramics. Open year-round, free admission. 1333 Lakeshore Rd., Burlington, 905-632-7796, www.burlingtonartcentre.on.ca
- Cambridge Galleries. Open 7 days a week, closed Sundays from Victoria Day to Labour Day. Queen's Square, 1 North Square, Cambridge, 519-621 0460, www.cambridgegalleries.ca
- Canadian Clay and Glass Gallery. Collection of historical and contemporary Canadian ceramic, glass and enamel art. Closed Mondays. 25 Caroline St.N., Waterloo, 519-746-1882.

www.canadianclayandglass.ca

- Carnegie Gallery. 10 King St. W., Dundas, 905-627-4265, www.carnegiegallery.org
- Gallery Stratford. Specializing in contemporary works on paper. Open Tues.–Sun.. 10–5. 54 Romeo St., Stratford, 519-271-5271, www.gallerystratford.on.ca
- Homer Watson House and Gallery. Open Tues.–Sun. 12–4:30. Home of one of Canada's first internationally recognized nineteenth-century artists, now a gallery and art education centre. 1754 Old Mill Rd., Kitchener, 519-748-4377, www.homerwatson.on.ca
- Kitchener-Waterloo Art Gallery. Open year-round. 101 Queen St. North, Kitchener, 519-579-5860, www.kwag.on.ca
- McIntosh Gallery. Closed Mon.; free admission. University of Western Ontario campus, 519-661-3181, www.mcintoshgallery.ca
- McMaster Museum of Art. Five exhibition galleries, a Paper Centre and Educational Access Gallery on the university grounds. Closed Sun. & Mon. Voluntary admission fee; free for students and seniors. Alvin A. Lee building, University Ave. at Sterling St. on McMaster University campus, 1280 Main St. W., Hamilton, 905-525-9140, www.mcmaster.ca/museum
- The McMichael Canadian Collection, 10365 Islington Ave., Kleinburg. Open daily 10–4. 905-893-1121, www.mcmichael.on.ca
- Museum London. Art and history museum in an architecturally distinguished structure documenting the culture of the region. Closed Mon.; admission by donation. 421 Ridout St. N, London, 519-661-0333, www.londonmuseum.on.ca
- Niagara Falls Art Gallery. Closed Sundays in summer; admission by donation. 8058 Oakwood Dr., Niagara Falls, 905-356-1514, www.niagarafallsartgallery.ca
- Niagara Historical Society & Museum, 43 Castlereagh St., PO

Box 208, Niagara-on-the-Lake, ON
L0S 1J0, 905-468-3912,
www.niagarahistorical.museum/

- Peel Heritage Complex. Houses the
Art Gallery of Peel, the Peel
Archives and the Whitney
Community Gallery. 9 Wellington
St. E., Brampton, 905-791-4055,
www.peelregion.ca
- Romance Collection Gallery, 177
King St., Niagara-on-the-Lake ON
L0S 1J0, 1-800-667-8525,
www.romancecollection.com

Excursions – Theatre

- 4th Line Theatre. Outdoor theatre on
farmland against a backdrop of
barns and meadows. Runs July
through August. Old Millbrook
School, 1 Dufferin St., Millbrook,
705-932 4445,
www.4thlinetheatre.on.ca
- Blyth Festival. Summer series of
original works by Canadian
playwrights. Runs June to
September. Blyth Memorial
Community Hall, 423 Queen St.,
(County Road #4), Blyth, 1-877-
862-5984, www.blythfestival.com
- Dofasco Centre for the Arts. Home
of Theatre Aquarius.190 King
William St., Hamilton, 905-522-
7529, www.theatreaquarius.org
- Drayton Entertainment. Presenting
musicals, comedies and dramas in
six historical venues around
southern Ontario. 1-888-449-4463,
www.draytonentertainment.com
- Drayton Festival Theatre. Former
town hall and opera house renovated
into a modern theatrical space. 33
Wellington St. S., Drayton, 519-638-
5511 or 1-888-449-4463,
www.draytonentertainment.com
- Gayety Theatre, 161 Hurontario St.,
Collingwood, 519-599 3915,
www.gayetytheatre.com
- Grand Theatre. 471 Richmond St.,
London, 1-519-872-8800,
www.grandtheatre.com
- Gryphon Theatre. Comedy, musicals
and theatre in a multipurpose venue.
Building C, Georgian College, 1

Georgian Dr, Barrie, 705-728-4613,
www.gryphontheatre.com
- Hamilton Place: Ronald V. Joyce
Centre for the Performing Arts and
The Studio. Internationally
acclaimed concert hall and a cabaret
space. 1 Summers Lane, Hamilton,
905-546-3100, www.hecfi.ca
- Huron County Playhouse.
Professional summer theatre in a
renovated barn. RR1 "B" Line, Grand
Bend, 519-238-6000,
www.draytonentertainment.com/
theatre_information/huroncountryplay
house/
- King's Wharf Theatre. Discovery
Harbour, 97 Jury Dr.,
Penetanguishene, 705-549-5555,
www.draytonentertainment.com/thea
tre_information/
- Kitchener-Waterloo Centre in the
Square. Multi-purpose venue for
opera, comedy, music and theatre.
101 Queen St. N., Kitchener, 519-
578-1570 or 1-800-265-8977,
www.centre-square.com
- Oakville Centre for the Performing
Arts. 130 Navy St., Oakville, 905-
815-2021, www.oc4pa.com
- The Red Barn Theatre. Over fifty
years' tradition of professional
summer theatre presented in a
converted nineteenth-century barn.
Temporarily holding performances
at Georgina's Stephen Leacock
Theatre due to fire in summer of
2009. 130 Gwendolyn Blvd,
Keswick, 1-888-733-2226,
www.redbarntheatre.ca
- Rose Theatre Brampton. State of the
art arts centre with two performance
halls. 1 Theatre Lane, Brampton, 905-
874-2800, www.myrosetheatre.ca
- St. Jacob's Country Playhouse, 40
Benjamin St., East Waterloo, 519-
747-7788, www.draytonenter
tainment.com/theatre_information/
- Schoolhouse Theatre. Nineteenth-
century schoolhouse renovated to
provide intimate cabaret atmosphere
and distinctive acoustics. 111 Albert
St., St. Jacob's, 519-638-5555,
www.draytonentertainment.com/
theatre_information/
- Shaw Festival, PO Box 774,

Niagara-on-the-Lake ON L0S 1J0, 1-800-511-7429, Fax: 905-468-3804. The only theatre festival in the world that specializes in plays by Bernard Shaw and his contemporaries, and plays about his era (1856–1950). Runs April through November. bxoffice@shawfest.com, www.shawfest.com

- Stratford Shakespeare Festival, PO Box 520, Stratford ON N5A 6V2, 1-800-567-1600, Fax: 705-271-3731. One of the world's premier repertory theatre companies, presenting a challenging roster of the best plays ever written. Runs April through November. www.stratfordfestival.ca

- Theatre Aquarius, 190 King William St., Hamilton ON L8R 1A8; 905-522-7529, Toll Free: 1-800-465-7529, www.theatreaquarius.org

Excursions – Historical

- Bell Homestead. Canadian homestead of Alexander Graham Bell, inventor of the telephone. Open Tues.–Sun. 9:30–4:30; adult admission $6.75, students and seniors $3.75, children 6 years and under admitted free. 94 Tutela Heights Rd., Brantford, 519-756-6220, www.bellhomestead.ca

- Brubacher House. Mennonite farmhouse documenting the region's nineteenth-century Pennsylvania German cultural and architectural history. Open May–Oct., Wed.–Sat., 2–5. Admission by donation; tours also available by appointment. North Campus Rd, North Campus, University of Waterloo, Waterloo, 519-886-3855, www.grebel.uwaterloo.ca/aboutgrebel/bruhouse.shtml

- Buxton National Historic Site & Museum. African Canadian history of the Elgin settlement at the terminus of the Underground Railroad. 519-352-4799, www.buxtonmuseum.com

- Castle Kilbride. Former mansion of the Livingston family and a landmark of Italianate design. Open Mar.–Dec., varying days; see website for details. Closed Mondays and holidays. Adult admission $6, students and seniors $5, children under 12 $3.50, preschoolers free; family rate for four $16. 60 Snyder's Rd. W., Baden, 519-634-8444, www.castlekilbride.ca

- Chatham-Kent Black Historical Society. Operating a heritage room and resource centre documenting the history of the area's black community after escaping slavery. Open Mon.–Fri., 9–5; tours available by appointment. W.I.S.H Centre, 177 King St. E., Chatham, 519-354-5248, www.mnsi.net/~wishc/heritageroom

- Chiefswood National Historical Site. May–Oct., open daily 10–3; Oct.–May, tours by appointment only. Adult admission $5, students $4, seniors and children under 12 free. Hwy. 54, blue tag #1037, Cainsville, 519-752-5005, www.chiefswood.com

- Doon Heritage Crossroads. A recreated rural village depicting two farms in the community in the early twentieth century. Open daily May to Labour Day, weekdays only, September to December 23, 10–4:30. 10 Huron Rd., Kitchener, 519-748-1914, www.region.waterloo.on.ca

- Guelph Civic Museum. Open daily 1–5. Adult admission $4, seniors, students and children $3, families $10 (reduced joint admission rates to McCrae House available). 6 Dublin St. S, 519-836-1221, www.guelph.ca/museum

- Hoodless Homestead. Childhood home of nineteenth-century women's issues activist Adelaide Hunter Hoodless. Open year-round, Tues. 10–4, or by appointment. 359 Blue Lake Rd, St. George, 519-448-1130, www.hoodlesshomestead.ca

- Joseph Schneider Haus. Kitchener's oldest dwelling, a Georgian farmhouse built by one of the area's first Pennsylvania German pioneers. Open daily July–Sept.; Wed.–Sun. Sept.–Dec. 23; closed Dec. 24–mid-Feb. 466 Queen St. S., Kitchener, 519-742-7752, www.downtown kitchener.ca/things/attractions

- Laura Secord Homestead. Restored home of the legendary War of 1812 heroine. Open May–Sept., seven days a week; Sept.–Oct. Wed.–Sun. only. Adult admission $4.50, $3.50 for children aged 6–12. 29 Queenston St., Queenston, www.niagaraparks.com/heritage-trail/laura-secord-homestead.html

- Mackenzie Heritage Printery and Newspaper Museum. Canada's largest printery museum preserving the story and the legacy of publisher and political agitator William Lyon Mackenzie, and the printing industry. Open May–Sept., seven days a week. Adult admission $4.50, $3.50 for children aged 6–12. 1 Queenston St., Queenston, www.niagaraparks.com/heritage-trail/mackenzie-printery-newspaper-museum.html

- McCrae House. Birthplace of Lt. Col. John McCrae, doctor, WWI soldier and author of the poem "In Flanders Fields." Open daily 1–5, closed Sat. Dec.–June. Adult admission $4, seniors, students and children $3, families $10 (reduced joint admission rates to Guelph Civic Museum available).108 Water St., Guelph, 519-836-1221, www.guelph.ca/museum

- Mohawk Chapel. Oldest Protestant church in Ontario. Open Wed.–Sun. in May, June, Sept., Oct.; daily July & Aug. Sunday services in summer at 10:30 a.m. 301 Mohawk St., Brantford, 519-756-0240, www.mohawkchapel.ca

- Niagara Apothecary, 5 Queen St., Niagara-on-the-Lake ON, www.niagaraapothecary.ca

- Niagara Historical Society & Museum, 43 Castlereagh St., PO Box 208, Niagara-on-the-Lake, ON L0S 1J0, 905-468-3912, www.niagarahistorical.museum/

- Uncle Tom's Cabin Historical Site and Josiah Henson House. Commemorates the life and contributions to the abolition movement and the Underground Railroad of Reverend Josiah Henson, whose memoirs inspired the classic novel. Open May–Oct. 10–4; seven days a week in July & Aug.; closed Mon. in May, June, Sept. and Oct. Adult admission $6.25, children under 6 free, family admission $20. 29251 Uncle Tom's Rd., Dresden, 519-683-2978 or 519-862-2291 (winter), www.uncletomscabin.org

- Wellington County Museum and Archives. Historical and cultural centre for Wellington County. RR#1, Fergus, 519-846-0916, ext. 221, www.wcm.on.ca

Excursions – Naturalists

- Ball's Falls. Restored 1800s hamlet with mill and historic buildings among waterfalls and hiking paths on the Bruce Trail. Open Apr.–Nov. Adult admission $5.50, students and seniors $4. RR#24, 905-788-3135, www.npca.ca/conservation-areas/ca-fees.htm#ballsfalls

- Bird Kingdom, 5651 River Rd., Niagara Falls ON L2E 7M7, 905-356-8888, Toll Free: 1-866-994-0090. Home to over 400 free-flying birds. Open 365 days a year, hours vary by season. www.birdkingdom.ca

- Bruce Trail Association. Conservancy group with hike information for Canada's oldest and longest continuous footpath, spanning the Niagara Escarpment. 1-800-665-4453 or 905-529-6821, www.brucetrail.org

- Butterfly Conservatory, 2565 Niagara Pkwy. Located on the grounds of the Niagara Parks Botanical Gardens, open daily from 9:00 a.m. year-round; closing time varies according to season; admission charge. www.niagaraparks.com

- Conservation Halton Foundation. Protection and management of six conservation areas around the Niagara Escarpment as well as a ski and snowboard centre. 2596 Britannia Rd. W., RR#2, Milton, 905-338-1168 or 905-847-7430, www.conservationhalton.on.ca
- Crawford Lake Conservation Area. Unique lake with surrounding boardwalk nestled atop the Niagara Escarpment near a recreated Iroquoian village. Hiking, cross country skiing and snowshoeing. Pets allowed on leash. Open year-round from 10:00 a.m.; closing time varies by season. Adult admission $6.50, children 5–14 $4.50. Guelph Line and Steeles Ave. near Milton, 905-854 0234, www.conservationhalton.on.ca
- The Floral Clock, located 10 km north of the falls on the Niagara Pkwy. www.niagaraparks.com
- Guelph Radial Trail. Runs northeast from Guelph along an abandoned electric railway route to meet the Bruce Trail, and features many glacial features. Hiking season April to November. 519-822-3672, www.guelphhiking.org
- Niagara Glen, Niagara Pkwy, Niagara Falls ON. A unique spot of beauty deep in the Great Gorge that has been a designated Nature Reserve since 1992. www.niagaraparks.com/nature-trails/niagara-glen-whirlpool.html
- Rattlesnake Point Conservation Area. Spectacular viewing points over scenic vistas from the edge of cliffs on the Niagara Escarpment. Hiking, cross country skiing, mountain biking and rock climbing. Pets allowed on leash. Open year round from 8:00 a.m.; closing times vary depending on season. Adult admission $5.50, children 5–14 $4, mountain biking day pass $7. Appleby Line north of Toronto. 905-878-1147, www.hrca.on.ca/ShowCategory.cfm?subCatID=1091
- Short Hills Provincial Park. Trail hiking, mountain biking, horseback riding and fishing in park approximately 4 km south of St. Catharines along the Niagara Escarpment. See website for fees. 905-774-6643, www.ontarioparks.com/english/shor.html
- St. John's Conservation Area. Hiking, fishing, wildlife viewing and day-use areas available. Open year-round. 905-788-3135, www.npca.ca/conservation-areas/st-johns/default.htm#activities
- Thames Valley Trail. 110 km path for hiking or cross country skiing along the Thames and North Thames rivers in the London area, linking Elgin and Avon trails. 519-645-2845, www.thamesvalleytrail.org
- Webster's Falls, Tews Falls and Spencer Gorge. Near Hamilton. Open sunrise to sundown; fee per vehicle $8, walking or biking $4.. 905-628-3060, www.conservationhamilton.ca/parks/visit/spencer.asp
- Woodend Conservation Area. Access to Bruce, Silurian and Hardwood Trails. Open year-round. 905-788-3135, www.npca.ca/c onservation-areas/woodend/default.htm

INDEX

Index

Index

Index

Index

Index

Index

Index

Photo Credits

2nd Look Graphics: 139B; A Little Sun Productions: 14B; Albright-Knox Art Gallery: 160B, 161; AME Restaurant: 81; Arpad Benedek: 13B, 12T; Art Gallery of Hamilton: 170; Art Gallery of Ontario: 42T&B, 43T&B; Bad Dog Theatre: 142; Bigworld: 10T; Breanne Thomas: 15T&B, 16T&B, 17T&B, 18T&B, 21B, 22T&B, 23T&B, 24T&B, 25T&B, 27, 28, 29T&B, 30T&B, 31T, 32T&B, 33, 35C&B, 38T&B, 39T&B, 40, 41B, 44T&B, 45T, 46T&C, 47, 52, 54T, 57T, 60T, 64B, 65C&B, 66, 68T&C, 69B, 70T&C, 73, 74T, 77, 78C, 79T, 81, 82T&B; 83T&B, 84C&B, 85, 86T&C, 87, 88T&B, 89, 92 (cherry beach), 93T, 94, 95, 96, 97T&B, 98B, 103T&B, 104T&B, 105T&B, 106, 114, 115, 116T&B, 117, 118, 119, 120T&B, 121T&B, 122, 123, 124, 125, 126T, 127, 128, 129, 130B, 131T, 133T, 137, 138, 139T; Brian Thibodeau: 13T; CanStage: 57B; CaribanaToronto.com: 111T(2); Cecilia Cotton: 100; Chris Gallow: 56, 58B; Christine Beevis: 150, 151T; City of Toronto: 112C&B; Cylla von Tiedemann: 58T&C; Dan Dragonetti Photography: 45B; David Cooper: 59B; David Hou: 62C; Derek Grime: 41T; Design Exchange: 50; Dragan Trifunovic: 98T; Dwayne Coon: 147, 149B, 153, 154, 156, 157, 158, 159, 166, 167, Eatertainment.com: 69T, 74B; Eldon House: 184; George Fischer: 19, 20B, 21T; Greg Tjepkema: 110T; Hamilton Place Theatre: 181; Henry Lin: 130T; 132, 134; Hillebrand Winery, Niagara: 168B; Image Net Media: 186B; Jackson-Triggs Winery, Niagara: 166T; Jamie Bradburn: 78B; Jo-Anne McArthur: 75, 76T; John Lauener: 26B; John Launer: 60B; Jon Dearden: 186T; Joseph Michael: 109T; Katharine Mulhern Contemporary Art Projects: 53; Ling Xia: 92B; Mark Robinson, Marcon Studios: 179; Mary Armstrong: 76B, 79B, 80T&C; Mary Marin: 140B; MBP Photo: 101; Michael Grills: 108T(2); Museum of Contemporary Canadian Art: 51T; Museum of London: 175; Narawon: 91; Neil Kinnear and Lesley Chung: 178; Nitin Sawant: 62B; NOW Toronto: 14C; One of a Kind: 108b(2); Park Hyatt Hotel: 135; Peter Spiro: 1, 14T, 31B, 93B, 107B; Preservation Gallery: 171; Richard Picton: 36T&B, 37T&B; Ron Tech: 140T; Sandy Bell, Vic MacBournie and John MacRae: 146, 148, 149T, 182, 183T, 187, 188B; Sara Levine Petroff: 54B, 55; Shin Sugino: 155; Simon Wilson: 151, 152, 188T, 189; Simone Castello: 131B; 133B; 136C&B; Simple Solutions: 141; SkyF: 185; Sony Centre: 62T; Stratford Shakespeare Theatre: 61B, 176, 177; Tarragon Theatre: 59T; Terry Manzo, David Smiley and Dwayne Coon: 75, 162; Textile Museum of Canada: 49T&B; The Sultan's Tent & Moroc Café: 71B; Tom Loonan: 160T; Tony Tremblay: 90, 113; Toronto Argonauts: 99; Toronto Music Garden: 67; Toronto Pride Parade: 102; Toronto Symphony Orchestra: 63, 64T; Trevor Schwellnus: 61T&C; Ultra Supper Club: 72; Victor PR: 34; Vladone: 20; Walter Dirks: 26T; Walter Willems: 51B; Wine Council of Ontario: 163; www.pixelhead.com: 109B, 110B.

Formac Publishing Company Limited acknowledges the financial support of the Government of Canada through the Book Publishing Industry Development Program (BPIDP) for our publishing activities.